Literary Lives

General Editor: **Richard Dutton**, Professor of English, Lancaster University

This series offers stimulating accounts of the literary careers of the most admired and influential English-language authors. Volumes follow the outline of the writers' working lives, not in the spirit of traditional biography, but aiming to trace the professional, publishing and social contexts which shaped their writing.

Published titles include:

Cedric C. Brown
JOHN MILTON

Peter Davison
GEORGE ORWELL

Richard Dutton
WILLIAM SHAKESPEARE

Jan Fergus
JANE AUSTEN

Caroline Franklin
BYRON

James Gibson
THOMAS HARDY

Kenneth Graham
HENRY JAMES

Paul Hammond
JOHN DRYDEN

W. David Kaye
BEN JONSON

Mary Lago
E. M. FORSTER

Clinton Machann
MATTHEW ARNOLD

Alasdair D. F. Macrae
W. B. YEATS

Joseph McMinn
JONATHAN SWIFT

Kerry McSweeney
GEORGE ELIOT

John Mepham
VIRGINIA WOOLF

Michael O'Neill
PERCY BYSSHE SHELLEY

Leonée Ormond
ALFRED TENNYSON

Harold Pagliaro
HENRY FIELDING

George Parfitt
JOHN DONNE

Gerald Roberts
GERARD MANLEY HOPKINS

Felicity Rosslyn
ALEXANDER POPE

Tony Sharpe
T. S. ELIOT
WALLACE STEVENS

Grahame Smith
CHARLES DICKENS

Janice Farrar Thaddeus
FRANCES BURNEY

Linda Wagner-Martin
SYLVIA PLATH

Gary Waller
EDMUND SPENSER

Cedric Watts
JOSEPH CONRAD

John Williams
MARY SHELLEY
WILLIAM WORDSWORTH

Tom Winnifrith and Edward Chitham
CHARLOTTE AND EMILY BRONTË

John Worthen
D. H. LAWRENCE

David Wykes
EVELYN WAUGH

Literary Lives
Series Standing Order ISBN 0–333–71486–5
(_outside North America only_)

You can receive future titles in this series as they are published by placing a standing order. Please contact your bookseller or, in case of difficulty, write to us at the address below with your name and address, the title of the series and the ISBN quoted above.

Customer Services Department, Macmillan Distribution Ltd, Houndmills, Basingstoke, Hampshire RG21 6XS, England

Byron

A Literary Life

Caroline Franklin
Senior Lecturer
University of Wales
Swansea

First published in Great Britain 2000 by
MACMILLAN PRESS LTD
Houndmills, Basingstoke, Hampshire RG21 6XS and London
Companies and representatives throughout the world

A catalogue record for this book is available from the British Library.

ISBN 0–333–67663–7 hardcover
ISBN 0–333–67664–5 paperback

First published in the United States of America 2000 by
ST. MARTIN'S PRESS, LLC,
Scholarly and Reference Division,
175 Fifth Avenue, New York, N.Y. 10010

ISBN 0–312–23152–0

Library of Congress Cataloging-in-Publication Data
Franklin, Caroline.
Byron : a literary life / Caroline Franklin.
p.   cm. — (Literary lives)
Includes bibliographical references (p.) and index.
ISBN 0–312–23152–0 (cloth)
1. Byron, George Gordon Byron, Baron, 1788–1824. 2. Poets, English — 19th
century — Biography. I. Literary lives (New York, N.Y.)

PR4381 .F7   2000
821'.7 — dc21
[B]
                                                                99–086622

This book is printed on paper suitable for recycling and made from fully managed and sustained
forest sources.

10   9   8   7   6   5   4   3   2   1
09   08   07   06   05   04   03   02   01   00

Printed and bound in Great Britain by
Antony Rowe Ltd, Chippenham, Wiltshire

For Marjorie Evans and in memory of
Ronald Victor Evans

Contents

Preface

> Literary lives are compiled for the bibliopolists, as puffs to sell their wares; they are nothing. When I die you will see mine, written by myself.
>
> (Byron in conversation with Edward Trelawny)[1]

Unfortunately, Byron's plan to preempt the future writing of his literary life failed, for his memoirs were eventually ceremoniously cast onto the fire by his literary executors to protect his posthumous reputation from more scandal. This literary life, though not the hagiographical puff Byron feared being compiled to sell its publisher's selections from the poetry, will steer clear of the poet's own pre-Freudian belief in the psychosexual origin of genius by setting his work in a professional rather than social context. This means going against the grain of the way Byron presented himself as an author. Though his memoirs were not published, Byron had already successfully instigated a cult of personality through the strongly autobiographical dimension in his poetry, which even today exerts a powerful hold over the way it is read. Though he was chiefly a narrative and dramatic poet, who often wrote rhetorically in a public voice, Byron's poetry was interfused with lyrical passages of introspection. The concept of a writer's inner self developed in British Protestant culture as a sort of secular soul, revealed in confessional disclosure and guaranteeing authenticity by its reference to a real individual.

However, because subjectivity was capable of making such a powerful truth claim, it was all the more vulnerable to accusations of egotism and also of prostitution of the sacred private self to the public at large. So whilst many continue to be seduced by Byron's personal magnetism, some critics have attempted to redress the balance by unmasking him as merely a cynical exploiter of the market. Undue distaste for the staggering contemporary popularity of writers like Byron and Dickens, however, is only the other side of the coin of the Romantic concept of genius, in its idealist assumption that a true artist chooses to write disinterestedly for posterity.

After all, the writer's selfhood or textual identity was plainly also a literary form of private property, a marketable asset whose copyright was sold to the publisher for the right to disseminate copies. When the subject of a text is the self then 'Byron' becomes a product or brand name. Self-mythologizing and an assertion of the transhistorical nature of art are features of Romantic poetry which attempt to deflect attention from this aspect of subjectivity. Laura Marcus observes, 'The Romantic and, following him, the post-Romantic autobiographer writes the self into the work and this suggests that authorial identity is not determined by the marketplace but is rather a function of conditions internal to the self'.[2] Such alienation is a normal feature of textuality, of course, for the whole point of texts is to transcend the specific time and place of their utterance.

The Romantic concept of a unique genius was a reflection of the increasing alienation of the artist from society in the nineteenth century, for a poet like Byron was now writing for enlarged and fractured reading publics, not known to him personally and not necessarily of his class and education. Though an aristocrat, he could no longer assume, like an Augustan writer, that he was speaking to reinforce the assumptions shared by the ruling class. He needed to shape an individuated authorial self through which to communicate to the reader. A turn to the autobiographical evolved from nineteenth-century concern with the biographical, the memoirs and historical accounts of great men which Byron himself liked to read and often cited in notes to his work. Such projections of heroic selfhood were all the more striking against a backdrop of political stasis. For the British party-political system was ossified and traditional dynastic power systems had been reinstituted in Europe after the defeat of Napoleon in 1815.

The last thirty years of structuralist and post-structuralist text-centred critical analysis have made it easier to distance oneself from Romantic idealizations of the author's psyche as sole instigator of meaning, his spontaneous inspiration and of the cult of personality, all of which Byron himself was instrumental in popularizing. But the advent of cultural materialism has also demonstrated the value of paying attention to the specific historical conditions which brought Romantic texts into being, and recreating the context in which they were first read. This will hopefully bring into focus the ideological significance of texts often masked by an exclusive focus on the personal, and clarify the otherness of those first readers' responses. This is not of merely archaic interest but a necessary defamiliarization process which should sharpen our own contemporary readings of the poetry, drenched as they are in the different preoccupations of our own historical moment.

In *The Archaeology of Knowledge* (1972) Michel Foucault observed of the cultural relations which determine a text's historical specificity:

> These relations are established between institutions, economic and social processes, behavioural patterns, systems of norms, techniques, types of classification, modes of characterization; and these relations are not present in the object; it is not they that are deployed when the object is being analysed; they do not indicate the web, the immanent rationality, that ideal nervure that reappears totally or in part when one conceives of the object in the truth of its concept. They do not define its internal constitution, but what enables it to appear, to juxtapose itself in relation to them, to define its difference, its irreducibility, and perhaps even its heterogeneity, in short, to be placed in a field of exteriority'.[3]

This literary life of Byron focuses on such fields of exteriority – those circumstances and interconnections which helped to bring texts into being in their particular historical moment. Strict chronology is sometimes sacrificed so that each chapter can focus on a different theme which particularly relates to specific texts but which may also have a more general application to the poetry as a whole. The usual procedure is for general social, political and cultural circumstances to be briefly indicated; then the relevance of a specific literary context is explored in detail, along with those generic and aesthetic traditions which the poet inherited and the way he modified them in the texts in question.

An introductory sketch briefly suggests the way Byron's family inheritance predisposed him to a fascination with the Gothic. Chapter 1 focuses on the way he deployed his rank as a writer, first as a provincial writer of occasional verse, and then as a Juvenalian satirist of the contemporary literary scene, when protesting against its domination by the periodical press. In the second chapter the symbiotic relationship between the orientalism of Byron's verse and its production by the publisher John Murray is explored. The personalities associated with the firm are described, and Byron's writing practice is set in the general context of the world of Regency publishing where coteries grew up to foster links between authors, critics, readers and reviewers. Byron's confused and changing attitudes to authorship and remuneration are seen adapting to the rapid commercialization and expansion of print culture. The third chapter considers Byron as a dramatist: the effect of his experience as head of the Drury Lane sub-committee and then of his reaction against Romantic 'bardolatry' in deflecting his ambition away from the stage and towards the production of avant-garde closet drama from abroad. Chapter 4 will consider Byron's self-projection as a poet of exile; the importance of his literary friendships in developing his scepticism into Romantic irony, and of his interaction with Italian culture in prompting the formal innovation to express this in his mature verse. Chapter 5 considers both those internal features of *Don Juan* and external factors which led to this text being peddled by radical publishers to the working-class, as well as the effect of its accretive method of composition and serial publication. Chapter 6 traces the story of Byron's alliance with P.B. Shelley and Leigh Hunt in founding *The Liberal* and his corresponding feud with the Lake Poets, especially Robert Southey, which produced the satiric masterpiece, *The Vision of Judgment.*

Suggestions for further reading

For those who would like fuller information on all facets of Byron's life as well as the literary, the standard scholarly biography is still Leslie A. Marchand's *Byron: a Biography*, 3 vols (1957), which gives a day by day account. A condensed version is available in one volume: *Byron: a Portrait* (1971). There are also studies focusing on specific periods of the poet's life, like Peter Quennell's readable *Byron: the Years of Fame* (1935) and *Byron in Italy* (1941), or the scholarly *Byron, Shelley and their Pisan Circle* (1952) by C.L. Cline. A meticulous account of Byron's collaboration with Leigh Hunt on *The Liberal* is given in William H. Marshall's *Byron, Shelley, Hunt and* The Liberal, (1960). For information on Byron's wife, marriage and the separation and its aftermath, consult Ethel Colburn Mayne's *The Life of Lady Byron* (1929), which is still unsurpassed. Margot Strickland gives brief entertaining biographies of the most important women in Byron's life in *The Byron Women* (1974), while his relationship with Teresa Guiccioli is examined in detail in Iris Origo's *The Last Attachment* (1949). Byron's bisexuality is studied by Louis Crompton in *Byron and Greek Love* (1985), both biographically and in the light of the wider historical context, together with literary analysis of the poetry. Byron's role in the Greek war of Independence is sensibly addressed by William St. Clair in *That Greece Might Still be Free* (1972). Fascinating light is cast on the poet by Doris Langley Moore's *Lord Byron: Accounts Rendered* (1974), which focuses on his finances. In *The Late Lord Byron* (1960) the same author details the immediate aftermath of the poet's death. His posthumous reputation in England is dealt with by Samuel C. Chew in *Byron in England: His Fame and After Fame* (1924), and the phenomenon of 'Byronism' is examined in *Byromania: Portrait of the Artist in Nineteenth and Twentieth Century Culture* ed. Frances Wilson (1999) and Andrew Elfenbein's *Byron and the Victorians* (1995).

The most direct way to sample the life and character of Byron, however, is to dip into *Byron's Letters and Journals,* edited by Leslie A. Marchand, 13 vols (1973–94), perhaps the most brilliantly entertaining letters in the English language. A one-volume selection is also available, *Byron: Selected Letters and Journals* (1982). The accounts of friends and contemporaries of the poet are, though necessarily slanted, of great interest, and range from the exhaustive biography of Thomas Moore, *Letters and Journals of Lord Byron: with Notices of his Life* (1830) to the brief but vivid essay by William Hazlitt in *Spirit of the Age* (1825). Extracts from many such accounts and the reported conversations of the poet have been assembled chronologically to give a succession of biographical portraits by Ernest J. Lovell in *His Very Self and Voice* (1954).

A more detailed chronology of Byron's life and works than is provided here will be found in Norman Page, *A Byron Chronology* (1988). For fuller information on the compositon and publication history of Byron's writing, consult the notes of *Lord Byron: the Complete Poetical Works*, 7 vols (1980–93), edited by Jerome J. McGann, and *Lord Byron: the Complete Miscellaneous Prose* (1991), edited by Andrew Nicholson. Also useful on the composition process of specific works are T.G. and E. Steffan and W.W. Pratt (eds), *Byron's Don Juan: a Variorum Edition,* 4 vols (1957); T.G. Steffan (ed.), *Lord Byron's Cain* (1968); and Thomas L. Ashton's *Byron's Hebrew Melodies*. The literary sources and antecedents of *Don Juan* are suggested by Elizabeth French Boyd in *Byron's Don Juan: a Critical Study* (1945), while Byron's indebtedness to Italian literature has been studied in Peter Vassallo, *Byron: the Italian Literary Influence* (1984). The literary significance of the poet's friendship with Percy Shelley is explored in Charles E. Robinson's *Shelley and Byron: the Snake and the Eagle* (1976).

The contemporary reviews of Byron's poetry have all been collected and reprinted in Donald Reiman (ed.), *The Romantics Reviewed,* 9 vols (1972). There is also a selection of responses to Byron's work from the whole of the nineteenth century in Andrew Rutherford, *Byron: the Critical Heritage* (1970). Byron's influence on European literature is traced in Charles E. Robinson (ed.), *Lord Byron and His Contemporaries*

(1982), and Paul G. Trueblood, *Byron's Political and Cultural Influence in Nineteenth-Century Europe* (1981).

Brief introductory books on Byron's poetry include Angus Calder's *Byron* (1987), Anne Barton's *Byron: Don Juan* (1992), and Bernard Beatty's *Byron: Don Juan and Other Poems, a Critical Study* (1987). More comprehensive accounts are M.J. Joseph's *Byron the Poet* (1964), Robert Gleckner, *Byron and the Ruins of Paradise* (1967), and Jerome J. McGann, *Fiery Dust: Byron's Poetic Development* (1968). Useful collections of essays include Bernard Beatty and Vincent Newey (eds), *Byron and the Limits of Fiction* (1988); Andrew Rutherford (eds), *Byron: Augustan and Romantic* (1990), and Jane Stabler (ed.), *Byron* (1998). There are also two recent issues of *Studies in Romanticism* devoted entirely to Byron: 27 (Winter 1988) and 31 (Fall 1992). For information on specific critical studies on Byron's poetry, consult Oscar José Santucho's and Clement Tyson Goode's *George Gordon, Lord Byron: a Comprehensive Bibliography of Secondary Materials in English 1807–1974, with a Critical Review of Research* (revised, 1997); and for an up-to-date account of recent scholarship, see Andrew Nicholson in Chapter 5 of Michael O'Neill (ed.), *Literature of the Romantic Period: a Bibliographical Guide* (1998).

Caroline Franklin, University of Wales, Swansea

Acknowledgments

My greatest debt is to scholars and biographers of Byron and historians of print culture in the Romantic period, on whose shoulders I have stood in writing this book. Particular thanks are also due to Peter Garside, Diego Saglia, John Russell Stephens and Michael Franklin, who read and commented on portions of the manuscript. I am grateful to Martin Procházka, editor of *Byron: East and West* (Prague: Charles University Press, 1999), for permission to include as parts of Chapters 1 and 2 material published as 'An English bard goes East: Authorship and authority in Byron's early poetry'. The library staff at Swansea and at the British Library have helped with their friendly interest as well as efficiency. The encouragement and professionalism of my series editor Richard Dutton and Charmian Hearne at Macmillan have facilitated the publication process, as has the hard work of all those who saw the book through the press.

List of Abbreviations

CPW	*Lord Byron: The Complete Poetical Works*, ed. Jerome J. McGann, 7 vols (Oxford, 1980–93). All quotations from Byron's poetry are taken from this edition.
L&J	*Byron's Letters and Journals*, ed. Leslie A. Marchand, 12 vols (Cambridge, Mass., 1973–94).
HVSV	*His Very Self and Voice: Collected Conversations of Lord Byron*, ed. Ernest J. Lovell, Jr (New York, 1954).
Life	Leslie A. Marchand, *Byron: A Biography*, 3 vols (New York, 1957).
Medwin	*Medwin's Conversations of Lord Byron*, ed. Ernest J. Lovell, Jr (Princeton, 1969).
Smiles	Samuel Smiles, *Memoir and correspondence of the late John Murray with an account of the origin and progress of the house, 1768–1843* (London, 1891).

Chronology

1788	Jan. 22 – George Gordon Byron born at 16 Holles Street, Cavendish Square, London; son of Captain 'Mad Jack' Byron and Catherine (née Gordon).
1789	Mother took lodgings in Aberdeen.
1791	Aug. 2 – Death` of father in France.
	Mother took apartment at 64 Broad Street, Aberdeen.
1794–8	Attended Aberdeen Grammar School.
1798	21 May – On death of the 5th Lord Byron ('the wicked Lord') George Gordon Byron became 6th Baron Byron of Rochdale.
	Aug. – Accompanied mother to ancestral mansion, Newstead Abbey, Notts.
1799	Sept. – Entered Dr Glennie's School, Dulwich.
1800	Summer at Newstead and at Nottingham. Fell in love with first cousin, Margaret Parker.
1801	April – Entered Harrow.
1802	Christmas holiday at Bath.
1803	July – Mother rented Burgage Manor, Southwell.
	Sept. – Fell in love with Mary Chaworth of Annesley Hall.
1804	Mar. – Friendship with the Pigots.
1805	2 Aug. – Played in cricket match against Eton.
	24 Oct. – Commenced studies at Trinity College, Cambridge.
1806	Sept. – Involved in Southwell amateur theatricals.
	Nov. – *Fugitive Pieces* privately printed.
1807	Jan. – *Poems on Various Occasions* privately printed.
	June – *Hours of Idleness* published. Became friends with J.C. Hobhouse and C. S. Matthews, and later with S.B. Davies and F. Hodgson.
	July – Wrote review of Wordsworth's *Poems*.
	Dec. – Left Cambridge.
1808	Jan. – Henry Brougham's review of *Hours of Idleness* published in *Edinburgh Review*.
	Mar. – *Poems Original and Translated* published.
	Oct.–Nov. – Continued satire [to be *EBSR*] had begun a year previously.
1809	Mar. – *English Bards and Scotch Reviewers* published.
	2 July – Departed with Hobhouse on Lisbon packet for Grand Tour. Visited Portugal, Spain, Gibraltar, Sicily, Malta, Albania, Greece, Turkey, Asia Minor. Wrote *Childe Harold*, *Hints from Horace* and *The Curse of Minerva*.
1810	17 July – Hobhouse returned to England.

Contextual Dates

<table>
<tr><td>1788</td><td>First attack of George III's insanity; impeachment of Warren Hastings. Published: Immanuel Kant, Critique of Practical Reason.</td></tr>
<tr><td>1789</td><td>Storming of the Bastille (14 July); Declaration of the Rights of Man. Published: William Blake, The Book of Thel, Songs of Innocence.</td></tr>
<tr><td>1790</td><td>Published: Edmund Burke, Reflections on the Revolution in France.</td></tr>
<tr><td>1791</td><td>Published: Thomas Paine, The Rights of Man, part I.</td></tr>
<tr><td>1792</td><td>September massacres; abolition of French monarchy; British defeat of Tipu Sultan in Mysore, India. Published: Mary Wollstonecraft, Vindication of the Rights of Woman; T. Paine, Rights of Man, part II (banned).</td></tr>
<tr><td>1793</td><td>Execution of French King and Queen and commencement of 'the Terror'; war with France. Published: William Godwin, An Enquiry Concerning Political Justice.</td></tr>
<tr><td>1794</td><td>Habeas Corpus suspended; treason trials of 41 radicals. Published: W. Blake, Songs of Innocence and Experience.</td></tr>
<tr><td>1798</td><td>France conquered Switzerland, Northern Italy and Malta; rebellion in Ireland. Published: Samuel Taylor Coleridge and William Wordsworth's Lyrical Ballads; Jeremy Bentham, Political Economy.</td></tr>
<tr><td>1799</td><td>Napoleon became consul; Anti-Combination Laws.</td></tr>
<tr><td>1800</td><td>First iron-frame printing press built; French conquered Italy.</td></tr>
<tr><td>1801</td><td>Act of Union; George III refused to grant Emancipation to Roman Catholics.</td></tr>
<tr><td>1802</td><td>Edinburgh Review and William Cobbett's Political Register founded.</td></tr>
<tr><td>1804</td><td>Napoleon crowned Emperor; Britain declared war on Spain.</td></tr>
<tr><td>1805</td><td>Battle of Trafalgar; death of Nelson. Published: Walter Scott, The Lay of the Last Minstrel; Robert Southey, Madoc; Henry Cary (tr.), Dante's Inferno.</td></tr>
<tr><td>1806</td><td>Deaths of William Pitt and Charles James Fox; Coalition ministry of 'All the Talents'. Published: Thomas Moore's Epistles, Odes and Other Poems, Mary Robinson, The Poems (3 vols); Elizabeth Inchbald, The British Theatre, 25 vols.(–1809).</td></tr>
<tr><td>1807</td><td>Abolition of slave trade in British dominions. Published: George Crabbe's Poems; T. Moore's Irish Melodies; Sydney Owenson Morgan, Lays of an Irish Harp; W. Wordsworth, Poems in Two Volumes.</td></tr>
<tr><td>1808</td><td>British campaign in Portugal but Convention of Cintra allowed French withdrawal. Leigh Hunt founded Examiner (–1881). Published: Felicia Hemans, Poems; Walter Scott, Marmion; J.W. von Goethe's Faust, part 1.</td></tr>
<tr><td>1809</td><td>Quarterly Review founded. Published: W. Blake, A Descriptive Catalogue; W. Wordsworth, Tract on the Convention of Cintra.</td></tr>
<tr><td>1810</td><td>French take Holland; London riots in support of parliamentary reform. Published: W. Scott, The Lady of the Lake; Robert Southey, The Curse of Kehama; George Crabbe, The Borough; Percy Bysshe Shelley, Original Poetry by Victor and Cazire, Zastrozzi, St Irvine, Posthumous Fragments of Margaret Nicholson.</td></tr>
</table>

1811	14 July – B. arrived in England.
	1 Aug. – B's mother died.
	3 Aug. – B's friend Charles Skinner Matthews drowned.
1812	Reviewed Spencer's *Poems*.
	27 Feb. – Maiden speech in House of Lords against the death penalty for Luddites.
	10 March – *Childe Harold's Pilgrimage* I and II published.
	21 April – Second speech in House of Lords on Roman Catholic civil rights.
	April – Liaison with Lady Caroline Lamb began.
	Oct. – Liaison with Lady Oxford began.
1813	Feb. – Reviewed William Henry Ireland's *Neglected Genius*.
	Mar. – *The Waltz* privately printed.
	May – Visited Leigh Hunt in gaol.
	1 June – Third and last speech in House of Lords in support of Major Cartwright.
	5 June – *The Giaour* published.
	July – Liaison with Augusta Leigh, his half-sister, began.
	Oct. – Romance with Lady Frances Webster began.
	2 Dec. – *The Bride of Abydos* published.
1814	1 Feb. – *The Corsair* published.
	6 Aug. – *Lara* published anonymously with Samuel Rogers's *Jacqueline*.
	9 Sept. – Proposed to Annabella Milbanke.
1815	2 Jan. – Married Annabella at Seaham, near Durham.
	April – *A Selection of Hebrew Melodies* published with musical score by John Braham and Isaac Nathan.
	May – *Hebrew Melodies* published by Murray.
	May – Became a member of the Drury Lane Sub-Committee.
	Nov. – Bailiffs entered B's house, no. 13 Piccadilly Terrace.
	10 Dec. – B's daughter, Augusta Ada born.
1816	15 Jan.– Annabella left B., taking Ada. They never met again.
	13 Feb. – *The Siege of Corinth* and *Parisina* published.
	March–April – Met Claire Clairmont.
	April – Second number of *A Selection of Hebrew Melodies* published.
	5–6 April – B's library auctioned.
	21 April – Signed deed of separation.
	25 April – B. sailed for the continent. Visited Belgium, Germany and Switzerland.
	1–6 May – Began *Childe Harold* III.
	9 May – Lady Caroline Lamb's novel *Glenarvon* published.
	27 May – Met P.B. Shelley for first time at Sécheron.
	14–18 June – The ghost story competition at the Villa Diodati.
	22 June – Toured Lake Geneva with P.B. Shelley.
	July–Aug. – Frequently attended the salon of Germaine de Staël at Coppet
	14 Aug. – M.G. Lewis arrived.
	26 Aug. – Hobhouse and Scrope Davies arrived.
	28 Aug. – The Shelley party departed for England.
	Aug.–Sept. – Tour to Chamouni, Mont Blanc and later the Bernese Oberland.

1811   Prince of Wales made Regent; Hampden clubs founded to campaign
        for democracy; insurrection in Columbia and Venezuela against Spanish
        rule. Published: L. Hunt, *The Feast of the Poets*; P.B. Shelley, *The Necessity
        of Atheism*.

1812   Anti-Luddite act passed and twelve regiments needed to quell unrest
        and food riots; Napoleon's retreat from Moscow; P.M. assassinated.
        Published: Anna Barbauld's *1811*; H. Cary (tr.) Dante's *Purgatory,
        Paradise*; George Crabbe's *Tales in Verse*; F. Hemans, *Domestic Affections
        and other Poems*; P.B. Shelley, *An Address to the Irish People* and *Proposals
        for an Association*.

1813   Wellington victor of Peninsular War; French expelled from Italy,
        Holland and Switzerland. Leigh Hunt gaoled for libel; R. Southey
        appointed Poet Laureate; Wordsworth accepted sinecure as Distributor
        of Stamps. Published: S.T. Coleridge, *Remorse*; James Hogg, *The Queen's
        Wake*; Mary Russell Mitford, *Narrative Poems on the Female Character*; T.
        Moore, *Intercepted Letters; or, The Twopenny Postbag*; W. Scott, *The Bridal
        of Triermain, Rokeby*; P.B. Shelley, *Queen Mab*.

1814   Abdication of Napoleon and exile to Elba; Peace with United States;
        Congress of Vienna; George Stephenson invented first locomotive;
        development of steam warship and steam printing-machine; Edmund
        Kean's debut. Published: George Daniel, *The Modern Dunciad*; L. Hunt,
        The Feast of the Poets; W. Wordsworth, *The Excursion*.

1815   Corn Laws; Napoleon escaped to France (March); Battle of Waterloo
        (18 June); Napoleon exiled to St. Helena; 'Holy Alliance' instituted.
        Published: W. Wordsworth, *Poems, The White Doe of Rylstone*; J. Hogg,
        The Pilgrims of the Sun; L. Hunt, *The Descent of Liberty, a Mask*; H.H.
        Milman, *Fazio*; W. Scott, *The Lord of the Isles*.

1816   Postwar depression; Spa Fields riot; exhibition of Elgin Marbles.
        Published: S.T. Coleridge, *Christabel and other Poems*; J. Hogg, *The Poetic
        Mirror, Mador of the Moor*; L. Hunt, *The Story of Rimini*; C. Maturin,
        Bertram; T. Moore, *Sacred Songs*, I; P.B. Shelley, *Alastor and Other Poems*,
        R. Southey, *The Poet's Pilgrimage to Waterloo, The Lay of the Laureate*; J.
        Wilson, *The City of the Plague*; W. Wordsworth, 'Thanksgiving Ode'; F.
        Hemans, *The Restoration of the Works of Art to Italy*; Margaret Holford,
        Margaret of Anjou; J. Taylor, *Essays in Rhyme, on Morals and Manners*; W.
        Cobbett, *Political Register* and 'Twopenny Trash' such as 'Address to the
        Journeymen and Labourers'.

5 Oct. – Departed with Hobhouse for Italy.

12 Oct. – Arrived in Milan.

10 Nov. – Arrived in Venice.

18 Nov. – *Childe Harold* III published.

Nov. – Affair with Marianna Segati.

Studied Armenian at monastery on Island of San Lazzaro.

5 Dec. – *The Prisoner of Chillon and Other Poems* published.

Hobhouse left for tour of Italy.

1817 12 Jan. – Birth of Allegra, B's illegitimate daughter by Claire Clairmont.

17 April – Set off for Rome.

29 April – Met Hobhouse and toured the antiquities together.

20 May – Departed for Venice.

16 June – *Manfred* published.

August – Met Margarita Cogni, a baker's wife.

Oct. – Wrote *Beppo*.

Sept. – Visit of Douglas Kinnaird, Lord Kinnaird, and W.S. Rose, and gift of Frere's *Whistlecraft*.

10 Dec. – Received news that Newstead Abbey sold to Thomas Wildman for £94,500.

1818 8 Jan. – Hobhouse returned to England.

28 Feb. – *Beppo* published.

28 Apr. – *Childe Harold* IV published.

3 July – Began *Don Juan*.

23 Aug. – Rode with P.B. Shelley on the Lido (incident in 'Julian and Maddalo').

24–29 – Visited by both the Shelleys.

1819 Feb. – Objections to *Don Juan* canto I in London.

2–3 April – Met Countess Teresa Guiccioli.

June – Visited Ravenna

18 June – Began *Prophecy of Dante*.

28 June – *Mazeppa* and *Ode on Venice* published.

15 July – *Don Juan* I and II published anonymously.

9 Aug. – Followed Guicciolis to Bologna.

Sept. – Returned to Venice with Teresa.

Oct. – Visit of Moore and gave him memoirs of life up to 1816.

24 Dec. – Followed Teresa to Ravenna and settled there.

1820 21 Feb. – Finished translation of Pulci's *Morgante Maggiore*.

March – Finished *Prophecy of Dante*. Wrote 'My Boy Hobbie O' on Hobhouse's spell in Newgate.

April – Became involved in planned revolt against the Austrians.

May – Crisis of the Guiccioli marriage.

July – Finished *Marino Faliero*. Teresa separated from her husband.

Aug. – Became initiated into secret revolutionary society of the Carbonari.

16 Oct. – Began *Don Juan* canto V.

9 Dec. – Commandant shot dead outside B's house.

1817 Demonstrations and petitions for parliamentary reform; Habeas Corpus suspended; renewal of parts of 1795 Treason Acts to proscribe 'seditious meetings'; death penalty for words inciting disaffection in armed forces; William Cobbett escaped to America; trial of William Hone; Pentridge rebellion; death of Princess Charlotte. Published: S.T. Coleridge, *Biographia Literaria, Sybilline Leaves, Zapolya;* John Hookham Frere, *Whistlecraft,* i–ii; F. Hemans, *Modern Greece;* John Keats, *Poems;* T. Moore, *Lalla Rookh;* W. Scott, *Harold the Dauntless;* P.B. Shelley, *A Proposal for Putting Reform to the Vote, Laon and Cythna* (withdrawn), R. Southey, *Wat Tyler* (piracy); John Wolcot ('Peter Pindar'), *Epistle to the Emperor of China;* William Hone's *Reformists' Register* and *Black Dwarf* founded; *Sherwin's Political Register* founded; *Blackwood's Edinburgh Magazine* founded.

1818 Trial and incarceration of Richard Carlile; strikes of spinners and weavers; Chile declared independence. Published: Bernard Barton, *Poems by an Amateur;* S.T. Coleridge, *The Friend* (3 vols); W. Hazlitt, *Lectures on the English Poets, A View of the English Stage;* F. Hemans, *Translations from Camoens;* L. Hunt, *Foliage;* John Keats, *Endymion;* H.H. Milman, *Samor, Lord of the Bright City;* T. Moore, *National Airs* I (–1827), *The Fudge Family in Paris;* T.L. Peacock, *Rhododaphne, or The Thessalian Spell;* P.B. Shelley, *The Revolt of Islam;* William Sotheby, *Farewell to Italy.*

1819 Peterloo Massacre; Six Acts to proscribe radical activity, including Blasphemous and Seditious Libel Act, fourpenny stamp tax imposed on newspapers; British acquisition of Singapore. Published: G. Crabbe, *Tales of the Hall;* F. Hemans, *Tales and Historic Scenes, Wallace's Invocation to Bruce;* L. Hunt, *Hero and Leander, and Bacchus and Ariadne, Poetical Works;* P.B. Shelley, 'Rosalind and Helen'; W. Wordsworth, *Peter Bell, the Waggoner.*

1820 Death of George III and accession of George IV; Cato Street conspiracy to assassinate government ministers; trial of Queen Caroline; revolutions in Spain, Portugal, Naples, Piedmont.
Published: Elizabeth Barrett, *The Battle of Marathon;* B. Barton, *Poems;* T. Bowdler, *The Family Shakespeare;* John Clare, *Poems Descriptive of Rural Life and Scenery;* George Croly, *The Angel of the World;* F. Hemans, *The Sceptic, Stanzas to the Memory of the late King;* J. Keats, *Lamia, Isabella, The Eve of St.Agnes, and other poems;* John Sheridan Knowles, *Virginius, a Tragedy;* Walter Savage Landor, *Idyllia Heroica Decem;* E.G.E. Lytton, *Ismael;* H.H. Milman, *The Fall of Jerusalem;* T.L. Peacock, 'The Four Ages of Poetry'; R.W. Proctor ('Barry Cornwall'), *A Sicilian Story, Marcian Colonna and other poems;* J.H. Reynolds, *The Fancy;* W. Scott, *Miscellaneous Poems;* P.B. Shelley, *The Cenci, Prometheus Unbound, Swellfoot the Tyrant;* W. Wordsworth, *The River Duddon, Memorials of a Tour on the Continent. London Magazine* founded.

1821 4 Jan. – Began 'Ravenna Journal'.
Jan. – Began *Sardanapalus*
10 Feb. – Finished first letter on Bowles–Pope controversy.
24 Feb. – Plan of Carbonari uprising failed and leaders betrayed.
25 Mar. – Wrote second letter on Bowles.
31 Mar. – Publication of 'Letter to John Murray Esq.' on Bowles controversy.
21 Apr. – *Marino Faliero* and *Prophecy of Dante* published together.
25 Apr. – *Marino Faliero* staged at Drury Lane.
27 May – Finished *Sardanapalus*.
12 June – Began *The Two Foscari*.
July – Promised Teresa he would discontinue *Don Juan*.
10 July – First Pietro Gamba then his father banished from the Romagna.
16 July. – Began *Cain*.
25 July – Teresa joined her father and brother in Florence.
6 Aug. – Shelley visited B. in Ravenna.
Aug. – Wrote *The Blues*.
Sept. – Wrote *The Vision of Judgment*.
9 Oct. – Began *Heaven and Earth*.
15 Oct. – Began 'Detached Thoughts'.
29 Oct. – Departed Ravenna for Pisa.
1 Nov. – Took up residence at Casa Lanfranchi, Pisa.
19 Dec. – Publication of *Sardanapalus, The Two Foscari* and *Cain*.

1822 28 Jan. – Death of Lady Noel, Byron's mother-in-law. Byron took on name of Noel Byron in sharing the estate.
Jan. – Resumption of *Don Juan* (canto VI).
Feb. – Sent £250 to Hunt for his voyage to Italy.
20 Apr. – Death of Allegra.
1 (?) Jul. – Leigh Hunt and his family arrived at Leghorn.
3 July – Leigh Hunt moved into Casa Lanfranchi.
July – Resumed composition of *Don Juan*.
8 July – P.B. Shelley and Edward Williams drowned in Bay of Spezia.
16 Aug. – Cremation of Shelley at Viareggio.
15 Sept. – Short visit of Hobhouse.
15 Oct. – Publication of first no. of *The Liberal*.
23 Nov. – Publication of *Werner* by Murray.
14 Dec. – Sent *Don Juan* canto XII to Kinnaird, i.e. seven cantos now unpublished.

1821 Death of Napoleon; death of Queen Caroline; Greek War of Independence began; suppression of Neapolitan uprising; Simon Bolivar victorious in Venzuelan war of liberation against Spain: Peru, Guatemala, Panama, Santo Domingo declared independence from Spain.
Published: J. Baillie, *Metrical Legends;* J. Clare, *The Village Minstrel;* F. Hemans, *Dartmoor;* L.E.L. (Laetitia Landon), *The Fate of* Adelaide; B.W. Proctor ('Barry Cornwall'), *Mirandola, a Tragedy;* J.H. Reynolds, *The Garden of Florence;* P.B. Shelley, *Epipsychidion, Adonais;* R. Southey, *A Vision of Judgment.*

1822 Suicide of Castlereagh; Liberal Tories Peel and Canning joined Liverpool ministry, Canning became foreign secretary; Brazil achieved independence from Portugal; Simon Bolivar won Ecuador's freedom from Spain; Greeks proclaimed independence.
Published: T.L. Beddoes, *The Bride's Tragedy;* Robert Bloomfield, *May Day with the Muses;* Caroline Bowles, *The Widow's Tale;* G. Crabbe, *The Poetical Works;* F. Hemans, *Welsh Melodies;* J. Hogg, *Poetical Works;* B.W. Proctor, *The Poetical Works;* S. Rogers, *Italy;* W. Scott, *Halidon Hill;* P.B. Shelley, *Hellas, A Lyrical Drama;* W. Wordsworth, *Ecclesiatical Sketches.*

1823   1 Jan. – No.2 *The Liberal* published.
10 Jan. – Finished *The Age of Bronze*.
Feb. – Finished *The Island*.
April–June – Friendship with the Blessingtons.
5 April – Visited by Edward Blaquiere.
6 May – Finished *Don Juan* canto XVI.
May – Elected member of London Greek Committee.
June – Quarrelled with Leigh Hunt and Mary Shelley.
24 July – Sailed for Greece on brig *Hercules,* with Pietro Gamba and Edward Trelawny.
3 Aug. – Landed at Argostoli, Cephalonia.
13 Nov. – Signed agreement for loan on £4000 to the Greek government.
22 Nov. – Arrival of Colonel Leicester Stanhope, agent for London Greek Committee.
29 Dec. – Embarked for Missolonghi.

1824   1 Jan. – Came ashore to tumultuous reception.
Jan. – Took 500 Suliotes into his service.
14 Jan. – Stanhope launched Greek newspaper, *Hellenica Chronica.*
22 Jan. – Wrote 'On This day I Complete My Thirty-Sixth Year'.
25 Jan. – Commissioned by Mavrocordatos to lead expedition against Lepanto.
5 Feb. – Arrival of William Parry, the fire-master.
15 Feb. – Suliotes disbanded. B. suffered severe convulsive fit.
21 Feb. – Departure of Stanhope for Athens.
19 April – Easter Monday. B. died of fever exacerbated by bleeding.

1823   Peel began reform of Penal Code; Huskisson initiated reform at Board of Trade; Mechanics' Institute founded; war between France and Spain. Published: F. Hemans, *The Siege of Valencia, The Vespers of Palermo, The Last Constantine*; L. Hunt, *Ultra-Crepidarius;* Charles Lloyd, *Poems;* Bulwer Lytton, *Delmour and other Poems;* T. Moore, *The Loves of the Angels, Fables of the Holy Alliance;* B.W. Proctor, *The Flood of Thessaly, The Girl of Provence;* P.B. Shelley, *Poetical Pieces.*

1824   Combinations Act repealed; unions permitted; National Gallery opened. Published: B. Barton, *Poetic Vigils;* R. Bloomfield, *The Remains;* Thomas Campbell, *Theodric and other poems, Miscellaneous Poems;* Josiah Conder, *The Star in the East;* L.E. Landon, *The Improvisatrice;* P.B. Shelley, *Posthumous Poems.*

Prelude: Byron's Gothic Inheritance

Byron is probably best known in literature as the creator of the 'Byronic hero'. This sinful, aristocratic character is surely first cousin to the Gothic villain, but viewed more sympathetically, often on account of his devotion to a woman or defiance of patriarchal tyranny, but chiefly because his point of view is so fully dramatized. From the time of his creation of Childe Harold, to the Giaour, Selim, Conrad, Lara, Manfred, Cain and others, Byron himself became identified in the public mind with these fallen heroes. In fact he often encouraged such speculation: for example, by specifically denying that he was romantically involved with the woman he had rescued at gunpoint from being ceremoniously drowned in the sea at Piraeus for adultery, an incident on which *The Giaour* was based. The very refutation, of course, sparked rumours that the hero of the poem *was* based on the poet himself.

Byron's heritage predisposed him to imagining himself into the part of the villain in the Gothic literature he read voraciously when a boy. This was hardly surprising, as Byron's family history seemed to predestine him to become a dissolute aristocrat himself, and to test the boundaries of what conduct was deemed destructive of the fabric of society. When Byron inherited his title and the ancestral mansion of Newstead Abbey in Nottinghamshire at the age of ten, he found himself likely to be the last incumbent, on whom it would inevitably fall to sell the house and lands which were already ravaged by the self-indulgence of his forbears.

Both his maternal ancestors, the Gordons of Gight, and his paternal line, the Byrons of Lancashire and Nottinghamshire, were prime examples of aristocratic families who were coming to the end of their power and influence, and could look back on a long history of lawlessness, self-indulgence and dissolution. Byron's mother, Catherine Gordon, had been the thirteenth of her line: an heiress who inherited the by-now decaying castle of Gight and its lands, near Aberdeen, which her family had won from banditry, brutal violence and feuds through the ages. Leslie Marchand has commented that this family had been 'among the most notorious of the Scottish lairds for their defiance of law and order' (*Life*, p. 16). Byron received a different version of family history, however from: '[m]y Mother (who was as haughty as Lucifer with her descent from the Stuarts, and her right line, from the *old Gordons, not* the *Seyton Gordons*, as she disdainfully termed the Ducal branch,) ... ' (*Life*, p. 34).

At the age of twenty, this plain and gauche Scottish heiress, Catherine Gordon, had been swept off her feet at Bath by a handsome Captain Byron whom she married a few months later on 13 May, 1785. By 1786 the couple was fleeing Scotland, for 'Mad Jack' managed to dispose of both her castle and her fortune of £23,000 in less than two years, and had also been disinherited by his father. Captain Byron had already starred in the scandal-sheets, for, at the age of twenty-two he had seduced and eloped with the Marchioness of Carmarthen, who subsequently married him when her husband divorced her and who brought with her an income of £4000 a year. Unfortunately this income disappeared when she died giving birth to a daughter, Augusta, in 1784. Hence the appearance of 'Mad Jack' at the marriage-market of Bath a year later.

The future poet was born in London on 22 January 1788, and his impoverished mother soon returned to Aberdeen with him, to live as frugally as possible on the meagre income that was left to her (£150 p.a.). She took a flat in Broad Street and henceforth had to learn to stomach her new role as a mere poor relation. Captain Byron only visited occasionally to scrounge from Catherine before first setting up a separate establishment from his wife then decamping altogether to live with his sister in France. There was a long-standing tradition amongst the Byrons of marrying their cousins, and his sister, Fanny, had married their cousin, Charles Leigh. Fanny's and Charles's son George would in the fullness of time marry *his* cousin too: Jack's daughter, Augusta. In stanzas on Donna Julia's family in *Don Juan*, such aristocratic inbreeding, it is suggested, 'spoils the breed' (I, 57). Yet, in 1813, when he met Augusta, having seen little of her during his childhood, the poet would fall in love and have a passionate affair with his own half-sister. Augusta then gave birth to a daughter, Medora, who grew up believing the poet was her father. The poet may have felt drawn by the habit of the Byron family to love his own female relations, and even to commit incest: that heinous sin most favoured by Gothic villains in literature. For, as he may well have suspected, his father seems to have been in love with his own full sister, with whom he lived in Valenciennes after she had left her husband. 'Mad Jack' certainly wrote Fanny passionate letters, though that incorrigible libertine also boasted of multitudes of mistresses: 'I believe I have had one third of Valenciennes...' (*Life*, p. 30).[1]

In 1791, when the news reached Aberdeen that the Captain had died of consumption at the age of thirty-four, poor Catherine's screams of grief were heard in the street outside. Nevertheless whenever she lost her temper with her spoilt son, she would always accuse him of following in the path of his wicked father and his forbears. The boy had been born with a clubfoot, and this, too, was treated as a stigma.

The Byrons had long been notorious for their extravagance, wild ways and eccentricity. Claiming Norman descent from the de Buruns, the family became prominent in the North of England, and their support for the Tudors made their fortune while their loyalty to the Stuarts lost it again. Sir John Byron had bought Newstead Abbey on the Dissolution of the Monasteries and his son was created Baron Byron of Rochdale in 1643 for his loyalty as a general of Charles I. They were a family renowned for their munificence, but it was in the eighteenth century that the Byrons became particularly notorious as examples of aristocratic profligacy and irresponsibility.

The four main culprits were the grandfather, great-uncle and father of Byron, along with the poet himself. Byron's grandfather was the least reprehensible of the four. Though a spendthrift and philanderer, John Byron was not such a hardened rake as his eldest son 'Mad Jack' and grandson the poet would become, though a story of his being found in bed with the chambermaid was published as a scandal-sheet in 1773. He followed the family habit of marrying a cousin: Sophia Trevanion, a friend of Hester Thrale. He became a sailor, and, though a most competent seaman, he was renowned for his bad luck with storms and so became nicknamed 'Foulweather Jack'. When only a sixteen-year-old midshipman on the *Wager*, he had been shipwrecked off the coast of Chile. He stayed loyal to the Captain after most of the crew deserted them, and succeeded in surviving against all the odds, eventually making his way home. Many years later he wrote a harrowing account of these adventures, *A Narrative of the Honourable John Byron...* (1768), on which his grandson would draw for graphic details of the shipwreck in *Don Juan*, Canto II:

> What could they do? and hunger's rage grew wild:
> So Juan's spaniel, spite of his entreating,
> Was kill'd, and portion'd out for present eating.
>
> (II, 70)

After participating in a disastrous episode of the Seven Years' War, John Byron had some naval successes, and was then given command of a voyage of discovery which took him around the world. Unfortunately, unlike Cook who was to repeat the exercise more fruitfully, Byron miraculously succeeded in missing almost all of the islands with which the Pacific ocean is dotted, though he solemnly recorded seeing giants near the Strait of Magellan. The Royal Society expressed its disappointment at his lack of scientific findings, though they recognized he had been beset by heavy seas as usual. By 1778 he had reached the rank of Vice-Admiral, but in action off the West Indies against the French, who were supporting the revolt of the American colonies, 'Foulweather Jack' was prevented by storms from achieving the victory everyone in Britain expected. His naval career was over.

Meanwhile, John's elder brother William, who had succeeded to the title at the age of fourteen, had graduated from mere eccentricity to murder in his efforts to bring notoriety to the family name. Byron inherited the title from this the fifth Lord Byron, his great-uncle William, known as the 'Wicked Lord'. A gambler and rake who once attempted to abduct the actress Miss Bellamy, William married Elizabeth Shaw, an heiress with £70,000, yet managed to dispose both of this and his own entire heritage. He built a miniature castle in the grounds of Newstead for parties, as well as two little forts from which he launched small warships and staged mock naval battles on the lake. In 1765, after dining well in a Pall-Mall club, he got into a tiff with his cousin and neighbour, William Chaworth, about who kept more game on his manor. They drew their swords in an empty, dark room, and whereas Chaworth's weapon merely got entangled in clothing, Byron ran his adversary right through when he came close to investigate. Chaworth died the next day and Byron was sent to the Tower.

As a peer of the realm Lord Byron was tried for murder in Westminster Hall by 119 lords, and before the royal dukes, the archbishops of York and Canterbury and the Lord Chancellor. Tickets were sold for six guineas each. He was found guilty of manslaughter but set free. After this disgrace, William became a recluse, especially after his wife left him, and his son eloped with his cousin, Juliana, the daughter of the Admiral, instead of marrying an heiress. He had the same bottle of claret served night after night, untouched, and ordered pistols to be laid out alongside the cutlery. He spent his time training crickets to crawl over his body. The unexpected deaths of first his son in 1776 and then his grandson, in 1794 left the way clear for the obscure little boy playing in the streets of Aberdeen to inherit the title and ancestral mansion.

But before that was to happen, the embittered old lord laid waste the estate. He felled the forest of oaks, had thousands of deer killed, leased out his coal mines in Rochdale for a nominal sum, and sold off all the family pictures and furniture; seemingly for spite as much as for money. Byron's publisher, John Murray, later described Newstead Abbey thus:

> Not a tree is left standing, and the wood thus shamefully cut down was sold in one day for £60,000. The hall of entrance has about eighteen large niches, which had been filled with statues, and the side walls covered with family portraits and armour. All these have been mercilessly torn down, as well as the magnificent fireplace, and sold. All the beautiful paintings which filled the galleries – valued at that day at £80,000 – have disappeared, and the whole place is crumbling into dust. No sum short of £100,000 would make the place habitable. ... I am far more surprised that Lord Byron should ever have lived at Newstead, than that he should be inclined to part with it; for, as there is no possibility of his being able, by any reasonable amount of expense, to reinstate it, the place can present nothing but a perpetual memorial of the wickedness of his ancestors.
>
> (*Smiles*, i. 253–4)

When the ten-year-old lord and his mother visited Newstead Abbey for the first time in 1798, they found much of the building roofless, and cattle stabled in the monastic hall, formerly the grand drawing-room. Nevertheless, they both fell in love with the romantic ruin and little George planted an oak in the grounds. The Abbey would inspire his poetry in the future:

> The mansion's self was vast and venerable,
> With more of the monastic than has been
> Elsewhere preserved: the cloisters still were stable,
> The cells too and refectory, I ween:
> An exquisite small chapel had been able,
> Still unimpair'd, to decorate the scene;
> The rest had been reform'd, replac'd, or sunk,
> And spoke more of the baron than the monk.
>
> Huge halls, long galleries, spacious chambers, join'd
> By no quite lawful marriage of the Arts,
> Might shock a Connoisseur; but when combined,
> Form'd a whole which, irregular in parts,
> Yet left a grand impression on the mind ...
>
> (*Don Juan*, XIII, 66–7)

In *Don Juan*, the poet set a mock-Gothic ghost story in Norman Abbey, described above: a fictionalized version of Newstead. This was the result of a curious interplay between the literal and the literary. Like William Beckford and Horace Walpole, Byron was inspired as a writer by his own picturesque mansion. But unlike them he had not built it himself. The mansion he inherited, Newstead Abbey, had already played its own part in the history of Gothic fiction: fiction which had in turn conditioned his imagination. The father of the Gothic novel and antiquarian, Horace Walpole, had himself fallen in love with the ruin in 1760:

> The great East [actually the West] window of the church remains and connects with the house; the hall entire, the refectory entire, the cloister untouched with the ancient cistern of the convent and their arms on it, a private chapel quite perfect ... [2]

What was more, the mistress of suspense, Ann Radcliffe, had been staying in the Nottingham area when she was writing *The Romance of the Forest* (1791). She had been inspired by Newstead and the stories she heard about the 'Wicked Lord' in depicting the ruined abbey and its libertine proprietor which feature in one of her most popular Gothic novels. The local people told tales of the old lord practising Satanism in the miniature castle; that he had once thrown his wife into the lake; that he had shot his own coachman and put the corpse inside the coach with his wife and driven it off himself.

Byron probably did not know that Newstead had provided the model for Radcliffe's haunted abbey. So it is doubly ironic that he viewed his family heritage through a Gothic lens. His own protagonists would often be troubled by sins from the past, like Manfred in Horace Walpole's *Castle of Otranto* (1764) or Schedoni of Ann Radcliffe's *The Italian* (1797). Like the novelists James Hogg and the future Robert Louis Stevenson, the Scottish Calvinism of his upbringing in Aberdeen had also influenced his Gothic preoccupation with man's dual nature and inevitable descent into sin. His mother, Aberdonian tutors and nurse, Agnes Gray, had made sure that as a small boy he was thoroughly familiar with the Bible, especially the Old Testament, and with Presbyterian precepts like predestination. His sense of sin was then further developed when this pious nurse's sister, May Gray, physically and sexually abused him. He was particularly haunted, as a boy, by John Moore's *Zeluco* (1786) and William Beckford's *Vathek* (1786): both novels featuring heroes drawn deeper and deeper into evil by malign forces of fate.

Heredity seemed to endow Byron with great gifts: of rank, intelligence, beauty and talent. But, even as a boy, his education and his reading predisposed him to associate his heritage of aristocracy with nameless sins committed in the past. His ambivalence about his family, status, and identity, caused him great personal anguish but also inspired him as a writer to infuse the themes of Gothic fiction with a new existential angst.

1
The Noble Poet and 'the Trade': Juvenilia and Juvenalia

'Perhaps the chief cause of most of Lord Byron's errors is, that he is that anomaly in letters and in society, a Noble Poet.'
(Hazlitt, *The Spirit of the Age*, 1825)

It is a sort of privilege of poets to be egotists; but they should 'use it as not abusing it;' and particularly one who piques himself (though indeed at the ripe age of nineteen), of being 'an infant bard,' – ('The artless Helicon I boast is youth;') – should either not know, or should seem not to know, so much about his ancestry.
(Henry Brougham, *Edinburgh Review*, 11 January 1808)

William Hazlitt's denunciation of Byron as a pampered egotist in *The Spirit of the Age* (1825) is suddenly interrupted by a row of asterisks, followed by the dramatic statement: 'We had written thus far when news came of the death of Lord Byron, and put an end at once to a strain of somewhat peevish invective, which was intended to meet his eyes, not to insult his memory'. Hazlitt presumably thought that this facade of extempore writing, parading its supposed 'sincerity', would be an appropriately Byronic way of refusing to write a hagiography for the most popular poet of the age. The integrity of the critic's judgement was not to be swayed by the fact that Byron had been a fellow liberal, or that he was about to become an icon of revolutionary freedom, having given his fortune and his life for the Greek insurgents' uprising against the Ottoman empire.

It may seem perverse to begin a literary life of a poet with his death, but the point I want to make is that Hazlitt's obituary, written in 1824, reprises exactly the sneers of the critic Henry Brougham, in the famous *Edinburgh Review* article which greeted Byron's literary debut in 1808. To both these notable liberals a noble poet was a contradiction in terms.

Hazlitt explained away the popularity of the verse by suggesting that Byron's magnetic poetic personality was merely the projection of aristocratic individualism. While this may have temporarily seduced a middle-class audience, aspiring to gentility, Hazlitt predicted it would ultimately prove irrelevant to the democratic nation-state of the future.

It is a crucial factor that Byron's literary career began in 1807, when the Ministry of All the Talents collapsed and the Whig party split into factionalism. The Tories were back in government after this brief interlude as they had been and would be for the whole of Byron's lifetime and beyond. The lack of an effective political opposition gave huge impetus to the public sphere of print culture. Ever since the French Revolution the intelligentsia had been intoxicated by the realization that ideas could influence political events. John Murray's friend Isaac D'Israeli wrote in 1794 that 'within the present century a great *Revolution* was effected in the human mind. Philosophers ceased to be isolated. It is but of late that people have been taught to *read*, and still later, that they have learned to think'.[1] The government maintained its influence in the daily press, keeping the radicals at bay through the stamp and paper tax. But the Whigs dominated the weeklies and the provincial press, and over the opinion-forming quarterlies the Whig *Edinburgh Review* reigned supreme with a circulation of 10,000. As Walter Scott wrote to George Ellis, 'No genteel family can *pretend* to be without it because, independent of its politics, it gives the only valuable literary criticism which can be met with'.[2] It is no exaggeration to say that the *Edinburgh* took the first step in the process which would lead to the foundation of English Literature as an academic discipline. By the 1880s it would be studied in schools and universities. For Francis Jeffrey elevated the status of critics from hacks to professional reviewers by making them independent of Constable, the proprietor, and by paying them handsomely, not for bookseller's puffs, but for scholarly judgements in lengthy essays. Under the protection of anonymity, the best writers and thinkers of the age flocked to write for the journal. With no equivalent to the French Academy, the great quarterlies became the forum of the 'public sphere' in nineteenth-century Britain.

So, after the collapse of the Whigs, frustrated young radicals threw their energies into periodicals to influence public opinion. The Hunt brothers (Byron's publishers in the 1820s) founded the brilliant weekly, the *Examiner*, in January 1808, to offer a more radical approach than the *Edinburgh*. Leigh Hunt defined its object as 'to assist producing reform in parliament, Liberality of opinion in general (especially freedom from superstition) and a fusion of literary taste into all subjects whatsoever.

It began with being of no party, but Reform soon gave it one'. In the very same month, we can see the way the *Edinburgh Review* itself had moved to the left from the way the crusading lawyer and reformer, Henry Brougham, bothered to review the unremarkable first book of poetry by an unknown nineteen-year-old peer, whose arrogant preface gave him an irresistible opportunity to demonstrate his contempt for the aristocracy. Brougham, a friend of the Hunts, would go on to defend them in two cases of seditious libel. But in 1815 he would jump at another opportunity to cut Byron down to size by taking Lady Byron's part in the separation negotiations despite being retained by the poet. For Byron's rank and his pride in it made him a target, not a natural ally, of the radicals with whose politics he had much in common.

In the 1980s Malcolm Kelsall and Michael Foot did battle over Byron's politics: one defining his attitudes as those of an aristocratic Whig, the other vindicating the poet as a radical hero. Byron's contradictory pronouncements about the reformers provided plenty of fuel for debate. But rather than fixing the author as a static entity whose personality and views exist prior to his textualized opinions, here we will focus on the provisional, contingent nature of the author as he represents himself in his different texts: texts which themselves were brought into being by his interaction with the intensely combative literary public sphere of his time. Particularly when considering Byron's debut, it is more pertinent to ask what the reformers in the literary world thought of him than what he thought of the reformers. The fact that they were from the outset prejudiced against him as an aristocrat and reluctant to accept his liberalism as any more than an affectation made him an outsider. The story of his literary career shows how Byron adapted to this role: by creating in his Oriental tales a gallery of aristocratic heroes and maverick renegades who made common cause with the people against their rulers, and romanticizing the solitary exile and lone wanderer in *Childe Harold's Pilgrimage* and *Cain*.

As with other Romantic poets, a reactionary and static political climate had caused the liberal peer reluctantly to turn his energies inwards to literary introspection, instead of embracing activism. 'I do think the preference of *writers* to *agents*...the mighty stir made about scribbling and scribes by themselves and others – a sign of effeminacy, degeneracy, and weakness. Who would write, who had anything better to do?'[3] Yet his rank gave the egotism of Byron's poetry a social dimension, for though he portrayed the Byronic hero as a unique and towering individual, the ambivalent character also functions as a representative of his class, which was losing its power both politically and ideologically in the age of the French revolution.

Class and poetry

Byron himself made class a determining factor in his relationship with his readers, reviewers and publishers. The very title of *Hours of Idleness* (1807), his first poetry to be submitted 'to the public eye', suggests aristocratic disdain for Grub Street and the bourgeois work ethic. He abandoned his earlier preference for anonymity and allowed his name and title to emblazon the title page. In a toe-curlingly self-conscious preface, Byron also drew particular attention to his rank in the very act of repudiating special treatment:

> It is highly improbable, from my situation, and pursuits hereafter, that I should ever obtrude myself a second time on the Public; nor even, in the very doubtful event of present indulgence, shall I be tempted to commit a future trespass of the same nature. The opinion of Dr. Johnson on the Poems of a noble relation of mine, 'That when a man of rank appeared in the character of an author, his merit should be handsomely acknowledged', can have little weight with verbal, and still less with periodical censors, but were it otherwise, I should be loth to avail myself of the privilege, and would rather incur the bitterest censure of anonymous criticism, than triumph in honours granted solely to a title.[4]

This arrogant defensiveness sets the tone for Byron's contradictory pronouncements about authorship for much of his career. On the one hand he demands to be judged as a writer on the strength of his literary merits in the cut-throat competition of the marketplace. Yet he also reminds the contemporary reviewer that the great critic Dr. Johnson thought a nobleman should be congratulated for bothering to take an interest in literature at all. It is clear that Byron feels it is demeaning for a peer of the realm to have dealings with 'the Trade' of Regency publishing and to prostitute his talents before the *hoi polloi*, the newly burgeoning 'reading public'. The young Lord's insecurity was no doubt exacerbated by acute awareness of his unimpressive status within the stratified world of the Regency aristocracy. After a lower-middle-class upbringing with his widowed mother in Aberdeen, he had, at the age of ten, unexpectedly inherited the title from his great uncle, 'the wicked Lord', along with a ruinous, largely roofless, mansion and debt-ridden, ravaged estate. As a young man it became clear to Byron, as he began to run up huge debts of his own, that he would have to sell his ancestral estate in Nottinghamshire. The only alternative seemed to be marrying for money to 'repair the ravages of myself and prodigal ancestry' (*L&J*, ii. 85).

Byron paradoxically embraced 'the Trade' of publishing books in order to gild his tarnished title. His middle-class precursor in adventurous poetry set him an example. The lawyer Walter Scott's literary output, nostalgic for Scotland's feudal past, paid for the building of a fantasy baronial hall named Abbotsford. A self-made man(or) impressed the Tory government, and he was created a baronet in 1820, but was bankrupted six years later by the fall of Constable and Ballantyne. The sixth Baron Byron of Rochdale, on the other hand, had no desire to devote himself to his estate. But he did wish to revalidate the tarnished title he had inherited, by accruing honour and acclaim for the name of Byron through literary renown. But he was haunted by the fear that aristocratic honour would be negated if it were tainted by commerce. Byron felt that all contact with 'the Trade' of book selling was something of a contamination. Even when he became successful he would regularly threaten to leave off writing ('this poem will be the last for some years'; 'I was and am quite in earnest in my prefatory promise not to intrude any more'; 'and so Good Night to my authorship', etc.). As he explained in the preface to *Hours of Idleness*, his 'situation' (as a peer) demanded some more prestigious way of entering the history books (*L&J*, iv. 13; 44–5). However, his lameness (he had a club foot) had fostered his natural bookishness as a child, and as an adult prevented him from starring in any but fictional roles as a man of action. (In 1821 he would write: 'Now let us be literary; – a sad falling off, but it is always a consolation. If "Othello's occupation be gone," let us take to the next best; and, if we cannot contribute to make mankind more free and wise, we may amuse ourselves and those who like it' *L&J*, v. 272.) His commitment to Liberalism had been sparked by his Whiggish mother, who dreamed of his making his name as an orator. But crucially, Byron's career as a Whig politician in 1812–13 would fizzle out when it became apparent that his egotism made him impatient with the mundanity of collaborative party politics ('parliamentary mummeries'). He was also understandably disillusioned by a system in which the Tories' reign seemed everlasting. Apart from the short-lived coalition government of 1807 they had governed for the whole of his lifetime. Then, in 1812, the very year of Byron's first parliamentary speech, the Prince Regent, in a Carlton House banquet, publicly repudiated his former Whig allies who had hoped for favour when he inherited the throne.

There is no doubt Byron adopted a lifelong face-saving pose of dilettante and man of the world. He liked to pretend that he casually scribbled a few verses 'to divert the dull moments of indisposition, or the monotony of a vacant hour' perhaps at midnight after returning home from a fashionable party. 'I do not think publishing at all creditable either to men or women, and (though you will not believe me) very often feel ashamed of it myself' (*L&J*, ii. 121). Hazlitt's jibe that an aristocratic poet is an anomaly reflects Byron's own consciousness that a peer's role had traditionally been that of patron not minstrel and certainly never a paid hack. It comforted him therefore to confer his payments for copyrights on needy literary friends like the novelist Robert Charles Dallas or the poet Thomas Moore and thus at least to combine both roles. 'I never will receive money for my writings,' he declared in 1811.[5] When, in 1814, he became the 'Napoleon of rhyme' lionized by the cream of the Whig aristocracy, the Holland House set, he felt it necessary to justify his occupation to Lady Melbourne as a combination of therapy and charity:

> It is a relief to the fever of my mind to write – & as at present I am what they call popular as an author – it enables me to serve one or two people without embarrassing anything but my brains – for I shall never avail myself of the *lucre* – & yet it would be folly to make presents to a bookseller – whose accounts *to* me last year are just 1500 guineas *without* including *Childe Harold* ...
>
> (*L&J*, iv. 15)

But it is obvious how much he revelled in his earning power as a sign of success with the populace at large.

The provincial poet

How far was Byron a dilettante at the beginning of his career? It is true that not only the preface but even the title *Hours of Idleness*, supposedly supplied by the publisher, is reminiscent of the Della Cruscans, a clique of amateur writers of amorous verse fashionable at the end of the eighteenth century. But, even as an insufferably haughty teenager, he showed awareness of audience, readiness for robust competition with fellow poets, and engagement with the notoriously savage Regency reviewers. These characteristics signalled his speedy metamorphosis into a thoroughly professional writer, in all senses except that of receiving remuneration. For example, in the preface to *Hours of Idleness* he declares himself aware that to circulate his privately printed occasional verses to a provincial circle of friends back in Nottinghamshire is a very different proceeding from writing to 'please everybody, because they who have no connection, or even knowledge of the author, will be sure to find fault if they can'. Within a few years he would remedy this hard fact of life by transforming the capitalist contractual relationship between unknown writer and suspicious reader/consumer into one of disarming confessional intimacy. But for now even to submit his verses to the common reader's scrutiny was to 'cross the Rubicon': to symbolically leave the baronial hall and enter into the republic of letters. Even while denying that he, a mere interloper, can possibly 'enter the lists' with other Scottish poets and mountain-dwellers the nineteen-year-old Byron makes sure the reader registers at least the possibility of a comparison with the hugely popular poet of the day, Walter Scott, and perhaps with William Wordsworth too. Above all, even while repeatedly referring to his rank, he nevertheless challenges the anonymous 'periodical censors' to judge his verse not on the author's title but on his merits. He is excited by the entrepreneurial aspect of authorship: forging an image, creating a readership, making a name for himself.

Fugitive Pieces

The collection of poetry offered to the public had already been carefully sifted. Byron had first of all distributed to friends in Nottinghamshire, Harrow and Cambridge *Fugitive Pieces* (1806) and then a revised version, *Poems on Various Occasions* (1807). Both had been printed by Samuel Ridge of Newark at the author's expense, the volumes handsomely produced with engraved emblems decorating some pages. *Hours of Idleness* looks similar, but the contents and tone were very different from the earlier incarnations. The changes he made were his considered response to his friends' and neighbours' reactions to the earlier books. So right from the beginning of his career we see Byron experimenting with exciting the response of his readers. He was a sociable man who would always involve his friends and lovers in the material business of writing and publishing. When he first decided to have a volume of poems privately printed, he had sent manuscript copies of his poems as he wrote them to his friends, John and Elizabeth Pigot, his neighbours at Southwell, the small Nottinghamshire town where Byron and his mother lived when Newstead Abbey was rented out. They helped him; Elizabeth by copying them out and her medical student brother by seeing them through the press when Byron was away. Byron already liked shocking bourgeois sensibilities by striking poses of aristocratic libertinism. He began his lifetime habit of having the printer make separate broadsheet copies of risqué or scurrilous poems to be circulated only privately amongst his closest friends. But he was also susceptible to criticism and advice. At a late stage he had the printing of the projected book suspended while he gave it an 'entire new form'.[6]

The resulting *Fugitive Pieces* was a collection of occasional verse: mainly the fruit of Byron's social life, especially his earliest heterosexual affairs in London and Southwell. In a sense, Byron always would remain an 'occasional' poet, in that his writing was intensely reactive to and reliant on specific situations. The moods of the thirty-eight lyrics ranged from the flirtatious or passionate to the cynical or humorous. Much of their interest lay in the fact that Byron's provincial circle would recognize each other in the verses. Byron included a few erotic poems amongst them, one of which, 'To Mary', was probably a poem he had originally asked Pigot to have printed separately because it was 'improper for the perusal of ladies'. The speaker declares that though Mary was not his first mistress she was the dearest, before she plunged him into torment by taking a new lover. His only comfort is in taunting 'prudes', by boasting of the number of times the lovers committed sinful acts, flagrantly in the bright light of day:

> Now, by my soul, 'tis most delight
> To view each other panting, dying,
> In love's *extatic posture* lying,
> Grateful to *feeling*, as to *sight*.
> (ll. 45–8)

The prudes of Southwell duly reacted in shock and horror, pronouncing Byron 'a most profligate sinner, in short a young Moore' according to the poet (*L&J*, i. 103). The Revd J.T. Becher, Vicar of Rumpton and Midsomer Norton in Nottinghamshire, a respected avuncular adviser to whom Byron had sent a copy of *Fugitive Pieces*, remonstrated with him in verse on the prudes' behalf: 'Forbear to taint the Virgin's spotless mind'. On the same day that he received Becher's letter (26 November 1806), the eighteen-year-old Byron sent for all the copies he had distributed and, except for four which were retained, dramatically burned the whole printing. Nevertheless he also on that day sent Becher a defiant poem in reply: 'Answer to Some Elegant Verses sent by a Friend to the Author, complaining that one of his descriptions was rather too warmly drawn'. He also dissipated his anger by writing, for private circulation in manuscript to his intimates, a misogynist satire 'To a knot of ungenerous critics' lampooning the leader of 'the censorious throng', 'a portly Female'. Another revealing unpublished response, 'Soliloquy of a bard in the country', bitterly reflects that by stooping to write poetry Lord Byron has put himself at the mercy of the provincial gentry's criticism. For 'When Peers are Poets, Squires may well be wits' (l. 16) and a 'little parson' (Becher) in need of bread necessarily 'echoes back his Patron's voice again' (l. 19), while the 'coxcomb' local doctor (Dr Smith of Southwell) relays the scandal in order to be invited out to free dinners (l. 51). Meanwhile, Byron immediately began preparing a revised collection, *Poems on Various Occasions* (1807).

Poems on Various Occasions

Though the offending 'To Mary' (*CPW* no. 77) and also the frank 'To Caroline' (*CPW* no. 73) were now omitted, along with the last six stanzas of 'To Miss E.P.', the riposte to Becher appeared by way of manifesto:

> The artless Helicon, I boast is Youth;
> My Lyre, the heart; – my Muse, the simple Truth:
> Far be't from me, the 'virgin's mind' to 'taint'...
> ('Answer to Some Elegant Verses', ll. 23–5)

Another addition, 'The First Kiss of Love', proclaims passionate love as a revival of Eden in a fallen world and the only foundation of truth in art:

> I hate you, ye cold compositions of art,
> Tho' prudes may condemn me, and bigots reprove;
> I court the effusions, that spring from the heart,
> Which throbs, with delight, to the first kiss of love.
> (ll. 13–16)

A hundred copies of this octavo volume were distributed to friends early in January. The contents, swelled to fifty-one poems, were now divided into three sections: the more important poems were followed by schoolboy translations and imitations of classical authors, then came 'fugitive pieces' or ephemera. The first section had been arranged to roughly correspond with a biographical narrative: 'On Leaving Newstead' was followed by 'On a Distant View of the Village and School, of Harrow, on the Hill', then poems relating to school and male friendships gave way to the light occasional verse and love poetry which dominated the collection.

Byron had retained the passionate 'To Caroline' (*CPW* no. 79) and the risqué comic poem 'To a Lady, Who Presented to the Author a Lock of Hair, Braided with his Own, and appointed a night in December to meet him in the garden'. He used combative footnotes to contradict those 'candid readers' who had supposed the addressee was a certain local 'English damsel' and to rebut their 'very severe and indelicate censure'. He later wrote to his friend William Bankes 'We coincide in opinion that the "poesies Erotiques["] are the most exceptionable...'

(*L&J*, i. 111). Replying to the praise sent by his old school friend Edward Long, he affected to despise provincial opinion: '"*Odi profanum Vulgas*" [I loathe the vulgar crowd] [G]ive me the approbation of my Friends, & I would resign all the *Bays*, that ever ornamented the "*Sinciput & Occiput*" of Homer...the praise of a Friend, particularly a *Harrovian* is far preferable to the admiration of the "*Turba Quiritium*" [Citizen mob]' (*L&J*, i. 109). In spite of this bravado, he had taken some of Revd Becher's advice and omitted or moderated tendentious stanzas in some poems and substituted fictitious names for those of the Southwell women. However, perhaps because he nevertheless saw himself as validating poetic truth through expressing the passions, Byron asked Pigot, when back at his studies in Edinburgh, to present a copy to Henry Mackenzie, veteran author of that classic of the cult of sentiment, *The Man of Feeling* (1771).

Hours of Idleness

In spite of the changes he had made, Southwell was shocked at *Poems on Various Occasions*. Mr Leacroft broke off all contact with Byron in protest at the depiction of his daughter Julia, now addressed as Lesbia. This stormy reception of Byron's earliest verse by provincial society in Nottinghamshire proved a useful lesson, indicating that, in consequence of the Evangelical movement, even a mild degree of eroticism was now deemed unacceptable. Byron complained to Edward Long 'I am surrounded here by parsons and Methodists' (*L&J*, i. 115). Becher's exhortations eventually prevailed, however, for when he prepared to present his poetry before the public at large as *Hours of Idleness*, Byron changed the character of the volume decisively. The final volume comprised forty poems of which only twenty-eight were reprinted from *Poems on Various Occasions* and twelve were new, including some elegiac pieces on his lost childhood. He exchanged risqué liveliness for the disillusionment and melancholy which were to become his trademark for the next decade. He also included a preface pleading his youth and amateur status in mitigation of critical censure.

Byron's judgement seemed borne out by the comparative success of the book. It sold well and was reviewed by seventeen journals, being favourably received by eleven of them.[7] However, even after the omission of so many of the love poems, the *Eclectic Review* still warned its readers that the presence of 'voluptuous themes and visions' made the volume 'unsuitable for any refined reader or well regulated family'.[8] The minor writer R.C. Dallas, a distant relation by marriage, 'felt irresistibly impelled' to introduce himself with a complimentary letter,

When he read the *Edinburgh Review*, Byron became incandescent with rage. He later recalled:

> When I first saw the review of my 'Hours of Idleness', I was furious; in such a rage as I have never been in since. I dined that day with Scrope Davies, and drank three bottles of claret to drown it, but it only boiled the more.[13]

It was all the more infuriating because, beginning his literary career in the early dazzling days of the *Edinburgh Review*, Byron himself nursed the ambition to call literary cant to the bar like its witty barrister critics. He had already experimented with satire as a seventeen year-old in 'On a change of masters, at a great public school'. The new headmaster at Harrow – nicknamed 'Pomposus' – was scorned in verse by the young peer as a 'Barbarian' and in an unpublished poem likened to a mere shopkeeper. Then he had tried his hand at reviewing. He had regretted Wordsworth's decline into 'childishness' in a Jeffrey-like piece on the elder poet's *Poems* for the July 1807 issue of *Monthly Literary Recreations*, the journal printed by Ben Crosby, the London agent of his Newark publisher. In October he confidently began a Popean literary satire for his second publication, which had already reached 'above four hundred lines' by 22 December.

Juvenalian satire

Byron was reading Juvenal at this time, identifying with the Roman's impassioned aristocratic rhetoric on the decline both of literature and society. He particularly admired William Gifford's translation of Juvenal into heroic couplets. In 1807, Byron's friend Francis Hodgson published his translation of *The Satires of Juvenal*. Byron's Cambridge friend, John Cam Hobhouse, had written an imitation of Juvenal's eleventh satire, which was originally intended to have been published together with Byron's, but which eventually came out in a volume called *Imitations and Translations* (1809) to which Byron contributed nine poems. It is often assumed that writing poetry is a solitary occupation, but, as we will see, Byron often formed the hub of a like-minded literary circle. What is more this Juvenalian circle represented a wider tendency, for fifteen volume-length imitations of Juvenal were published in Britain between 1791 and 1821, while there were nine translations of Juvenal's entire works between 1785 and 1829. Gary Dyer comments that Juvenalian satires tended to be dominated by conservative ideology, and that this surge of interest in Juvenal 'is deeply implicated in the ethos of the years from the French Revolution to the coronation of George IV'.[14]

English Bards and Scotch Reviewers

In February 1808 Byron's chagrin to be scornfully dismissed by (as he thought) the magisterial editor Francis Jeffrey in the most prestigious journal of the day and a Whig organ to boot put all the other favourable notices he had received on *Hours of Idleness* out of mind. In a move which would become characteristic of his career, he channelled his violent reaction to criticism of his first book into the shaping of the next. Now Byron entirely forgot the Aberdonian childhood he had just lyrically represented as roving 'a careless mountaineer on the Highlands of Scotland', and his plan of producing a volume entitled 'The Highland Harp', inspired by a Hebridean tour to collect Erse traditions and poems (*L&J*, i. 132). He allied himself with the *English* poets and vowed revenge on all 'Scotch reviewers'. For the literary establishment was dominated by Scots at that time, in both publishing and reviewing and he was now determined to enter it, and by force if necessary. His satire was rapidly expanded to the manuscript of 540–4 lines which he gave to Dallas on his twenty-first birthday for the printer. Its lofty survey of the low state of literature was now twinned with a searing condemnation of contemporary critics. The title pointed to this bifurcated target, for Byron changed it from *British Bards* to *English Bards and Scotch Reviewers*.

The exciting prospect of imminent publication inspired Byron to produce a plethora of additions and emendations, until he begged Dallas, 'Print soon, or I shall overflow with more rhyme' (*L&J*, i. 194). Indeed, when the poem appeared anonymously in March 1809 it was 696 lines long. The manuscript was turned down by Dallas's own publisher, Longman, on account of its 'asperity' and was finally accepted by the less prestigious James Cawthorn. The first edition of *English Bards and Scotch Reviewers* was anonymous. Once bitten, Byron tested the response of the reading public before putting his name to the successful second edition. Byron later recalled his trepidation as to how it would be received by the public:

> For the first 4 days after it was announced, I was very nervous about its fate. Generally speaking, the first fortnight decides the public opinion of a book. This made a prodigious sensation, more perhaps

than any of my works, except 'The Corsair'. In less than a year and a half it passed through four editions and rather large ones. To some of them, contrary to the advice of my friends, I affixed my name. The thing was known to be mine, and I could not have escaped my enemies in not owning it; besides it was more manly not to deny it. There were many things in that satire which I was afterwards sorry for, and I wished to cancel it.

(*Medwin*, p. 144)

Second edition

Byron's audacious attack on that self-appointed literary judge Jeffries, the critic, who had created for himself a mediating role between the writer and his public, was a gamble which seemed to have paid off. His appeal to the readership over the head of Jeffrey to recognize the satiric poet as the true judge of contemporary literature was a bid for authority to be returned to the author. He therefore quickly capitalized on his success by putting his name to a second and even further expanded edition of 1050 lines, for the print run of a thousand copies was sold by the end of April.[15] Buoyed up by success, he was now even less inclined than before to listen to Dallas's appeals for moderation. So to this second edition the newly confident Byron added a self-vindicating preface, augmented from that which he had added to the second issue of the first edition, portraying himself heroically combatting a modern monster: 'As to the *Edinburgh Review*; it would, indeed, require a Hercules to crush the Hydra; but if the Author succeeds in merely "bruising one of the heads of the serpent", though his own hand should suffer in the encounter, he will be amply satisfied.' (*CPW*, i. 229). In this second edition, as Frederick Beaty remarks, Byron used Juvenal's first satire, and the commentary from Madan's *New and Literal Translation of Juvenal and Persius*, to guide him in providing the satire with a frame, intended to improve its coherence and provide a justificatory precedent.[16] He announces that the self-made critic is his chief target:

> A man must serve his time to every trade
> Save Censure; Critics all are ready made
>
> (ll. 63–4)

A new conclusion celebrates the defiant revelation of the author's identity:

> And now at once I tear the veil away:-
> Cheer on the pack! the Quarry stands at bay,
>   (ll. 1043–4)

Before he left the country on his Grand Tour, Byron appended to the second edition a high-spirited postscript aimed at his chief tormentors. He declared he could think of no reason why Hewson Clarke, who had been a Cambridge contemporary of his, should have any animosity against him 'except a personal quarrel with a bear, kept by me at Cambridge to sit for a fellowship, and whom jealousy of his Trinity contemporaries prevented from success'. As for Jeffrey, he informed him he would unfortunately not be in Britain when the next number of the *Edinburgh Review* came out, 'But I yet hope to light my pipe with it in Persia' (*CPW*, i. 263).

Further editions

The poem was so popular that Cawthorn brought out two further editions while Byron was abroad. But the poet only grumbled that if the print runs had been smaller the poem would have boasted an even larger number of editions.[17] When he returned from his travels, Byron made some minor additions to the poem in preparation for the fifth edition which was to be brought out in December 1811, and he was eager to print a sequel, *Hints from Horace*. However, he subsequently suppressed the poem. The poet who had ambitions for a political career in the House of Lords took the hint, conveyed by Lord Holland's tame poet, Samuel Rogers, that the leader of the Whigs would be obliged if the poem were withdrawn. Nevertheless, the unscrupulous Cawthorn had to be restrained from issuing pirated copies for some years. This was hardly surprising, as, according to the reviewer of the *Literary Journal* in 1818, copies of the poem were exchanging hands for from four to five guineas.[18] Byron would find himself for some time to come making apologies to several of its targets who were to become friends: Walter Scott, Thomas Moore, Samuel Rogers, Lord and Lady Holland and Samuel Taylor Coleridge.[19] He even made his peace with Francis Jeffrey by letter. In 1816, Byron read the satire through and made

demands a generalized persona or mask to speak to and for the public at large. The speaker of the new poem is definitively a writer. His declared object is 'not to prove that I can write well, but, *if possible*, to make others write better' according to the preface appended to the second edition. The mock-modesty is better managed here than in the *Hours of Idleness* preface, as the reason given for indulgence towards the writer is not his youth but his moral intentions. In taking on the traditional role of satirist, Byron now assumed not the authority of a peer of the realm, but the right of the plain man of society to stand up in the commonwealth of letters and brand those hacks who were corrupting public taste: 'An author's works are public property: he who purchases may judge, and publish his opinion if he pleases; and the Authors I have endeavoured to commemorate may do by me as I have done by them'. The poet likens himself to a doctor in his attempt to diagnose the disease infecting literature since the days of Dryden and Pope, and the disappearance of the 'polish'd nation' who had inspired them with its praise (l. 111). He readily admits he is merely a provincial 'country practitioner' in comparison with an expert satirist like William Gifford, to whom he would willingly give way, 'Then sleep my pen for ever!' (l. 703).

The speaker does hint occasionally at his literary identity, admitting: 'I poured along the town a flood of rhyme,/ A school-boy freak' (ll. 48–9). He did not deserve the drubbing he received but concedes: 'Not that a Title's sounding charm can save/ Or scrawl or scribbler from an equal grave' (ll. 53–4). He candidly confesses that as one 'of a thoughtless throng' lured by 'every path of pleasure's flowery way', he is not the ideal spokesman for morality. But in the absence of Gifford, even an aristocratic rake may step fearlessly into the breach:

> Altho' some kind, censorious friend will say,
> 'What art thou better, meddling fool, than they?'
> And every Brother Rake will smile to see
> That miracle, a Moralist in me!
>
> (ll. 697–700)

But he nevertheless affirms: 'Lords too are Bards: such things at times befall' (l. 719). At the close of the first edition he even portrays himself as a heroic patriot writing for the good of his country:

> Zeal for her honour bade me here engage
> The host of idiots that infest her age.
>
> (ll. 993–4)

Byron is signalling in his first satire that he is definitely entering the literary arena; that he is no dilettante. He begins with an apostrophe to 'Nature's noblest gift – my grey goose-quill!' (l. 7). The poem was clearly written to establish the authority of a young writer through attacking the triteness of the competition, and to wreak revenge against 'biased' Whig reviewers who had ridiculed his first book with particular venom because of his class. It champions the role of the poet against that of the journalist, whose status had been elevated by the *Edinburgh*. Ironically, Francis Jeffrey was just as wary of being soiled by contact with 'the Trade' as Byron. He wrote to Cockburn: 'From the very first, I have been anxious to keep clear of any tradesman-like concern in the Review, and to confine myself pretty strictly to intercourse with *gentlemen* only, even as contributors'.[24] It is difficult to overstate the authority of these journals in the first quarter of the nineteenth century. They were becoming arbiters of taste; mediators between the newly-expanding reading public without a classical education and print culture, including a flood of poetry.

Byron's poem denounces the Edinburgh reviewers as 'young tyrants' and 'usurpers on the Throne of Taste' (ll. 83–4). It attempts to wrest back from Jeffrey the job, formerly that of wits like Dryden or Pope, of sifting the literary sheep from the goats. The poet actually compares his own role as satirist with that of Jeffrey:

> I pursue
> The self-same road, but make my own review:
> Not seek great JEFFREY's yet like him will be
> Self-constituted Judge of Poesy.
>
> (ll. 59–62)

The attack on the authority of the *Edinburgh Review* and its lawyer editor, Francis Jeffrey, thus forms the centrepiece of the satire. Critics like Jeffrey are also satirists of a sort, but, unlike the present writer, their fustian prose does not carry on that British tradition of poetry which models itself on the classics. This is his recipe for a 'self-made' periodical critic:

> Take hackneyed jokes from MILLER, got by rote,
> With just enough of learning to misquote;
> A mind well skilled to find, or forge a fault,
> A turn for punning, call it Attic salt;
> To JEFFREY go, be silent and discreet,
> His pay is just ten sterling pounds per sheet:
> Fear not to lie, 'twill seem a sharper hit,

> Shrink not from blasphemy, 'twill pass for wit;
> Care not for feeling – pass your proper jest,
> And stand a Critic hated, yet caress'd.
>
> (ll. 65–74)

Almost all the contemporary reviewers of Byron's satire quoted the personal invective against Jeffrey, beginning:

> Health to immortal JEFFREY! Once in name,
> England could boast a judge almost the same:
> In soul so like, so merciful, yet just,
> Some think that Satan has resign'd his trust,
> And given the Spirit to the world again,
> To sentence Letters, as he sentenced men.
>
> (ll. 438–43)

Dallas commented that 'as this seems to have been the inspiring object of the Satire, so these lines were most fluently written, and required least correction afterward' (*Dallas*, pp. 38–9). Jeffrey is scorned as 'a party tool' who uses reviewing for propaganda purposes, hoping that, when they seize power, patronage from the Whigs will transform him from an Edinburgh lawyer to a Judge Jeffries of more than mere literature:

> Who knows? if chance his patrons should restore
> Back to the sway they forfeited before,
> His scribbling toils some recompence may meet,
> And raise this Daniel to the Judgement Seat.
>
> (ll. 450–3)

As the *Eclectic Review* pointed out, the ironic refrains 'Health to immortal JEFFREY!' (l. 438), 'Health to great JEFFREY!' (l. 460), allude to the famous lines of Charles Churchill on William Warburton, Bishop of Gloucester in Dedication to the *Sermons* (1765).[25] Churchill, together with John Wilkes, had founded the *North Briton*. His satire was best known for his attacks on the Scots ancestry of the Tory Earl of Bute, in Whig accusations that the latter was attempting to increase Crown power over Parliament. Byron's allusions to the Whiggish anti-Scottish propaganda of the previous century could be taken as hinting that the Scottish reviewers were operating as a conservative element within the Whig party, which in turn kept the status quo in place by its failure to mount an effective opposition. This would certainly be the basis of the onslaught against the *Edinburgh Review*, mounted by James and John Stuart Mill in the first two numbers of the Utilitarian *Westminster Review*, founded in 1824 to campaign for radical reform. But that was a long way ahead, and in 1808–9 the *Edinburgh* was itself politically progressive, though aesthetically conservative. Byron's poem does suggest the much-vaunted independence of the *Edinburgh Review* is a screen for its pandering to the vanity of the aristocracy at Holland House:

> Long, long beneath that hospitable roof,
> Shall Grub-street dine, while duns are kept aloof.
> See honest HALLAM lay aside his fork,
> Resume his pen, review his Lordship's work,
> And grateful for the dainties on his plate,
> Declare his landlord can at least translate!
> Dunedin! View thy children with delight,
> They write for food, and feed because they write:
> And lest, when heated with the unusual grape,
> Some glowing thoughts should to the press escape,
> And tinge with red the female reader's cheek,
> My lady skims the cream of each critique;
> Breathes o'er the page her purity of soul,
> Reforms each error, and refines the whole.
>
> (ll. 546–59)

However, the satire of Holland House is not specifically written from a radical point of view. It could equally be compared with Tory satires such as Eaton Stannard Barrett's *All the Talents* (1807), which comments on the *Edinburgh Review*: 'It is sometimes just, often erroneous, always insolent; and owes most of its popularity to this perfection, which it always exerts far too freely, unless the book be written by a *fellow-countryman*, or a *Lord*. ... [I]t has had the vanity to declare that it possesses ALL *the literary* TALENTS of the country. Happy is that country in having scribblers who call themselves wise!' ('Dialogue the Third', note to p. 77). The *Edinburgh Review* had also been parodied in 1807 by Edward Copleston in his *Advice to a Young Reviewer, with a Specimen of the Art*, and John Ring's *The Beauties of the Edinburgh Review; alias the Stinkpot of Literature*.

The (anti)climax of the poem was the mock-heroic account of the famous duel between the greatest editor and the most fashionable poet of the day, when Jeffrey and Moore are discovered to have no lead in their pistols! (We see how seriously Regency writers took their satires in the fact that Moore later challenged Byron to another duel over this accusation.) Caledonia's kilted goddess saves her favourite Jeffrey but advises him not to thirst for gore, but to concentrate the efforts of 'the oat-fed phalanx' on their intellectual stranglehold over England. Just before she vanishes in a Scottish mist, she warns:

> Yet mark one caution, ere thy next Review
> Spread its light wings of Saffron and of Blue,
> Beware lest blundering BROUGHAM destroy the sale,
> Turn Beef to Bannocks, Cauliflowers to Kail.'
>
> (ll. 522–5)

The implication is that the Scots hacks only write their Whig journal for their keep (its covers were the party colours of buff and blue), but they will lose their living if they let young hotheads take over. Byron's note explained: 'Mr Brougham, in No. XXV of the Edinburgh Review, throughout the article concerning Don Pedro de Cevallos, has displayed more politics than policy: many of the worthy Burgesses of Edinburgh being so incensed at the infamous principles it evinces, as to have withdrawn their subscription' (*CPW*, i. 409).

The Don Cevallos article

The review article alluded to, actually written by both Jeffrey and Brougham, had brought Tory fear of the influence of the *Edinburgh* to a head. It demolished a propagandist account of the French usurpation of the Spanish throne by Ferdinand VII's secretary of state, and castigated the Spanish royal family's previous appeasement of the invaders. Even more controversially, the reviewers voiced their conviction that, despite an initial setback, Napoleon would eventually crush the popular Spanish revolt against the French invasion.[26] They lambasted both the self-seeking Spanish royal family and self-serving British foreign policy, in contrast to the bravery of the true Spanish patriots. The reviewers mischievously conclude with the hope that the example of the revolutionary 'lower orders' in Spain will reinvigorate true ideals of liberty and inspire radical reforms in Britain. The democratic tone of this article, combined with its defeatist attitude towards Napoleon, outraged public opinion in 1808, in Holland House as well as Tory strongholds. Twenty-four prominent readers, including Walter Scott, cancelled their subscriptions, and Sidney Smith reported to Lady Holland that some even removed back numbers of the *Edinburgh* from their libraries and fumigated the shelves! Lord Buchan kicked the offending number out into the street in his rage.[27] A rash of pamphlets appeared, accusing the *Edinburgh* of being pro-Bonaparte and of fomenting revolution in Britain, such as the anonymous 'A short methodical abstract, calm consideration and consequent appreciation of the *Edinburgh Review* on the exposition of Pedro de Cevallos' (1808?), Mentor [pseud.], 'The Dangers of the *Edinburgh Review*' (1808); Senex [pseud.], 'A letter to the young gentlemen who write in the *Edinburgh Review*' (1809); and R. Wharton, Esq., MP, 'Remarks on the Jacobinical tendency of the *Edinburgh Review*' (1809).

The Don Cevallos article was widely seen as a salvo which announced the determination of the *Edinburgh Review* to radicalize the Whigs. The Tories were sufficiently alarmed to immediately give John Murray the go-ahead in his plan of setting up a rival periodical, the *Quarterly*, to combat the influence of the *Edinburgh*. Byron's attack on the *Edinburgh Review* earned him glowing plaudits from the right-wing periodical the *Anti-Jacobin Review*, which considered Jeffrey 'has libelled most wickedly one of the most loyal of men, Don Pedro de Cevallos, for which he is execrated by every honest man in the country'.[28] The *Anti-Jacobin Review* was not alone in assuming the anonymous author to be a Tory. In fact Byron was a member of the Cambridge Whig club, and had taken his seat on the opposition benches of the House of Lords only a few days before the poem was published.

Augustan aesthetics

Byron's attempt to recover Jeffrey's judicial role for the poet of the Popeian tradition led him into paradoxes not just over politics but also aesthetics. His speaker's stance implies that the poet and his readership share common aesthetic and moral standards. But the Augustan consensus on what constituted excellence in poetry had already been undermined by Romantic writers like Wordsworth and Coleridge. In fact, Romanticism challenged the very idea that there could be a consensus. Moreover, his wider purpose of condemning many of his contemporaries for abandoning the tradition which he now adopted actually brought Byron into contradiction with the poem's personal attack on Jeffrey. These aims are open to the charge of inconsistency, because Francis Jeffrey's views on literature were, in fact, as Augustan as Byron's own.[29] For the very reason that the *Edinburgh Review* had alienated many Romantic writers besides Byron was precisely because Jeffrey himself held by these same Augustan standards and castigated them accordingly. From its inception the periodical committed itself to progressive economic and political views based on the values of the Scottish Enlightenment. However, Jeffrey took a conservative stance towards the new poetry which continuously rolled off the presses for the first twenty-five years of the century.

In 1802, in the very first review in the very first issue of the periodical, Jeffrey had turned a review of Southey's *Thalaba* into a manifesto condemning the 'Romantic' extravagance of the Lake Poets. 'Poetry has this much, at least, in common with religion, that its standards were fixed long ago, by certain inspired writers, whose authority it is no longer lawful to call in question'. This is typical of the reliance on traditional precepts, upon which the newly-authoritative critics of the nineteenth century based their right to act as intermediaries, helping new readers discriminate between the flood of new publications. Admittedly, Jeffrey's views were not strictly neo-classical. Like Byron, he felt that a poet should write with feeling, and he denounced stilted artificiality. He also wrote in support of the enthusiasm led by Coleridge and Gifford for the 'romantic' British dramatists of the sixteenth and seventeenth centuries. In fact many critics have noted the similarities between Jeffrey's and Byron's specific comments on contemporary poetry. Like Jeffrey, Byron condemns Scott's use of the supernatural in *The Lay of the Last Minstrel*:

> While mountain spirits prate to river sprites,
> That dames may listen to the sound at nights;
>
> (ll. 155–6)

A long note by the future author of *Manfred* castigates the poem's 'incongruous and absurd' premise. Likewise, the poet soon to become famous for his Byronic heroes denounced:

> The golden-crested, haughty Marmion,
> Now forging scrolls, now foremost in the fight,
> Not quite a Felon, yet but half a Knight,
> The gibbet or the field prepared to grace;
> A mighty mixture of the great and base.
>
> (ll. 166–70)

Scott's verse is also linked with Gothic 'Tales of Terror' which make money by pandering to the depraved taste of the populace: 'The poem was manufactured by Messrs Constable, Murray, and Miller, worshipful Booksellers, in consideration of the receipt of a sum of money, and truly, considering the inspiration, it is a very creditable production' (*CPW*, i. 402). Now 'MILTON, DRYDEN, POPE, alike forgot,/ Resign their hallow'd Bays to WALTER SCOTT' (ll. 187–8).

Southey's pretentious epics in hexameters are next to be mocked and, as in the *Edinburgh Review*, his exotic superhero Thalaba is the main butt, deemed the 'Illustrious conqueror of common sense' from whom 'startled Metre fled before thy face' (ll. 217–20). From the would-be successor to Homer, Byron turns to a poet who goes to the other extreme, looking for the sublime in the ordinary incidents of humble life: 'That mild apostate from poetic rule,/ The simple WORDSWORTH' (ll. 236–7). Like Jeffrey, Byron cannot comprehend why Wordsworth literally descends to the level of an idiot in the 'Christmas stories' of *Lyrical Ballads*. Though both Jeffrey and Byron admired the realism of Crabbe and the down-to-earth raciness of Burns, both were suspicious of Wordsworth's theory of poetic diction in the preface to the second edition of *Lyrical Ballads* (1800) and the 'obscurity' of Coleridge (l. 258). In 1807, Wordsworth's new volume of poems was mercilessly attacked by Jeffrey, and featured in other literary satires which probably influenced Byron, such as Richard Mant's *The Simpliciad* (1808).

The 1816 sale catalogue of Byron's library, sold when he left Britain for ever, contained a complete set of the *Edinburgh Review*. Byron later, in *Don Juan*, openly declared his admiration of its editor and Jeffrey, in his turn, let the poet know that he had not written the *Hours of Idleness* review. So close were Byron's and Jeffrey's comments on contemporary poets that it has been suggested that the satirist was actually influenced by the reviews of his chief target in composing his other salvos. Though this indeed seems possible, it is also true that Byron and Jeffrey shared a common heritage in that both were imbued by the scepticism, pragmatism and common-sense values of the Scottish Enlightenment. Each held to a sociological view of the development of poetry through history, and valued the power of literature to influence public opinion. Out of the Augustan stress on universal rather than particular human emotions, the *Edinburgh Review* was evolving a theory of realism which was in accord with its progressive politics and economic theory. Byron's public school training in rhetoric taught him that poetry should produce action in the world ('words are *things*') and in his satire of

Wordsworth and Coleridge he showed distrust of the imagination in favour of experience.[30] However, he had also been strongly influenced by the cult of sentiment, so his satiric strictures against self-indulgent subjectivity function as displaced denunciations of his own juvenilia. As Jerome McGann and Robert Gleckner have noted, the sort of sentimental poetry particularly derided in *English Bards and Scotch Reviewers* included verse which had strongly influenced his own *Hours of Idleness*, such as Charlotte Dacre's *Hours of Solitude* (1805) and Thomas Moore's *The Poetical Works of the late Thomas Little* (1801).[31] After reading Brougham's review he had written to Becher, 'I think *I* could write a more sarcastic critique on *myself* than any yet published' (*L&J*, i. 163). *English Bards and Scotch Reviewers* was as much an indirect repudiation of his own occasional verse and dilettante stance as it was of other literary dunces. Never again would Byron publish a collection of personal lyrics. Most of the *Hebrew Melodies* (1815) are spoken by personae, and his subsequent occasional poems were usually either distributed privately to Byron's inner circle or published as interpolations or codas to the narrative verse, where they could often be taken as spoken by the characters.

Although literary historians have sometimes simplified Byron's career into a development from the romantic (*Childe Harold*, the *Oriental Tales*) to the satiric (*Beppo, Don Juan*), it is apparent that even with his first two books Byron veered between these modes. Both the occasional lyric, produced for a select circle of friends, and the literary satire, assuming the aesthetic and moral standards traditionally held by an élite, were essentially Augustan genres. Both books were reminiscent of a previous age when poetry was not, in the words of Wordsworth's 'democratic' Preface to the second edition of *Lyrical Ballads*, simply written in 'the language of men', but showed its aristocratic provenance as the product of the shared culture of a relatively small circle of 'select' readers. However, whereas a provincial collection of 'occasional' lyrics presents poetry as an ephemeral and sometimes collaborative genteel entertainment, a literary satire reflects the ideological divisions and cut-throat competition between professional writers for the marketplace. Byron's decision to follow his collection of lyrics with an attention-grabbing literary satire therefore signalled his defiant decision to adopt the profession of writer.

2
The Traveller from the East meets the 'Emperor of the West': Byron and Murray

Murray is a happy fellow, living in the light of his own glory. The *Review* is the greatest of all works, and it is his own creation. He prints ten thousand copies and fifty times ten thousand read its contents in the East and in the West.

(Robert Southey)

> Along thy sprucest book-shelves shine
> The works thou deemest most divine,
> The Art of Cookery and mine,
>   My Murray.

(Byron)

Byron told Edward Trelawny the air of Greece made him a poet. '*How I wrote there!*' he reminisced in a letter to Murray in 1821 (*L&J*, viii. 221). He began *Childe Harold's Pilgrimage, A Romaunt* on the last day of October 1810 in Jannina and he finished the first draft on 28 March. When, back in London, his prospective publisher suggested he write two more cantos, he replied: 'But to do that, I must return to Greece and Asia; I must have a warm sun and a blue sky; I cannot describe scenes so dear to me by a sea-coal fire' (*L&J*, ii. 92). Was Byron therefore a materialist poet? Keats certainly thought so: 'He describes what he sees – I describe what I imagine. Mine is the hardest task'.[1] Coleridge, bilious with sour grapes, saw the poem as no more than a versified guide book: 'A man accustomed to cast his words in metre and familiar with descriptive Poets and Tourists, himself a picturesque Tourist, must be troubled with a mental Strangury, if he could not lift up his leg six times at six different Corners, and each time piss a Canto'.[2]

How far is the poem Byron wrote on his travels dependent on his actual life experience? Certainly he makes truth to life the touchstone of his authority as a poet. 'What should I have known or written, had I been a quiet mercantile politician, or a lord in waiting? A man must travel, and turmoil, or there is no existence' (*L&J*, v. 70). His invocation to the muse proudly proclaims itself to be actually composed at Delphi. He later interrupts his retrospective account of Spain to hail Parnassus which is before his eyes as he writes (i. 60–4). But, as Diego Saglia has pointed out, 'Place is both a thing "out there" and a spectacle filled with historical and cultural meanings that the poet has to decipher before inserting them in a wider tale of Humanity and History'.[3] The traveller-poet combines the subjective and the objective in bringing together the observing self and the place, and he foregrounds the act of writing as the site of this interaction.

Though travel provides inspiration for the Orientalist writer, it would be naive to suppose that he meets experience as a *tabula rasa*. His preconceptions and even the forms and modes of writing are provided by his existing knowledge of other texts: travel books, histories and poetry. Byron's notes testify to his use of the Orientalist canon: Richard Knolles, Demetrius Cantemir, Barthelemi D'Herbelot, Sir Paul Rycaut, Baron De Tott, Lady Mary Wortley Montagu, Sir John Chardin, Thomas Hyde, Sir William Jones, and others.[4] And, of course, despite the impression of immediacy, the poem was extensively revised by Byron on his return to England, and influenced by his literary advisers there.

Throughout the eighteenth century, travellers to the Ottoman Empire had puzzled over the question of whether the present-day Christian inhabitants of the area they liked to call Hellas were the descendants of the ancient Greeks. If so, they were quite ignorant of their ancient heritage, and classically-educated Western commentators philosophized over them as melancholy evidence of cultural degeneration and over ivy-clad ruined temples as exemplars of the transience of human greatness. In the second half of the century, disgust for the inhabitants began to turn to pity and indignation at Turkish tyranny. Occasionally, poetry based on actual travels to the Levant appeared, such as William Falconer's *The Shipwreck, a Poem in Three cantos by a sailor* (1762), to which Byron alludes in his notes to *Childe Harold*; Joseph Dacre Carlyle's *Poems, suggested chiefly by scenes in Asia-Minor, Syria, and Greece* (1805); and Waller Rodwell Wright's *Horae Ionicae* (1809), which was complimented in *English Bards* (ll. 867–80) by the poet, before he set off for Asia Minor to see if he could do better.[5]

Byron's *Childe Harold's Pilgrimage*, therefore, crystallised an important transition in Philhellenist and Romantic Orientalist literature, in that it so emphatically foregrounded the narrator's own subjective impressions of the scenery and his personal experience of contemporary cultures rather than his classical erudition. Byron thus opened up Philhellenism to readers who had not received an élite male education. What was more, growing awareness of the inevitable defeat of Napoleon infused his Philhellenism with frustrated political idealism, so that melancholy musings on mutability are energized by a call for direct political action to liberate the birthplace of democracy from tyranny:

> Hereditary bondsmen! know ye not
> Who would be free themselves must strike the blow?
> (Childe Harold's Pilgrimage, II, 76)

There is no doubt that Byron and his friend John Cam Hobhouse travelled to Southern Europe specifically to obtain material for their writing. Byron wrote sarcastically to a friend that 'Hobhouse has made woundy [sic] preparations for a book at his return, 100 pens two gallons Japan Ink, and several vols best blank is no bad provision for a discerning Public' (L&J, i. 208). They would produce respectively *A Journey through Albania and other provinces of Turkey in Europe and Asia, to Constantinople, during the years 1809 and 1810* (1813) and *Childe Harold's Pilgrimage, A Romaunt* (1812).[6] When their books were in press on their return, Byron worried that 'the *Captain's* [Hobhouse's] prose being as it were connected with my rhimes, & coming out at the same time, should make us appear such pestilent scribblers… – Why, we shall want a press to ourselves' (L&J, ii. 81). The two friends represented contrasting faces of Philhellenism: Hobhouse was an indefatigable antiquarian, producing exhaustive prosaic accounts of the antiquities and the topography, while Byron sought out a lonely spot to conjure up atmospheric visions of the past. In retrospect we can see how they represent the utilitarian and the mythmaking strands of British Philhellenism, which would eventually unravel in the mismanaged attempts of the London Greek Committee to fund and support the Greek Revolution of the 1820s.

The Napoleonic wars dictated their route. They could not follow the conventional Grand Tour through France to Italy, and seized a last-minute chance to cross the Iberian peninsula and vicariously experience the war itself, travelling in the wake of the British army, and stopping to view the scenes of recent battles. This gave Byron a chance to follow up his exploitation of the Don Cevallos controversy in *English Bards* by providing readers with his immediate impressions of the Peninsular campaign like a poetic war correspondent. The friends wore magnificent scarlet dress uniforms to associate themselves with the British forces.

Then they sailed to Malta by way of Gibraltar and Sardinia, and thence to Greece in a British frigate, the *Spider*. They experienced some real action near the Ionian islands when privateers were captured and they were fired upon by a Turkish brig. On arriving in the Ottoman Empire, they travelled extensively in northern Albania, a feudal country which few Europeans had visited unless for a military or diplomatic purpose. Hobhouse records that they took with them on their trek four large and three smaller trunks, their own beds and bedding, and packhorses loaded with sacks containing an 'indispensable' canteen and other necessaries. Despite these precautions, Hobhouse solemnly warned the reader: 'Properly speaking, the word comfort cannot be applied to anything I ever saw out of England' (*Journey*, i. 47). The climax of their adventure was their sojourn at the court of the formidable warrior, Ali Pasha, Vizier of Albania, who was known as 'the Mohammedan Bonaparte', having become strong enough to challenge the Sultan's control.

Hobhouse had begun to keep a journal as soon as they arrived in the Ottoman Empire, because, unlike Spain and Portugal, Albania had hitherto featured in no English travel books. There were not even any maps, he tells us. There were no topographical poems either, of course. Byron took down phonetic transcriptions of the war songs they heard, as this dialect of Arnaout was 'not a written language', and had them translated on their return to Greece, where he also collected some Romaic folksongs. After travelling to Constantinople and extensively in the Balkans, Hobhouse returned home, and Byron stayed on alone in that part of the Ottoman Empire the Philhellenists called Greece from July 1810 until he returned home a year later. Instead of travelling, he settled in Athens to saturate himself thoroughly in the Romaic language and culture. He met there many antiquarians and Philhellenes of various nationalities. Greece made him a poet, not merely by providing picturesque scenery, but by inspiring him with the political ideal of Philhellenism.

Byron's personal experience, heavily advertised in the extensive notes and appendices to the poem, gave novelty to the familiar genre of the topographical poem. He declared: 'If we see no nation but our own, we do not give mankind a fair chance; – it is from *experience*, not books, we ought to judge of them. There is nothing like inspection and trusting to our own senses' (*L&J*, i. 195). William Gifford later commented, 'We have never had descriptions of Eastern manners before. All that has been hitherto attempted was done without actual knowledge' (*Smiles*, i. 220). Wearing his dress uniform and using his rank, Byron had drawn on his role as a member of the British ruling class in his travels, associating himself with the diplomats, traders and soldiers of its Empire. Yet he acquired expensive Oriental costumes and swords with which to dazzle London society masquerades. The poem, too, allowed the reader to try on the Western role of aristocratic traveller/explorer with his appropriating colonial gaze, but also to cross-dress by slipping into the exotic garb of the Other, the primitive Eastern warrior.

He also provided a mysterious, melancholy hero, young and of high birth but already disillusioned with life. His readers were understandably inclined to identify Harold with his creator, the handsome lord in Hamletian mourning recently returned from his travels. For, with the protagonist of *Childe Harold*, Byron returned to an aristocratic point of view, but this time his poem emphasized the way the modern Western nobleman had degenerated from the austere warlord of former ages into a mere wastrel like Harold, whose life is devoted to 'concubines and carnal companie/ And flaunting wassailers of high and low degree' (I, 2). Byron could claim moral authority in the portrayal of the aristocrat as Byronic hero, a disillusioned sceptic devoid of a meaningful role. He later quizzed the Evangelical Dr Kennedy: '[I]t is a doctrine of yours, is it not? that the human heart is corrupted, and therefore, if I shew that it is so in those ranks, which assume the external marks of politeness and benevolence – having had the best opportunities, and better than most poets of observing it, am I not doing an essential service to your cause?'[7]

The Napoleon of rhyme had established the territory of his first literary empire: Philhellenism, and its amelioration of aristocratic and colonial guilt.

* * *

Byron was decidedly nervous about his new poem. He made a play of being reluctant to show it to Dallas when he first returned from his travels, and when the latter praised it he protested that 'It was any thing but poetry' (*Dallas*, p. 116). Nevertheless he made a present of the manuscript to Dallas which ensured the latter's pecuniary interest in publication, and he allowed himself to be persuaded into deferring Cawthorn's publication of *Hints from Horace*, until *Childe Harold* came out. Byron's apparent arrogance masked a genuine need for reassurance which led him to seek opinions on the manuscript not only of trusted friends like John Cam Hobhouse and R.C. Dallas, but also of poets he admired like Waller Rodwell Wright.

Byron's was nervous about the poem because its frank egotism (the original manuscript was entitled 'Childe Burun') might expose him to more caustic attacks in the press. He admitted to Dallas: 'I much wish to avoid identifying Childe Harold's character with mine, & that in sooth is my second objection to my name on the T[itle] Page. ... My plaguy Satire will bring the North & South Grubstreets down upon the "Pilgrimage" ' (*L&J*, ii. 75–6). He was reluctant to put his name to the new poem. The publication of further aggressive satires like *Hints from Horace*, *The Curse of Minerva* and *The Waltz* seemed safer than exposing himself again to ridicule through confessional lyricism. His return to sentiment and the subjective could only be attempted if he was sufficiently reassured – preferably by the approval of the ultra-conservative literary judges of the age.

John Murray

Perhaps the greatest paradox of Byron's literary life is that most of the verse of the most dashing Liberal poet of the nineteenth century emanated from the coterie of the publisher of the *Quarterly Review*, John Murray. The *Quarterly* supported the King, the Anglican Church and the war against Napoleon. Through Canning it had secret links direct to the Tory government. It was the scourge of most Liberal writers. Percy Bysshe Shelley, William Hazlitt, Leigh Hunt, Samuel Rogers, Walter Savage Landor, and Lady Morgan all suffered under the lash of its editor, William Gifford, or the acerbic reviewer, John Wilson Croker. Reading a *Quarterly* review of his poems was popularly supposed to have brought on Keats's fatal tubercular collapse. Croker's diatribe on her anti-war poem, *1811* (1812), was credited with extinguishing Anna Barbauld's poetic career. Only Byron was spared, being, as it were, the tame poet of the publishing house. Leigh Hunt sardonically observed in his reminiscences that the *Quarterly* coterie had 'stroked [Byron's] mane, patted his withers, and coaxed him to canter along the road quietly with them'.[8]

It is usually supposed that it was quite accidental that Byron's *Childe Harold's Pilgrimage* first came to be offered to Murray in 1812. Byron did tell his literary agent, R.C. Dallas, to take the manuscript first to the more well-established Miller, but it was unlikely that the publisher of Lord Elgin would accept a poem attacking Elgin for removing the marbles from the Acropolis. The later realization that he had just turned down the most sensationally saleable poem of the age probably speeded the elderly Miller's decision to retire. To rub salt in the wound, his prestigious premises at 50 Albemarle Street, his copyrights and stock were purchased by Murray himself in September 1812. It was Byron's popularity which had set the seal on the young publisher's prosperity and spurred him to take on the mortgage. Murray boasted to his relatives:

> My house is excellent; and I transact all the departments of my busi-
> ness in an elegant library, which my drawing-room becomes in the
> morning; and there I am in the habit of seeing persons of the high-
> est rank in literature and talent, such as Canning, Frere,
> Mackintosh, Southey, Campbell, Walter Scott, Madame de Staël,
> Gifford, Croker, Barrow, Lord Byron, and others; thus leading the
> most delightful life, with means of prosecuting my business with
> the highest honour and emolument'.
>
> (*Smiles*, i. 266)

It was in this drawing room that, in the proudest moment of his life,
Murray introduced Scott to Byron in 1815, having effected a reconciliation between them after *English Bards and Scotch Reviewers*. He
commissioned a painting to commemorate the event. In its fireplace,

Meeting of Byron and Scott in 1815. (L to R): Isaac D'Israeli, John Murray, Sir
John Barrow, George Canning, William Gifford, Walter Scott and Byron.
[Reproduced by kind permission of John Murray (Publishers) Ltd]

after his death, Byron's memoirs were ceremoniously cast into the flames.

Only when Miller refused it, did Dallas carry the MS to John Murray. But it seems likely that Byron had set himself up to be invited into the Murray coterie when he published his satire. *English Bards and Scotch Reviewers* had come out in March 1809 just a month after the launch of the *Quarterly Review*. The poem's target was the *Edinburgh*'s editor, Francis Jeffrey, and the poet repeatedly calls upon William Gifford, the editor of the *Quarterly*, to restore true literary judgement to a corrupt culture. In 1809, Jeffrey's and Brougham's Don Cevallos article frightened the government into supporting John Murray's plan to found the Tory *Quarterly*, in the hope of countering the *Edinburgh*'s influence and fostering patriotic support of the government.[9] The periodical enlisted the pens of Walter Scott, Robert Southey and other Romantic writers whom Jeffrey had alienated, while Murray also secured the poetry of Byron for his list. For Byronism emerged from the fracture between philosophical Whiggism and aesthetic experimentation at this time. The eventual defeat of Napoleon and with him the ideas which inspired the French Revolution, together with the stagnation of the British Whigs, produced a flowering of literature in which frustrated political idealism turned inward, extolling instead the freedom of individual subjectivity. But the *Edinburgh* was slow to appreciate Romantic poetry, and castigated subjectivity as a truth which is merely particular and individual, in contrast to those universal emotions of humanity sanctioned both by classical theory and the new Utilitarian emphasis on realism and social utility.[10]

John Murray was eager to capitalize on the disaffection of moderate or Whiggish writers who had been attacked by the *Edinburgh*. It was natural therefore that Murray would interest himself in the young poet who had, in his scourging of the *Edinburgh*, paid such pointed tribute to the *Quarterly*'s prospective editor, William Gifford. Byron may well have known, through literary gossip, that the *Quarterly* was to be launched at virtually the same time as his satire on its rival periodical. He and Gifford may well have met; they were both members of the Alfred club. Anyway, in a meeting with Dallas on Byron's return from his Grand Tour, Murray told Dallas he regretted he had not had the opportunity to publish *English Bards and Scotch Reviewers*, and expressed an interest in publishing something from the author (*Dallas*, pp. 120–1). Indeed, Byron refers to a scheme of Murray publishing 'all my rhymes together, including my satire' as early as 23 June 1810 (*L&J*, i. 248).

On his part, Byron needed respectability and allies after his onslaught on the powerful *Edinburgh*, if he was to be accepted by the newly-expanded reading public. He also had to make compromises either in self-censorship when composing, or in mutually agreed adjustments to his manuscripts, in order to keep Murray as his publisher as long as he did. The poet and his publisher often clashed over the precise limits of his unorthodoxy, and this process began with *Childe Harold*. When Murray objected to some tendentious stanzas critical of the government's conduct during the Peninsular War, Byron replied grandly: 'I am afraid I can alter nothing ... for even the *Æneid* was a *political* poem & written for a *political purpose*, ... but if there are any alterations in the structure of the versification you would wish to be made, I will tag rhymes, & turn Stanzas, as much as you please (*L&J*, ii. 90–1). But in fact he was persuaded to make various small changes including the softening of stanzas criticizing the Convention of Cintra, the omission of some of the stanzas attacking individuals like Wellington, Elgin and Beckford, and the rephrasing of a freethinking passage.

Murray made a very fair offer: to print *Childe Harold* at his own expense and share any profits with Dallas, the copyright to be disposed of later depending on its success. Dallas congratulated himself for eventually obtaining £600 for it (*Dallas*, pp. 121–2). The poet would often call in on his publisher on his way back from fencing practice: 'while Murray was reading passages from the poem, with occasional ejaculations of admiration; on which Byron would say, "You think that a good idea, do you, Murray?" Then he would fence and lunge with his walking stick at some special book which he had picked out on the shelves before him. As Murray afterwards said, "I was often very glad to get rid of him!" (*Smiles*, i. 207). Perhaps this anecdote reveals Byron's unconscious rivalry with other writers!

John Murray II was not very much older than the poet, and, though he had assured George Canning that he was 'no adventurer', he embodied the romance of enterprise as Byron did that of travel. He was as determined to raise the status of bookseller from tradesman to gentleman as Byron was to make the profession of poet worthy of an aristocrat. In that they were made for each other. *Childe Harold's Pilgrimage* was also the ideal poem for Murray's firm, which had already published Mitford's *History of Greece* and which would go on to specialize in travel literature in the later nineteenth century, forming with Thomas Cook and Baedeker the holy Trinity of tourism. Murray's handbooks for travellers of the mid nineteenth century – when the nobleman's grand tour was replaced by the middle-class Cook's tour – would be peppered with quotations from *Childe Harold*.[11]

The symbiotic relationship, posited by Edward Said, between European imperialism and first utilitarian then fashionable Orientalism can be confirmed from the origin of this firm. Murray's father, a Scottish retired lieutenant of marines, had set up the Fleet Street shop in 1768, and specialized in sending books abroad to his fellow officers, expatriates in the colonies and to East India Company officials.[12] John Murray II came of age in 1801 and perpetuated this tradition by concentrating on textbooks for and by the services and professional classes, such as medical books, memoirs and voyages. He was appointed publisher to the Admiralty and brought out the Navy List. He expanded his range to include such writers as Jane Austen, Madame de Staël, Thomas Malthus, Robert Southey, Samuel Rogers, James Hogg, Thomas Moore, Edward Gibbon, Charles Lyell, and Washington Irving, but was still the obvious choice for the *Despatches* of the Duke of Wellington, and the travels of Mungo Park, Sir John Ross, and Sir William Parry.

John Murray II was much more ambitious than his father. He followed in the footsteps of the trailblazing Scottish publisher, Archibald Constable. Constable's policy was to attract the best authors through handsome payment, and so put his firm at the centre of literary Edinburgh. This heralded a new age when the publisher replaced the patron as mediator between authors and the reading public, and the literati met in his premises rather than a salon. By 1825 a journalist could write:

> A literary man of the present day would as soon think of seeking patronage from the Emperor of Austria, or setting forth the talents and the virtues of the Spanish Ferdinand, as of placing his hopes of a hearing with the public upon the foremost nobleman in the land ... this change has brought the publishers of books into an attitude of the greatest importance and honour; – it has made them the connecting link between the people of every land where intellect has not the same unbounded scope.[13]

Through Constable, Edinburgh ('the Athens of the North') broke the monopoly of London on 'the Trade' and for twenty years took the initiative in raising the status of the profession of letters. Constable launched the *Edinburgh Review* in 1802, promising to expect no special treatment of his publications by the contributors, and ensuring professionalism by generously paying the editor £200 p.a. and anonymous contributors ten and sometimes twenty guineas a sheet. Murray became for a time the *Edinburgh*'s London agent and later modelled the *Quarterly Review* on these principles. The partnership between Constable and Scott (nicknamed the Czar and the Wizard of the North respectively) in the production of bestselling poems like *The Lay of the Last Minstrel* (1805) also became the model for that of Murray and Byron. Constable and Scott were drawn together by their antiquarianism, which inspired the poet to produce modern versions of the medieval ballads and romances he had collected. In a comparable way, Byron and Murray collaborated in mediating the traveller's experience of the exoticism of the East.

After the success of *The Lay*, Constable had amazed the literary world by offering £1050 for the copyright of the as yet incomplete *Marmion,* in which Murray took a quarter share of the risk.[14] Though Murray was a more prudent businessman, he was no less generous and was dubbed by Scott 'the Emperor of the West', and known also as 'the Prince of Booksellers'. Over the years of his association with Byron, Murray paid out about £15,000 for copyrights, either to those upon whom the poet conferred them, or later when he became reconciled to payment, to Byron himself. He paid £600 for the copyrights of the first two cantos, and £2000 for the third canto of *Childe Harold,* £1575 for the first two of *Don Juan* with the *Ode to Venice,* and £2710 for the rights of *Sardanapalus, The Two Foscari* and *Cain.*[15]

Remuneration

Byron's attitude to remuneration changed throughout his career. His fear that, if he accepted payment, it would be thought he had sacrificed his independence from his bookseller's interests vied with pride that he could command huge sums. When Murray offered 1000 guineas for *The Giaour* and *The Bride of Abydos,* the poet wrote in his diary: 'I won't. It is too much: though I am strongly tempted, merely for the say of it. No bad price for a fortnight's (a week each) what? – the gods know. It was intended to be called poetry' (*Smiles*, i. 222). Murray was understandably annoyed when Byron first refused because it was too much, then requested the money 'for the say of it', merely to confer it on the sycophantic Dallas. Finally, after a brief squabble with the publisher, he left the money with Murray. He accepted five hundred guineas for the copyright of *The Corsair* and again gave it to Dallas. At the end of 1815, Byron was in such severe financial difficulties that he planned to sell his library. When Murray heard of this he sent the poet a cheque for £1500, offered to send another in a few weeks, and even to sell the copyrights for his poetry and send Byron the proceeds. Byron returned the cheque but was moved by the publisher's impulsive generosity. Murray then sent him two notes amounting to a thousand guineas for *Parisina* and *The Siege of Corinth.* Byron returned them, as 'what is right is right, and must not yield to circumstances'. However, later he reverted to his infuriating unprofessionalism over money, by writing to ask for it back in order to donate £600 to the impecunious philosopher William Godwin, and to divide the remainder between the Irish playwright Charles Maturin and Coleridge. Murray and Gifford were outraged, especially as they disapproved of Godwin's revolutionary views. Gifford fumed: 'A downright robbery is honourable to it' (*Smiles*, i. 356). Eventually, Byron was so pressed by his own debts that he accepted the money for himself, probably the first time he had done so. Only two years previously he had encouraged Dallas to make a public statement denying that the poet had ever received remuneration, after the Tory press had attacked his mercenary motives in much the same terms he had himself earlier satirized Scott.

When in 1816 Byron left Britain for good, after the scandal of his failed marriage, he changed his mind entirely about payment. He made Douglas Kinnaird his agent, who informed Murray that his offer of fifteen hundred guineas for the third canto of *Childe Harold's Pilgrimage* was refused. But this time the publisher was startled to discover it was because Byron had decided the poem was worth two thousand! From then on Byron drove hard bargains with his long-suffering publisher, as he now not only accepted but threw himself with gusto into the role of paid professional. Byron recollected to Medwin that Murray once quoted his own lines satirizing mercenary writers from *English Bards* back at him, 'But I have altered my mind considerably upon that subject; as I once hinted to him, I see no reason why a man should not profit by the sweat of his brain, as well as that of his brow, &, besides, I was poor at that time and have [*sic*] no idea of aggrandizing booksellers' (*Medwin*, pp. 168–9).

The glittering rewards earned by Scott and Byron fired men and women of letters with the possibility either of making a living or at least of supplementing a modest income through the profession of authorship and journalism. In 1814 a new Copyright Act, supported by Southey, bettered the author's situation further, by extending the term of copyright to twenty-eight years or the life of the author, whichever was the longer.[16]

It is no coincidence that the word 'genius' was at this time undergoing a shift in usage from 'individual characteristic' to a creative intelligence of a higher order than that of common humanity, deriving from supernatural inspiration. For we are seeing a star system in the making. Scott's biographer, John Gibson Lockhart, remembered the insatiable demand for the poetry of Scott and Byron when a young student at Oxford, 'how the booksellers' shops there were beleaguered for the earliest copies, and how he that had been so fortunate as to secure one was followed to his chambers by a tribe of friends'.[17]

Price of books

Demand exceeded the supply of secular books in the first quarter of the century which for the first time overtook religious titles in number. Poetry by Walter Scott, Byron, Samuel Rogers and Thomas Moore was particularly popular.[18] The majority of these books were highly-priced, costing two guineas for a quarto and twelve shillings or more for an octavo. The conservative book trade was slow to introduce mechanization; the Napoleonic wars made materials expensive; but, crucially, the manufacturing and commercial class who had benefited from trading in war supplies were prepared to pay highly for literature as a luxury item.[19] Charles Knight, writing in 1854, believed that the publishers had deliberately maintained a narrow market with high prices.[20] A printer told the select committee of the House of Commons on the Copyright Acts in 1818 that 'Books are a luxury, and the purchase of them has been confined to fewer people'.[21] Byron complained to a friend that quarto 'is a cursed unsaleable size' (*L&J*, ii. 113), but Murray knew better, having learned from the example of Scott that sumptuous first editions of fashionable literature could sell in large numbers to the rich, followed by cheaper reprints and omnibus editions for the middle class. It was not until the mid 1820s that the proportion of highly-priced books began to decline in relation to medium-priced publications aimed at the 200,000 whom Jeffrey in 1812 had estimated to constitute 'the middling classes of society'. John Murray reported that: 'the public are absolutely indignant' that they had to wait until 1830 for a mid-priced collected edition of Byron's works, for he had been delayed in buying up all the remaining copyrights.[22] By the 1820s, a few visionaries had the dream of extending readership even further. In 1826 Brougham set up the Society for the Diffusion of Useful Knowledge to provide the working classes with cheap educational books, and the same year Constable attempted to exploit a mass readership of fiction, and bankrupted himself in the process. But in 1812 such concepts were unthinkable. It was then not useful knowledge but 'the viewless wings of poesy', the most prestigious of genres, which genteel readers wanted: eager to soar above both religious and secular didacticism. A poem like *Childe Harold's Pilgrimage*, combining the exotic adventuring of an explorer with the social cachet of the aristocrat's Grand Tour, particularly appealed to the entrepreneurial classes, unable to travel because of the Napoleonic Wars.

The publication of *Childe Harold*

The story of *Childe Harold*'s publication on 1 March 1812 is well known. Byron later recalled, 'I awoke one morning and found myself famous'. Murray had been assiduous in publicizing the new poem and in ensuring that worthies like Lord Holland received presentation copies. In three days the first edition of 500 copies had been sold and a new edition in octavo was set up, which itself soon went. Dallas called on Byron to find him 'loaded with letters from critics, poets, authors, and various pretenders to fame, all lavish in their raptures' (*Dallas*, p. 229). Four and a half thousand copies were sold in six months. He would be lionized by high society, and even the Prince Regent made a point of complimenting the poet. Though *The Waltz* (1812), his anonymous satire on fashionable London, failed and was disowned, his series of Oriental tales, *The Giaour* (1813), *The Bride of Abydos* (1813), *The Corsair* (1814), and *Lara* (1814), featuring Byronic heroes as moodily magnificent as Harold, were each rapturously received. Six thousand copies of *The Bride* were sold in a month, and Murray reported on *The Corsair*: 'I sold, on the day of publication, – a thing perfectly unprecedented – 10,000 copies' (*Smiles*, i. 223). Twenty-five thousand copies were sold within a month. Perhaps no poet has ever had such success as Byron.

Composition: revision and amendments

Byron always associated passion with composition (*L&J*, viii. 146). In 1821 he would write to Thomas Moore: 'I feel exactly as you do about our 'art', but it comes over me in a kind of rage every now and then, like ••••, and then, if I don't write to empty my mind, I go mad. As to that regular, uninterrupted love of writing, which you describe in your friend, I do not understand it. I feel it as a torture, which I must get rid of, but never as a pleasure' (*L&J*, viii. 55). He defined poetry as 'the lava of the imagination whose eruption prevents an earthquake' (*L&J*, iii. 179). Nevertheless, he admitted that his apparent spontaneity was often the result of long thought on a subject, 'Extemporising verses is nonsense; poetry is a distinct faculty, – it won't come when called, – you may as well whistle for a wind; a Pythoness was primed when put upon her stand. I must chew the cud before I write. I have thought over most of my subjects for years before writing a line ... You might as well ask me to describe an earth-quake whilst the ground was trembling under my feet'.[23]

Byron developed a habit of having a few copies of his first draft of a poem printed in order to circulate it to his inner circle of literary confidantes. This most egotistical of writers was also most open to readers' reactions. 'Second thoughts in every thing are best, but, in rhyme, third and fourth don't come amiss' (*L&J*, ii. 150). Then the length would increase through accretion and revision, and the printer would run off some copies of the final version for their comments before the publication date. Sometimes this process even continued after publication, through the revision or additions to several editions, as happened with *The Giaour*. This was a verse tale based on a real incident from his travels in which Byron had rescued at gunpoint a Turkish woman sewn up in a sack and about to be ceremoniously drowned for adultery. The first MS draft had been 406 lines and the first published edition 685, but by the seventh the poem had swelled to 1334 lines. Eventually, the poet wrote to Murray, 'I have but with some difficulty *not* added any more to this snake of a poem – which has been lengthening its rattles every month' (*L&J*, iii. 100). Some critics have assumed this method of composition to be the slipshod practice of a dilettante, too lazy to ensure coherence and unity. But it was rather that the poet was aiming at a daring experiment in abandoning his original straightforward plot. He was testing readers' reactions in assessing how far he could go in breaking down narrative into evocative fragments narrated from differing points of view for the reader to piece together.

Ian Jack has described as 'concentric circles' those different audiences which made up Byron's readership, from the inner circle who read the drafts in manuscript or private printings to those who could afford to pay highly for the first edition in quarto, broadening out to the wider reading public who bought a subsequent and probably revised cheaper edition.[24] The ripples of fashion thus radiated outwards from a small audience of literati, known personally to the poet, like that which had appertained in the early eighteenth century. The published text then stimulated the 'public sphere' of educated and wealthy readers, who communicated with the middle class through the periodicals, which enthusiastically recommended Byron to their readers. Later, from about 1816, radical publishers would use extracts from Byron's poems in their papers and even pirate cheap copies for the working classes. For example, William Hone issued a prose version of *The Corsair* in 1817, to help make a martyr of Jeremiah Brandreth, the leader of a Nottinghamshire uprising, whose defence counsel, at his trial for treason, had compared him to Byron's hero.[25]

William Gifford

Byron supposedly exploded in wrath at hearing that Murray had shown the poem to the satirist William Gifford before accepting it. For, after the drubbing he had received in the *Edinburgh*, it would be embarrassing if it was suspected he wanted special treatment in the *Quarterly Review*, which Gifford edited: 'I will have no traps for applause' (*L&J*, ii. 75). But, as we have seen, for many years, Byron *was* to be the only Whig writer not to be lashed by the new periodical. Byron much later admitted, 'Murray has long prevented 'The Quarterly' from abusing me' (*Medwin*, p. 170). Murray reported William Gifford's reaction to *The Giaour*: 'The new edition of his poem contains passages of exquisite beauty…equal to anything that I have ever read. What is he about? Will he not collect all his force for one immortal work?' (*Smiles*, i. 219–20). If it was a paradox that the poetry of Byron should be published by John Murray, then the close literary relationship between the poet and the editor of the *Quarterly Review* is even stranger.[26] It was not only that the young aristocratic rake and the lowborn elderly pedant would seem to have little in common, but that a Whig poet who would execrate Robert Southey as a turncoat and William Wordsworth as a sinecure-holder could adopt as his 'literary father' a government tool like Gifford requires explanation. Though Gifford was a respected classicist and editor of English Renaissance dramatists, he was most famous as the brutal former editor of the *Anti-Jacobin*, a periodical supported by the Tory government, which from 1797–8 used fairly unsubtle satire to attack writers of pro-revolutionary or Liberal views. For his services, Gifford received government pensions. The founding of the *Quarterly* was a reprise of this counter-revolutionary policy, and brought together, as members of its editorial coterie, other ex-*Anti-Jacobin* stalwarts. These included Scott's friend, the foreign minister George Canning, who had been partly responsible for the mismanagement of Sir John Moore's expedition to Spain; his friend the classicist John Hookham Frere, whose diplomatic career ended after his advice to Sir John Moore in 1808 was found to have contributed to the disastrous retreat; and the diplomat and antiquarian George Ellis, to whom Scott had dedicated Canto V of *Marmion*. Such men, with Gifford, had a vested interest in rebutting the *Edinburgh*'s criticism of Government policy in the Peninsular War, and promoting patriotism through the new *Quarterly Review*. Yet Byron was sufficiently impressed by their respect for literary tradition and reputation as satirists of affectation that he allowed Murray to consult them as literary advisors on his work. He respected Gifford's judgement above all. Gifford had been a less talented humorist in the *Anti-Jacobin* days, and inclined towards unsubtle partisan abuse, but could be relied upon to perform the drudgery of editorship of the *Quarterly* under the watchful eye of Scott and Murray. Why did Byron have reverence for such a man?

It is possible that Byron, famously hypersensitive on the subject of his own club foot, felt an affinity with the hunchbacked and infirm scholar who had surmounted early hardship and poverty, as detailed in the dignified autobiography appended to his 1802 translation of Juvenal. Add to this Byron's own identification with the conservative diatribes of Juvenal on the degeneration of contemporary society and literature in *English Bards and Scotch Reviewers*. But most telling is the young poet's admiration for Gifford's mockery of the sentimental verse of the Della Cruscans, in his *Baviad* (1791) and *Maeviad* (1795). When Byron wrote to thank Gifford for his praise of *The Giaour*, he assured him: 'Any suggestion of yours even were it conveyed in the less tender shape of the text of the Baviad or a Monk Mason note in Massinger would have been obeyed – I should have endeavoured to improve myself by your censure ...' (*L&J*, iii. 64). In other words, Byron wishes to profit from the harshness of Gifford, as dealt out in merciless lashings inflicted on contemporary poets or former scholars of the Renaissance dramatists he had edited. He willingly submits to him as a literary disciplinarian. He described Gifford as his 'literary father and myself as his prodigal son' (*L&J*, xi. 117, 123).

Though he was one of them, Byron believed that contemporary Romantic poets were bent 'upon a wrong poetical system' (*L&J*, v. 265–6), and quixotically defended Pope against the strictures of Bowles, and the tenets of neo-classical drama against Romantic quasi-Shakespeareanism. He saw Gifford as defending the standards established by a classical literary tradition; standards with which he wanted to remain in contact. He was only too well aware of the affinities of his own early verse with that of the Della Cruscans, and perhaps consciously or unconsciously guarded against future criticism of excess subjectivity or slovenly writing by the expediency of keeping an in-house watchdog.

The extent of Byron's trust in Gifford's judgement is not only evidenced by the way he asks for the editor of the *Quarterly* to be shown each publication in advance and instructs Murray that in all points of difference between Gifford and any other adviser, he would choose the former. He goes further. As well as making innumerable changes according to Gifford's advice, Byron invited Gifford to choose which was better from alternative passages in *The Bride of Abydos* and later *Beppo, Marino Faliero* and *Cain*; he gave him permission to omit or alter any lines he pleased in *The Siege of Corinth*; and Byron entirely rewrote the third act of *Manfred* on account of his disapproval. The poet said he would give Gifford and two other advisers the final decision whether to publish or burn the MS of the fourth canto of *Childe Harold*. For his part, Gifford seems to have been as genuinely impressed by Byron's verse as he was by his title. He was so delighted with *The Corsair* he was able to repeat several passages from memory; and Murray reported that Gifford thought the author of *Childe Harold* I and II 'would last far beyond any poet of the present day' (*Smiles*, i. 223–5). He stayed up all night reading *Childe Harold III* and commended the first act of *Marino Faliero* as 'sterling genuine English'. After his self-imposed exile in 1816, Byron relied on Gifford even more heavily as a meticulous reader of his manuscripts and even a proof reader, when the poet felt too lazy to perform this chore.

Byron rarely communicated directly with Gifford. Murray acted as go-between, ostensibly to spare the elderly Gifford from the chore of writing to Byron. But this also allowed Murray tactfully to edit the dialogue of both editor and poet. For example, Murray summarizes for Byron the editor's suggestions for improving *The Siege of Corinth*, which he supposedly read 'with great delight', but Gifford's actual note to Murray had concluded darkly: 'I lament bitterly to see a great mind run to seed, and waste itself in rank growth' (*Smiles*, i. 357–8). At other times, particularly later in his career, it was Byron who would angrily refuse to tone down controversial passages. But he always apparently exempted Gifford from his execrations: 'I care for none of you except Gifford, and he won't abuse me except I deserve it, which will at least reconcile me to his justice' (*L&J*, viii. 218). It was Murray's tact which kept the Byron/Gifford relationship open as the line of communication between the poet and his publisher's circle. Murray's salving of Byron's outbursts with doses of flattery, and his perseverance, even after Gifford had become disillusioned by the poet's sexual disgrace and increasingly radical politics, staved off the inevitable break between poet and publisher for some years. The Murray circle thus mediated between Byron and a mass readership in the years of fame (1812–16): influencing what he wrote by suggesting subject-matter; by timing publications to foster rivalry with other poets like Walter Scott; by circulating drafts to gauge the likely reactions of readers and reviewers; and by focusing on sections of the reading public through the price charged for editions.

Subjectivity and the reader

Byron's texts themselves attract the reader by their particular success in obscuring the capitalist process of book production foregrounded in this chapter, firstly by substituting the rhetoric of intimacy for the contractual roles of producer/consumer, and secondly by paradoxically presenting the idealization of pre-modern societies within the gilt-embossed covers of a luxury volume. The book, *Childe Harold's Pilgrimage*, which the Duchess of Devonshire observed was gracing everyone's drawing-room table in 1812, contained within its handsome covers a heterogeneous collection of texts. The epic travel poem itself was a hybrid of narrative and lyric genres, interrupted by interpolated songs and framed by lively prose notes in the ironic voice of the poet of *English Bards*. In addition, the first edition contained fourteen and, from the second edition on, twenty additional lyrics, arranged as if to correspond with the themes of the narrative. This blurred the distinction between the fictional Childe Harold as singer of the interpolated songs and the overall author 'Lord Byron'. Many of these lyrics had implied female narratees. Five were addressed to 'Florence', having been inspired by Byron's love affair with Mrs Constance Spencer Smith in Malta, and six were addressed to a mysterious 'Thyrza', whose tragic early death could be inferred to be the cause of Harold's misery.

There was also an appendix containing a lively and eclectic collection of examples and translations of the Romaic language. This included, amongst other items: the first printed text of the famous war song of the Greek patriot, Konstantin Rigas, and Byron's own translation of it; an appeal in Romaic for Philhellenes to help John Marmarotoures, Byron's tutor in the language, publish in England a Romaic translation of Barthélemy's *The New Anarcharsis;* parallel passages from St John's gospel in classical Greek and Romaic; and a set of phrases useful for the traveller who wished to follow in Byron's footsteps, such as 'I love you with all my heart' and five different 'affectionate expressions'. There was even a facsimile of a letter to Byron from the Bey of Corinth, to illustrate the Turkish epistolary style. This appendix was designed to introduce the British reader to the culture of the modern Christian population now living in that part of the Ottoman empire corresponding to ancient Greece, and to highlight their intellectual and political oppression by the Turks, for they could only publish books in their language abroad.[27] The apparatus of factual notes and heterogeneous appendix which framed the main text could be construed differently by readers from a wide ideological spectrum: as a helpful guide for future travellers; as a collection of linguistic curios for those with a smattering of schoolboy classical Greek; as guarantor that the poem is grounded in the author's lived experience; but also combining with the rhetoric of the poetry to politicize its Philhellenist sentiments.

Childe Harold's Pilgrimage inaugurates an intimate relationship between author and reader; more personal than any which had so far appeared, outside Rousseau's *Confessions*. It is not employed straight away for the poem begins by employing Augustan ironic humour, similar to that of James Thomson's *The Castle of Indolence* (1748). Harold is jauntily introduced in cod archaisms as a recognizable parody of the author, a cynical rake who leaves his 'monastic dome' to relieve his *ennui* with travel:

> Whilome in Albion's isle there dwelt a youth,
> Who ne in virtue's ways did take delight;
> But spent his days in riot most uncouth.
> (*Childe Harold's Pilgrimage* I, 2)

But in the revision process the character's melancholy *weltschmertz* was allowed to escape the confines of his own lyrical effusions, into the additional lyrics, and infuse at times the narrator's voice. The narrator increasingly speaks in the first person of his deepest feelings, and the second canto ends with his grief:

> All thou could'st have of mine, stern Death! thou hast;
> The parent, friend, and now the more than friend:
> (*Childe Harold's Pilgrimage* II, 96)

For, as he explained in the notes, an extraordinary number of deaths within a short time had devastated Byron on his return home. These included his mother, his college friend Charles Skinner Matthews, his Harrow schoolmate John Wingfield and the Cambridge chorister, John Edleston.

A dialectic is thus set up between the sceptical protagonist and his alter ego, the confessional poet. In the Preface and the addition to it, appended to the fourth edition, Byron insisted that 'Harold is the child of imagination' and intended as 'the sketch of a modern Timon' rather than a self-portrait. Nevertheless, by putting interpolated lyrics into the mouth of the character similar to those included over the poet's name, and by including first-person anecdotal prose notes referring the reader to his actual experience abroad, Byron was himself inviting interest in the way his writing could be perceived as drawing on and fictionalizing his own life story. The Byronic hero Harold is an insider in the Establishment through birth and education, yet emotionally as well as geographically detached from Britain. The poet portrays himself, also, as a Romantic voice in the wilderness or a lonely face in the crowd: 'Then must I plunge again into the crowd...' (*CHP* II, 97). This is alienation with which each individual reader could easily identify, himself aware of being transformed into an anonymous consumer in an industrialized modern economy.

Gender

The poem addresses itself quite specifically to both male and female readers at different times. To an extent this is a matter of mixed genres. The epic narrative itself is a masculine quest for adventure, while many of the lyrics have female addressees.[28] The poem functions as a masculine *bildungsroman*, with its scenario of the grand tour which supplemented the young nobleman's classical education, its tributes to male friends in the prefaces and notes, and elegies to dead youth – both the personal friends of the poet and those who died on the battlefield. His lengthy farewell to female relations and mistresses signals the way Harold's epic journey functions as a celebration of masculine freedom from domestic constraints. Like an on-the spot-war reporter, he then journeys through the ravaged Peninsula, giving vivid eye-witness accounts of the campaign: contrasting the passivity of the Portuguese with the fierce independence of the Spaniards in their stand against Napoleon. As he treks East and leaves effeminate modern civilization behind, he traverses sublime mountainous scenery to reach the authentically male warrior cultures of the Ottoman empire.

Byron followed Scott in what may have been a conscious attempt to masculinize poetry, which was seen by Gifford's coterie as having been unduly feminized by the sentimental lyrics of the Della Cruscans and popular women poets like Charlotte Smith. But the poem is not merely adventurous narrative. It comprises a serious attempt on the poet's part to focus his attention squarely on the cultural construction of masculine identity, a force both for good and for evil. Picturing the battles of the Peninsular War (I, 35–44), a Spanish bullfight (I, 68–80), the subjugation of women in a polygamous Moslem court (II, 55–66), and the male camaraderie of a Suliote camp (II, 67–84), Byron probes the intermingling of heroic idealism and vicious brutality in male warrior cultures of Europe, past and present.

Although the implied reader is often specifically male in the public discourse of the narrative, the lyrics of the private voice like 'To Ianthe' and 'To Inez', and those appended to the poem, often have specifically female narratees. Ianthe is an idealised adolescent girl, whose purity overawes the poet and proscribes any sexual relationship. Instead she is invited to 'glance o'er this page' (l. 31) as a substitute. This poem, which opens *Childe Harold*, constitutes an overtly seductive invitation to the virgin readers Byron had already been warned against corrupting by moralists like the Rev. Becher and R.C. Dallas. The fictional Harold uses similar tactics. He repeatedly repudiates sexual relationships with women like 'Florence', and declines even to dance with the female addressee of 'To Inez', while simultaneously inviting their sympathy by his melancholy. This pose of the disillusioned libertine certainly attracted contemporary female readers. The feminist follower of Mary Wollstonecraft, Lady Caroline Lamb, and bluestocking Annabella Milbanke were representative of a host of contemporary women readers smitten by a Byronic hero they imagined to be modelled on the writer himself. Byron was 'Mad, bad and dangerous to know', as Lady Caroline excitedly confided to her diary. 'His poem sufficiently proves that he *can* feel nobly, but he has discouraged his own goodness', wrote the solemn Miss Milbanke, Caroline's husband's mathematical cousin.[29] Both pursued the poet. Lady Caroline acted the part of a Byronic heroine, dressing as a pageboy to visit him in a tempestuous adulterous affair. Then the virginal Annabella encouraged him to marry her so that she could reform him. In his guilt over his affair with his own half-sister, Augusta, when they were snowed up together at Newstead, Byron eventually succumbed to the disastrous union in 1815. Both Caroline and Annabella ruined their lives in the vain attempt to become Childe Harold's lost love.

As Louis Crompton has pointed out, for such contemporary female readers the misogyny of the poem's opening was mitigated by the inclusion of the 'Thyrza' lyrics – Haroldian elegies to the poet's true love, who died at a tragically young age before they could meet on his return from the East.[30] Three of these love lyrics were published with the first edition, and a further three added to the end of the second edition. We now know that the 'Thyrza' lyrics were actually elegies composed after Byron learnt of the death of the Cambridge chorister, John Edleston, with whom he had experienced an intense romantic friendship. But the feminized name of the addressee, the absence of masculine pronouns and the feminine characteristics of the beautiful young singer allowed the poems to be read as evidence of Harold/ Byron's capacity for an idealized romantic love for a woman.

> The kiss, so guiltless and refin'd,
> That Love each warmer wish forbore;
> Those eyes proclaim'd so pure a mind,
> Ev'n passion blush'd to plead for more.
> ('To Thyrza', *CPW* no. 166, ll. 33–6)

The search for 'Greek love' was probably one of the poet's primary motives for travelling East (*L&J*, i. 206–7), and certainly part of the reason he stayed behind in Greece after Hobhouse's return to Britain. The 'Thyrza' poems express yet another (private) strand of Philhellenism within the heterogeneous volumes of *Childe Harold's Pilgrimage*.

The poem reached out to its contemporary readers with an attractive combination of the familiar and the new. They would be familiar with other topographical poems like Wright's *Horae Ionicae* (1809), and the mock-Spenserianisms of Thomson and Beattie. But the Augustan conventions of such poems had been infused by Byronic meditative melancholy, in changes of gear from the narrative mode to lyrical emotional intensity. The outer narrative of the journey was thus complemented by an inner psychological quest. The poem moved from the known to the unknown, also, in its Orientalism. It bridged the Occident and the Orient, journeying from the Moorish exoticism of Spain to the heart of the Moslem Ottoman empire itself.

Childe Harold's Pilgrimage I and II was a literary phenomenon, going through countless editions and being translated into all the major European languages during in the nineteenth century, becoming perhaps the most bestselling and best-known poem in English Literature. From the time of its publication until his death Byron was a 'star' whose every deed and word was liable to be assiduously scrutinized and recorded by contemporaries. When he was lionized in London, strange women wrote to offer themselves to him; when the scandal of his libertinism was at its height in 1815, they ostracized him. Once, a woman was so overcome at being in the same room as the satanic lover that she fainted away when his name was announced and was carried out unconscious past the bemused poet. Now when he travelled abroad, he found he had metamorphosed from tourist to tourist attraction, his home being scrutinized by visitors through field glasses, villagers clustering to watch his carriage passing down the street.

Byron's Orientalist poetry 1812–16 was crucially influential in popularizing literary Philhellenism and thus preparing the ground for the political schemes of expatriate Westernized Greeks to found a modern nation-state based on democratic principles. They needed a myth of nationhood to import to the indigenous peoples who fought among themselves as much as against their Turkish overlords, and whose Christianity rather than ethnicity defined their identity. Byronism played a vital role in the years leading up to the Greek revolution of 1821. Together the poet from the East and the 'Emperor of the West' had produced a literary sensation.

3
The Acting of Tragedy and the Tragedy of Acting: Byron, Drury Lane Theatre and Romantic Drama

> Gods! o'er those boards shall Folly rear her head
> Where GARRICK trod, and SIDDONS lives to tread?
> On those shall Farce display buffonery's mask,
> And HOOK conceal his heroes in a cask?
> Shall sapient managers new schemes produce
> From CHERRY, SKEFFINGTON, and Mother GOOSE?
> While SHAKESPEARE, OTWAY, MASSINGER, forgot,
> On stalls must moulder, or in closets rot?
> (*English Bards and Scotch Reviewers* (1809), ll. 586–93)

It appears to me that there is room for a different style of the drama; neither a servile following of the old drama, which is a grossly erroneous one, nor yet *too French*, like those who succeeded the older writers. It appears to me, that good English, and a severer approach to the rules, might combine something not dishonourable to our literature'.

> (*L&J*, viii. 78)

Byron is the most important British dramatist of the Romantic period. First as the commissioner of others and later as a playwright himself, he attempted to instigate a revival of blank verse tragedy. Though he had some success in his attempt to encourage the staging of the 'legitimate' dramas of others, Byron was so disillusioned with the London theatre that in his own eight plays, he wrote for 'the closet' or the private reader. Only *Marino Faliero* was staged in his lifetime, and he ordered his publisher to get the production stopped. Nevertheless, five of his plays were adapted for the stage after his death, during the nineteenth century, and *Werner* was regularly performed as a popular vehicle for William Charles Macready. His tragedies inspired the art of others, such as paintings by John Martin and operas by Gaetano Donizetti and Guiseppe Verdi. Byron's ambivalent attitude to the theatre serves to exemplify that of the canonical male Romantic poets, who all attempted to write blank verse for the stage because of their wish to emulate Shakespeare, yet were then inhibited by the 'anxiety of influence'. Another difficulty was that the only two London theatres allowed to present 'legitimate' drama each seated over 3000 spectators, and were often given over to lavish spectacle, and thus did not readily lend themselves to experimental plays of ideas dependent on the power of the spoken word.

As they do not contribute to the progress towards dramatic realism of the nineteenth-century theatre and because they focus on introspection at the expense of plot development, Romantic dramas like Byron's have been considered failures as plays by some theatre historians. Yet George Steiner has written that Byron's dramas are 'of the first interest to anyone concerned with the idea of tragedy in modern literature ... The range of technical audacity is extreme. We move from the strict neo-classicism of *Marino Faliero* to the near surrealism of the late mystery plays.'[1] The genre of tragedy traditionally depended on the audience's belief in providence and the convention of a noble protagonist was the product of a hierarchically ordered society. Modernity destroyed these conditions of reception, for Enlightenment rationalism led to a secular world view and to the emergence of the ideals of republicanism and democracy when the American War of Independence and the French Revolution destroyed the old social order. Attempts at tragedy written during the Romantic period therefore fell short of sublimity, for the hero's troubles often lacked public significance, and stress on his remorse was a bathetic substitute for divine retribution. By setting most of his plays in courtly or patriarchal societies of the past, and featuring manifestations of the divine or supernatural in three of them, Byron was more successful than most of his contemporaries in approaching true tragedy. Traditional tragedy had articulated an essentially aristocratic viewpoint, now increasingly irrelevant to modern Britain, but his class gave Lord Byron a unique perspective to represent as tragedy the loss of aristocratic ideals through the fall of the Byronic overreacher.

Critics like John P. Farrell and Jeffrey N. Cox have gone on to make the essential point that Romantic dramatists actually extended the paradigms of traditional tragedy in adapting it to represent their own historical moment.[2] Written in despair after the collapse of republicanism in France and the restoration of the monarchy, plays like Byron's *Cain* and Shelley's *The Cenci* take as their subject-matter the tragedy of an individual's failure to realize his/her visionary ideals through destruction of the traditional social and moral hierarchy. Thus when the protagonist commits a violent revolutionary act on behalf of humanity he/she attempts heroism yet also risks descent into meaninglessness. Cox comments:

> We can agree with Steiner that the romantics were barred from writing tragedies of the closed world and yet realize that they forged a new mode of tragic drama by depicting the travails of the extraordinary individual as he plumbs the ever-deepening recesses of the self and hurls himself into the rush of history. The romantic tragedy of the open world portrays modern revolutionary man's heroic attempt to order the chaos of the liberated self and to shape history freed from divine control.[3]

Byron's tragedies on the modern impossibility of heroism do not lead towards nineteenth-century plays of social realism but they do anticipate some of the concerns of the twentieth-century existential drama of Samuel Beckett and the Theatre of the Absurd. The specific historical conditions that produced them were first his concerted attempt to reform the theatre of his own time by instituting the acting of poetic tragedy, then his turn away into an *avant-garde* 'mental theatre' of ideas through which to examine the tragedy of revolutionary action. We will therefore consider first Byron's involvement with the Drury Lane Theatre in 1815, and then we will have to abandon biographical chronology to jump ahead to the 1820s and his search for a mode of writing tragedy.

*   *   *

On the evening of 24 February 1809 the magnificent fifteen-year-old Theatre Royal in Drury Lane, with a seating capacity of 3611 making it the largest in Europe, was razed to the ground by fire. Byron watched the conflagration from a nearby house-top, though he thought the most dramatic view of the fire was from Westminster Bridge where it was reflected in the Thames (*L&J*, ii. 207). According to legend, its proprietor, the dramatist and Whig politician Richard Brinsley Sheridan was sipping a drink, calmly seated outside the Piazza Coffee House near the conflagration. When reproached for his excess of *sang froid* he retorted: 'A man may surely be allowed to take a glass of wine by his own fireside'.[4] Sheridan was ruined, for the building was under-insured.

His poor management was to blame for he had not maintained the fire precautions designed by his architect, Henry Holland. He had allowed the metal safety-curtain to be removed and neglected to keep the rooftop reservoirs filled with water.[5] Only five months earlier, the Theatre Royal in Covent Garden had suffered exactly the same fate.

The duopoly

With the simultaneous demise of both patent theatres the whole question of their duopoly came up for discussion. Ever since the Restoration two patentees only had been permitted to present regular plays both past and present, composed solely of dialogue. Charles II originally granted the patents to two courtier-dramatists, Sir William Davenant and Thomas Killigrew in a move which permitted drama while regulating it closely. Since 1737 the Licensing Act had given the Lord Chamberlain the power to censor all forms of drama and to enforce the duopoly through fines. From the period of the French Revolution through to the rise of working-class radicalism in the 1820s, strict censorship prevented dramatists dealing with politics, religion or any controversial topics. By the early nineteenth century, both patents had become converted to shares owned by wealthy noblemen, who were paid large sums by the two theatres for their licences. The only other venue allowed to stage 'legitimate' drama was the Theatre Royal in the Haymarket, which opened in the Summer when both patent theatres were closed. Other theatres, like Sadler's Wells, Astley's, and the Royal Circus were only permitted to stage musicals, ballets, operas, pageants, and pantomimes which supposedly contained minimal dialogue. Lord Dartmouth, Lord Chamberlain from 1804–10, was not particularly sympathetic to the patentees' privileges, and turned a blind eye to the fact that the dialogue sometimes dominated.[6] By the 1820s the best of the minor theatres, like the Adelphi and the Olympic would plainly outstrip the patent houses.

In 1809 the relationship between Covent Garden and Drury Lane theatre could be likened to that between the Whig and Tory parties: ostensibly they were in competition yet in fact they shared a monopoly of power, rooted in the same adherence to traditional property rights. However, as in politics, belief in the two-party system to achieve a balance between competition and stability was eroding. With the growth of a more radical liberalism, voices were raised in favour of freeing the theatre from control. As we will see, Byron was not one of these. Initially, he allied himself with Whig paternalism. Yet by the 1820s, when he was writing most of his plays, he was to find himself at the centre of debate on the freedom of the press.

The third theatre scheme

In 1809, while plans were in train for the rebuilding of the two patent theatres, a scheme was proposed to petition the King for permission to build a third Winter theatre in the East end of London. It was to be named the London Theatre Royal. It would be smaller in size than the Patent theatres, for its aim would be to reinstitute 'legitimate' drama, prioritizing cultural improvement over commercial gain. The plan was supported by the sentimental dramatist Richard Cumberland, five Members of Parliament and the Lord Mayor of London.[7] The petitioners intended to bring forward a Bill in the House of Commons should they get royal permission. Their desire to break the duopoly was to be the first measure in a bid for the freedom of the London stage. A flood of pamphlets was generated on the subject, one of which was by Byron's guardian, the Earl of Carlisle: *Thoughts on the Present Condition of the Stage, and upon the Construction of a New Theatre* (1809).

By Autumn 1809 an immense new Covent Garden in the Greek-revival style had opened its doors, only to become the site for outright class warfare in the 'Old Price' riots. The theatre, with its division into pit, box and gallery had traditionally been a microcosm of society, and of the British Whig constitution balancing the claims for government by monarchy, oligarchy and democracy. The management had attempted to stem the rising influence of the lower orders in the audience by raising the prices, cutting back on the galleries and extending the boxes, to attract back the aristocracy, who were abandoning the increasingly rowdy theatre in favour of the opera. Leigh Hunt commented in *The Examiner* that: '...a whole circle of the Theatre taken from them to make privacies for the luxurious great is a novelty... offensive to the national habits'.[8] The lower classes rioted in the auditorium and the management responded in kind by sending in toughs to sort them out. Riots lasted from 18 September to 17 December, when the management capitulated by reverting to the original entrance fees and removing some of the extra tier of private boxes which had decreased the amount of gallery seats available.

Supporters of a third Patent theatre commented in Parliament that, despite the fact that it had absolutely no competition, Covent Garden was not half full. They attributed this to its huge size, and argued that, though London had undoubtedly grown larger, theatregoers would prefer more and smaller theatres.[9] The paradox appeared to be that the only theatre licensed for a play with dialogue was a building so immense that it was difficult to hear it, or to see the expressions on the actors' faces. Leigh Hunt described such performances as like 'being invited upon one side of Salisbury Plain to hear Handel performed on the other'.[10] The proprietor, Henry Harris, later declared that he made no profit whatsoever from 'legitimate' drama from 1809–21, his losses only offset by the Christmas pantomime.[11] He faced growing competition from the burlettas and operas offered by the minor theatres and needed to make large profits to cover his huge overheads. Covent Garden, like Drury Lane when it was rebuilt, inevitably responded by mounting magnificent spectacles for which its huge size was eminently suited. These included such bread and circuses as a jingoistic celebration of Nelson's victories with special stage effects invented by Philippe de Loutherbourg, and a lavish recreation of the coronation of George IV.

During the spring of 1810 debate raged, and when the Privy Council turned down the Petition on legal advice, the campaign continued in Parliament. Sheridan made a passionate defence of the sacredness of ancient property rights in response. The campaigners retorted that Drury Lane had still not been rebuilt.[12] Both sides agreed on the present degraded state of the stage, but the petitioners blamed it on the size and commercialism of the patent theatres while their opponents ascribed it to the poor taste of the audience. Leigh Hunt commented, in a review of *Quadrupeds, or the Manager's last Kick*, a burlesque on Covent Garden's reliance on performing animals, 'It is in vain … that they [the patent theatres] effect … to throw the blame of their spectacles and hippodramas upon the vitiated state of the public taste. It was the vitiated state of their own wants that induced them to grasp at profit in this manner … '.[13]

The petitioners put forward an impressively detailed plan for a non-profit-making joint-proprietorship of subscribers to build and manage a third theatre. They doubtless would have carried the day, had not Samuel Whitbread, the brewer, come to Sheridan's aid. A defence of the duopoly and concrete plans to reopen Drury Lane were now much more convincing coming from a wealthy businessman than the ruined playwright. However, even when the Bill had failed, the petitioners went on to charge the patentees on 7 February 1812 with degrading the drama by exhibiting animals on stage, but they were outvoted 58–34. The campaign for theatrical freedom was dead for the forseeable future.

Rebuilding of Drury Lane

The success of the patentees still left the problem of how to resurrect the Drury Lane Theatre. Sheridan himself was bankrupt, and much to his dismay was kept out of the scheme. He eventually died in a garret on 7 July 1816, and Byron composed a commemorative poem which was recited in the theatre. Samuel Whitbread, the leader of the Whigs in the House of Commons, who had successfully opposed the London Theatre Bill in 1810, drew extensively on the third theatre petitioners' ideas in proposing that a joint-stock company be set up to settle with the creditors and fund the rebuilding; that a committee be appointed to supervise the project; and the theatre was to be managed by a sub-committee of five.

Whitbread and the Whigs wanted to make Drury Lane Theatre a showcase of national culture. It would therefore endorse the Patent as an example of the Whiggish principle of 'liberty', in the ancient sense of a privilege granted to responsible property-owners, who answered to 'the people' at large, rather than to the profit motive. Their primary aim was a return to 'legitimate' drama, in a 'national theatre' which would favour British drama over endless translations of the sentimental German dramatist, August von Kotzebue, and reject the commercialism which had put child actors, performing animals and gimmicks before intellectual content.[14] These aims were stated in *Proposals for Rebuilding the Drury Lane Theatre* (1811) and engendered cartoons, satires, and much sarcastic comment in the Tory press. For at a time when the Opposition confidently expected that George III would soon be declared incapable, and that the Regent would back his Whig friends in a change of government, party politics dominated the resuscitation of the Drury Lane Theatre. The committee was dominated by Whigs, even including James Perry, the editor of the Whig newspaper, the *Morning Chronicle*.

The launching of a National Theatre when 'bardolatry' was at its height was an attempt to gain cultural authority, for the Whigs' patriotism had been constantly impugned in the press because of their support for appeasement during the Napoleonic wars. At a period when Charles Lamb, William Gifford, and Samuel Taylor Coleridge were rediscovering, editing and lecturing on Renaissance dramatists, the Golden Age of drama was being co-opted by reactionaries as the heart of a nationalistic canon of English Literature. The repudiation of neoclassicism by contemporary Romantic poets and dramatists was jingoistically interpreted as a refutation of French influence. This made it all the more difficult for would-be reformers to steer between the Scylla of pseudo-Shakespeareanism on the one hand and the Charybdis of French exploration of republican ideology in neoclassical drama on the other.

Byron and the Whigs

The phenomenal success of *Childe Harold's Pilgrimage* in 1812 had granted the poet his entrée to Holland House, the salon of the great Whig magnates, which a peer with such raffish ancestry as Byron could never have achieved by rank alone. He took the women by storm: in particular, those of Melbourne House, where he conducted a tempestuous adulterous affair with Lady Caroline Lamb; proposed (the first time unsuccessfully) to Caroline's husband's cousin, the heiress Annabella Milbanke; while making an intimate confidante of Lady Melbourne, the mother of the man he had cuckolded: William Lamb, the future Prime Minister. Then Byron joined the liberal wing of the Whigs under the guidance of his new 'autumnal' mistress Lady Oxford (she was forty) and her *eminence grise* Sir Francis Burdett. Byron had demonstrated his political allegiance by his maiden speech in the House of Lords on 27 February against a Bill proposing the death penalty for Luddite framebreakers, who were protesting against their worsening poverty in Nottinghamshire, his home county. He made a second speech on 21 April on behalf of Roman Catholic civil rights, and on 1 June 1813 he would make a speech in favour of the veteran Major Cartwright's petition for parliamentary reform. But, from his maiden speech, it had been immediately obvious that Byron was neither an orator nor a politician and could best support the attempt to oust the Tories as a poet and possibly a future dramatist.

Probably remembering Byron's call for a reform of the stage in *English Bards and Scotch Reviewers*, which incorporated praise of Sheridan, Lord Holland asked Byron in August 1812 to enter a poetry contest to write an address to be delivered on the opening night of the new Drury Lane Theatre. But the arrogant literary lion refused the indignity of 'contending against all Grubstreet' (*L&J*, ii. 197). When he alone was commissioned after almost a hundred attempts had been rejected, the noble poet graciously agreed. The appointment of Byron to write the Drury Lane address marked his adoption of the unofficial role of Shadow Poet Laureate. His special treatment was commented on ironically in the press and in a cartoon by George Cruikshank. James and Horace Smith brought out a delicious spoof volume of *The Rejected Addresses*, parodying all the poets of the day. Byron considered 'Cui bone', in the style of *Childe Harold's Pilgrimage*, one of the best. *The Genuine Rejected Addresses* preceded by that written by Byron were also published in 1812.

Byron felt that Lord Holland and Samuel Whitbread castrated his indictment of public taste by removing an attack on Covent Garden's reliance on performing animals to pull the crowds, though he admitted 'the address will go off *quicker* without it though like the agility of the Hottentot at the expence of *one* testicle' (*L&J*, ii. 211–12). On 10 October 1812 the new Theatre was opened and Byron's enfeebled address was spoken by the actor Robert William Elliston. Byron presumably wrote the anonymous letter apologizing for its 'hurried composition' published in the *Morning Chronicle*.

Unfortunately, the new theatre was built on the same grandiose scale as its predecessor and was from the beginning burdened by its debts. Almost as soon as it reopened, it looked unlikely to cover its enormous running costs of £160 a night and to compete successfully with the proliferating illegitimate theatres. However, legitimate Regency patent theatres had one thing going for them. This was a galaxy of star actors. In January 1814 an unpromisingly short but charismatic actor named Edmund Kean made his debut in *The Merchant of Venice* and his new chiaroscuro acting style not only took the town by storm but restored Drury Lane's receipts to a healthy level. This was not to last, but at the time it seemed a promising omen for the high ideals of Whitbread's committee. On 18 May 1814 Byron met Kean after seeing him in *Othello* and wrote of the 'perfection' of his Iago: 'I am acquainted with no *im*material sensuality so delightful as good acting,' (*L&J*, iv. 115). A week later he sent Kean fifty guineas and presented him with a snuff-box and Turkish sword. On 26 November 1814 Byron saw Kean as Macbeth, and a week later dined with him at Kinnaird's. Kean was soon earning the enormous salary of £50 a week, justified by the record-breaking takings of £643 for the first performance of his Hamlet.[15] Coleridge famously commented, 'To see him act is like reading Shakespeare by flashes of lightning'.[16] Other Drury Lane actors pioneering the new passionate style included Frances Maria Kelly and the beautiful Charlotte Mardyn. Byron later pronounced that George Frederick Cooke was the most natural actor, John Philip Kemble was the most supernatural and that Edmund Kean was a medium between the two. However, he thought the more neoclassical Mrs Siddons, who had just retired, was worth them all put together (*L&J*, ix. 31). Even so unworldly a dramatist as Percy Shelley wrote characters with particular actors in mind, so charismatic were they.

Byron and the Drury Lane sub-committee

By the 3 May 1815 Whitbread was so worried about the financial basis of Drury Lane that he called a general meeting and proposed reverting to a commercial management.[17] He was opposed by James Perry and Byron's friend Douglas Kinnaird who clung to the ideal of a National Theatre putting on only 'legitimate' drama, though Whitbread protested that 'there was no national purse to which recourse could be had in emergency'. Richard Lansdown has pointed out that Kinnaird persuaded Byron to serve on the sub-committee in the interval immediately after this meeting and before the next as a last-ditch attempt to save the National Theatre idea, and that this coup succeeded in staving off Whitbread's proposal. Byron was duly appointed to the sub-committee, 'at the request of my friend Douglas Kinnaird, who made over to me a share of 500l, for the purpose of qualifying me to vote'.[18] Other members of the committee were Lord Essex, George Lamb, Douglas Kinnaird, and Peter Moore. Samuel Whitbread was the manager and George Raymond was the stage-manager. Despite the cachet of Byron's membership, the amateur management committee was an unmitigated disaster and would eventually be wound up in 1818–1819 amidst much ill-feeling and recrimination.[19] On 6 July 1815 Whitbread would commit suicide. Byron sardonically commented to Thomas Moore: 'I perceive Perry [editor of the *Morning Chronicle*] attributes his death to Drury Lane, – a consolatory encouragement to the new committee'.

Byron was certainly an avid theatre-goer and boasted 'When I was a youth – I was reckoned a good actor' (*L&J*, ix. 37). He had played the part of Penruddock in *The Wheel of Fortune* and Tristram Fickle in *The Weathercock* in private theatricals at Southwell in 1806. He too was inspired to do all he could to instigate a flowering of drama in this age which abounded with poetic talent. Byron thought Whitbread 'a great and very good man' (*L&J*, iv. 302) and he threw himself into his apportioned role with gusto, which was to find or commission new plays. He first looked into the theatre's stock of plays: 'The number of *plays* upon the shelves were about *five* hundred; conceiving that amongst these there must be *some* of merit, in person and by proxy I caused an investigation. – I do not think there was one which could be conscientiously tolerated' (*L&J*, ix. 35). As well as this planning of the repertoire, each member of the sub-committee attended weekly meetings and undertook the day-to-day running of the theatre. Byron enjoyed fraternizing with the actors in the Greenroom: 'It is really very good fun, as far as the daily and nightly stir of these strutters and fretters go;

and, if the concern could be brought to pay a shilling in the pound, would do much credit to the management' (*L&J*, iv. 322–3). Byron and Kinnaird once donned costumes and went on stage as extras in a masquerade scene, and the poet heard: 'one leg of an elephant saying to another, "D-n your eyes, move a little quicker!'[20]

Byron told Thomas Moore that he wished he too was on the committee: 'It seems so hopeless a business, that the company of a friend would be quite consoling' ... 'All *my* new function consists in listening to the despair of Cavendish Bradshaw, the hopes of Kinnaird, the wishes of Lord Essex, the complaints of Whitbread, and the calculations of Peter Moore – all of which, and whom, seem totally at variance' (*L&J*, iv. 296–7). They had just been discussing whether to light the theatre by gas, and what economies they could make. Whitbread suggested raising the prices of the pit by sixpence but Byron imagined this could inspire a repetition of the 'Old Price' riots. He later recalled their constant disagreements: 'Then the Committee! – then the Sub-Committee! we were but few – and never agreed! – There was Peter Moore who contradicted Kinnaird – & Kinnaird who contradicted everybody – then our two managers Rae and Dibdin – and our Secretary Ward! And yet we were all very zealous – & in earnest to do good and so forth' (*L&J*, ix. 36). On 28 November 1815 he warned an aspiring author that the financial difficulties of the theatre 'render the strictest economy unavoidable – many of the offices have been done away with or retrenched' (*L&J*, iv. 334).

When the new season opened that autumn Byron had to deal with the unsolicited manuscripts of aspiring playwrights: 'Then the scenes I had to go through! The Authors and the authoresses – the Milliners – the wild Irishmen' ... 'to all of whom it was proper to give a civil answer – and a hearing – and a reading'. He tried to keep a straight face when a sixty-year-old dancing master called dressed in silk stockings to show off his legs in a request for a part; and later remembered the Irish dramatist 'Hibernicus' in whose play 'the unities could not fail to be observed for the protagonist was chained by the leg to a pillar during the chief part of the performance'. He confessed he often sent authors to Douglas Kinnaird because his friend was better at turning them down (*L&J*, ix. 36). He later constructed a rejection in verse out of the usual clichés for Murray to send Dr John Polidori:

> Dear Doctor – I have read your play
> Which is a good one in it's way
> Purges the eyes & moves the bowels

And drenches handkerchiefs like towels
With tears that in a flux of Grief
Afford hysterical relief
To shatter'd nerves & quickened pulses
Which your catastrophe convulses.
I like your moral & machinery
Your plot too has such scope for Scenery!
Your dialogue is apt & smart
The play's concoction full of art –
Your hero raves – your heroine cries
All stab – & every body dies;
In short your tragedy would be
The very thing to hear & see -
And for a piece of publication
If I decline on this occasion
It is not that I am not sensible
To merits in themselves ostensible
But – and I grieve to speak it – plays
Are drugs – mere drugs, Sir, nowadays – ...

(L&J, v. 258)

Commissioning drama

Byron enjoyed playing the role of patron, as the literary star of the sub-committee in 1815. He did his best to commission talent from the poets of the age. He suggested several times to Thomas Moore, author (and singer) of the popular *Irish Melodies*, that he write an opera (*L&J*, iv. 296–7; 302). He also wrote on 15 September 1815 to William Sotheby, suggesting he submitted a tragedy. 'You will be glad to hear that the Season has begun uncommonly well – great & constant houses – the performers in much harmony with the Committee & one another & as much good humour as can be preserved in such complicated & extensive interests as the D[rury] L[ane] Proprietory. – ' (*L&J*, iv. 312). Byron said Sotheby's would be the first tragedy of the new committee (*L&J*, iv. 314). He later recalled ironically, 'Mr. Sotheby obligingly offered *all* his tragedies and I pledged myself – and notwithstanding many squabbles with my Committe(e)d brethren – did get 'Ivan' accepted – read & the parts distributed – But lo! in the very heart of the matter – upon some *tepid*ness on the part of Kean – or warmth upon that of the Author – Sotheby withdrew his play' (*L&J*, ix. 35). So much for the committee's 'harmony' and 'good humour'! On 10 April 1817 Byron told Scrope Berdmore Davies that Sotheby was treated 'with atrocious cruelty' (*L&J*, xi. 165).

Byron was also in communication with Coleridge, whose lectures on Shakespeare he had attended in 1811–12. Coleridge had written to Byron in Easter 1815, asking for his assistance with the booksellers to publish two volumes, one of poetry and one literary autobiography.[21] Byron replied on 31 March, apologizing for his satire of Coleridge in *English Bards and Scotch Reviewers*, and suggesting that the older poet write a play for Drury Lane, even though this was before he had been voted on to the sub-committee. Byron had actually been instrumental in persuading Drury Lane to accept Coleridge's verse tragedy *Remorse* (D.L. 1813) which had proved a great success. Coleridge promised he would send an even better tragedy than *Remorse* by Christmas: 'All my leisure hours I have devoted to the Drama, encouraged by your Lordship's advice and favourable opinion of my comparative powers among the tragic dwarfs, which exhausted Nature seems to have been under the necessity of producing since Shakespeare'.[22] Coleridge was bubbling over with ideas for adaptations: *Richard II*, Beaumont and Fletcher's *Pilgrim*, and he could have produced a version of Fletcher's *The Beggar's Bush*, had not Douglas Kinnaird already embarked on his own adaptation, *The Merchant of Bruges* (D.L. 1815). On 18 October Byron replied promising he would act as 'a Negociator [sic] with the Trade' for Coleridge's poetry and encouraged him to include 'Christabel' in the volume he proposed to publish. He particularly urged Coleridge to finish his tragedy, '[I]t is a field in which there are none living to contend against you ... I say this *not* disinterestedly but as a *Committee* man' (*L&J*, iv. 319). At this time he asked Moore to review Coleridge's work favourably in the *Edinburgh Review*. Coleridge then sent Byron a copy of 'Christabel' which he passed on to Murray for publication, though he urged Coleridge to complete the fragment. On Byron's recommendation, Murray published *'Christabel', 'Kubla Khan', and other poems* (1816) with great success.

Coleridge had all sorts of plans for different dramatic productions, but hinted unsubtly that he needed an advance: 'Simply *enable* me to do it – & I will pledge my Honor & my Existence, that if I live, I will present you a tragedy by the beginning of December, and a Romantic Comic Opera by February – and in the interim correspond with Mr. Dibdin on the subject of a sort of pantomime'.[23] Byron's own dire financial situation was such as to 'drive him half mad' in November, as Hobhouse recalled.[24] He had married the heiress Annabella Milbanke on 2 January, but despite her £20,000 fortune he calculated his debts as at least £30,000 in 1815 and was constantly beset by duns. The strain would contribute to the breakdown of his marriage early in 1816. Nevertheless, Byron sent Coleridge a gift of £100 in February 1816 'at a time when I could not command £150 in the world', Byron later remembered.[25] To its author's chagrin, Coleridge's melodrama, *Zapolya*, an adaptation of Shakespeare's *A Winter's Tale,* was eventually rejected by the sub-committee, who compared it unfavourably with Charles Robert Maturin's Byronic melodrama, *Bertram.* This was after Byron had left England in 1816. Coleridge published in the *Courier* a savage attack on *Bertram* as an example of the 'moral Jacobinism' of the modern stage, and then incorporated it in his *Biographia Literaria* (1817) as chapter 23. Byron probably suspected that he himself was the indirect object of this attack on libertinism in modern literature, which came out just after the failure of his marriage, when rumours about his incestuous relationship with his half-sister Augusta were circulating. It is virtually certain that Coleridge's remarks inspired *Don Juan,* for Byron would take up Coleridge's suggestion that an author should attempt setting the myth in modern times, but, characteristically, he mocked and sub-verted the didacticism the older poet had in mind.

Byron was also keen to revive a tragedy of the most celebrated female playwright of the age. Joanna Baillie's avant-garde dramatic theory advocated focus not on action but on the moral psychology of the protagonist, each of whom was dominated by a different passion. Her plays would influence his own. 'I once thought of getting Joanna Baillie's 'De Montfort' [sic] revived; but the winding-up was faulty'.[26] He was referring to the last act which apotheosizes the hero's sister after his death, in defiance of tragic convention. He wrote to another Scot, 'the Great Unknown', but though Walter Scott declined to offer a play himself he recommended the Irish writer, Maturin, author of the Gothic novel, *Melmoth the Wanderer.* On 21 September 1815 Byron accepted Maturin's *Bertram; or, The Castle of St Aldobrand,* though he suggested that George Lamb or himself should adapt it for the stage. 'I talk to you of all this in the *hope* that it may be brought forward – but not in the certainty – Lamb & I are but two in 5 – & it is difficult to say what obstacles may not arise in the jarring interests of a theatre to pre-vent the representation of any piece whatever. I have been *vainly* – since my connection with it – endeavouring a trial of the revival of 'De Montfort' [sic] – Kean would be Bertram – but I know no woman for [Imogine?] – but Mrs. Siddons'. By now Byron was wary of the eternal wrangling of the committee system. He assured Maturin, as a mark of his good faith, that he would offer the play to Covent Garden if Drury Lane turned it down, and would try to get it published also. He also sent him fifty guineas on his own account (*L&J*, iv. 336).

Werner

By November, Byron began to think he would have to provide a tragedy himself. He wrote the first act of *Werner*, but 'Lady Byron's farce [i.e. the failure of his marriage] put it out of my head for the time of her representation' (*L&J*, viii. 237). It was an adaptation of Harriet Lee's popular 'German's Tale, or Kruitzner' from Sophia and Harriet Lee's *The Canterbury Tales* (1797–1805), and heavily influenced by Schiller. Byron did not complete it till 1822, perhaps by then thinking to recapture his depressed popularity. He claimed it was written for the reader not the stage (*L&J*, viii. 224). However, it was a melodrama in the style of the stage-plays of the day. Though rather turgid (Ellen Terry complained it was 'the dullest play that ever was'), with much cutting it was performed in Drury Lane six years after his death in 1830, as a star vehicle for Macready. The latter advertised it as 'advancing the drama as a branch of national literature and art'.[27] It became a staple of the theatre for thirty years, and Macready was commanded to perform it for the young Queen in 1837. There was such a crush, Victoria noted in her diary, that 'many people had to be *pulled* out of the Pit by their wrists and arms into the Dress Circle. I never saw such an exhibition'. She judged Byron's play 'fine but dreadful'.[28]

Revival of verse tragedy

Maturin's *Bertram* was the only successful outcome of Byron's involvement with Drury Lane. The play would be produced in May 1816, after Byron had left for the continent, and was counted a huge hit with twenty-two performances. It inspired a temporary revival of blank verse tragedy. Henry Hart Milman's *Fazio* followed at Covent Garden in 1818. Byron told Samuel Rogers regretfully, 'I tried during the directory to have it done at D[rury] L[ane] but was overruled'. Richard Lalor Sheil's *Evadne; or The Statue* (C.G. 1819) became a repertory favourite as did James Sheridan Knowles' *Virginius; or, The Liberation of Rome* (C.G. 1820) with Macready as protagonist. Kean starred in John Howard Payne's

Brutus, or The Fall of Tarquin (D.L. 1818), which had 52 performances, and Mary Russell Mitford's *The Foscari* (C.G. 1826) and *Rienzi* (D.L. 1828) followed later. These Whiggish plays, often set in classical or medieval Rome, managed some discussion of republican politics, being sufficiently distanced from contemporary Britain. They also implied support for Italian independence, which after 1815 had joined Philhellenism as a contemporary liberal cause particularly appealing to art lovers. Byron's two plays on the history of Venice, *Marino Faliero* (D.L. 1821) and *The Two Foscari* (1821), belong to this group, combining some subtextual references to British politics with the theme of Italian nationalism.

Ambivalence about the stage

Despite this temporary revival of verse tragedy, Byron felt that the committee and his role in it had been a failure. This failure coincided with the collapse of his marriage into acrimonious accusations and counter accusations in 1816. Rumours about his incest with Augusta and brutal treatment of his wife caused his ostracism by the *ton* and denunciations in the press, resulting in one of the greatest moral outcries of the century against an individual. Byron departed Britain never to return. So, although his hands-on experience at Drury Lane stimulated his desire to become a playwright, he shrank more than ever from exposing his work to the judgement of the vociferous *hoi polloi*. The lower classes were becoming an ever more prominent proportion of the audience, and Byron did not relish the conventional power of the first-night audience to hail or damn a play, hissing and cheering at will, and even hooting plays off the stage. On 31 March 1817, he wrote revealingly to Kinnaird: 'As to tragedy, I may try one day – but *never* for the *stage* – don't you see I have no luck there? – my two addresses were not liked & my Committeeship did but get me into scrapes…Unless I could beat them all – it would be nothing & who could do that?' (*L&J*, v. 196). Byron's ambivalence is obvious.

However by the 1820s it seemed more likely that the lower classes might support a play by Byron, susceptible of subtextual inferences towards radical politics, even if the respectable bourgeois disapproved. For the working class of the capital were now staging their own pageants in the streets in support of the rejected Queen Caroline and against censorship of the press. They were also clamouring for pirated copies of *Don Juan*, which they associated with theatrical pantomimes and burlesques based on the myth which abounded on the popular 'illegitimate' stage.

Page, stage and *avant garde*

We can see from the account of Byron's experience at Drury Lane that the would-be Regency dramatist was faced by a widening chasm between the vitality of popular shows and self-consciously literary drama focused on the written word. Even with regard to Shakespeare this was so. For the versions so popular on the stage were those which had been bowdlerized and sentimentalized according to Augustan taste. When *King Lear* was allowed to be shown again after the death of the mad King George III, the text was Nahum Tate's of 1681 complete with a happy ending. Critics like Lamb and Hazlitt were doubtful that the original plays were suitable for modern performance. The imaginative act of reading was idealized by the Romantics in preference to actualization. Longman and Murray therefore found it sufficiently profitable to publish new plays as well as established literature.[29]

'Illegitimate' theatre, meanwhile, had made a virtue out of necessity in developing new mixed forms combining music, dance and pictorial stage effects: burlesques, pantomime, and musical melodrama. The huge amounts spent on special effects, the star system, and multiple versions of popular stories appearing spontaneously are all familiar to us. They were the first manifestations of modern mass entertainment. The paternalistic attempt by the Drury Lane Committee to found a National Theatre, on the other hand, attempted to define spoken drama as morally-uplifting Art untainted by commerce. The literati looked back nostalgically to the Golden Age of Shakespeare, and tended to favour Gothicized pseudo-Elizabethan pastiche. Dramatists faced with this cultural divide between the meretricious and the ossified responded by forming an *avant garde* and by writing for posterity. '*My* object is not *immediate* popularity in my present productions', Byron wrote in 1822. ' … But *mark what I now say* – that the time will come – when *these* will be preferred to any I have before written' (*L&J*, ix. 92–3). The danger of this was falling into élitism. The fact that both Byron and Shelley were writing their dramas in exile, both aristocrats disgraced by sexual scandal and branded as political radicals, exacerbated their separation from the cultural mainstream. Both explored a variety of dramatic genres, as did Shelley's friend, the drama critic Leigh Hunt. They experimented in a search for form: Hunt making use of the archaic and aristocratic masque, turned inside out for satiric purposes; and Byron enlisting the Christian morality play to denounce authoritarian religion; while Byron and Shelley took popular Gothic fascination with incest to new depths, exploring the underworld of the psyche.

Byron's residence in Switzerland in 1816 also exposed him to the continental debate between the Classical and Romantic traditions of drama which, though disseminated in Britain by Coleridge and Hazlitt, originated in German theories of literature. In Madame de Staël's *De L'Allemagne* (1813), which Byron had praised in print, a distinction was drawn between the Northern, Romantic, Christian culture and Southern, pagan, classical traditions. In the summer of 1816, when he lived in Switzerland, he frequently visited Madame de Staël's salon at Coppet, and here met the dramatist and critic August Wilhelm Schlegel. The latter was at the forefront of the German idolization of Shakespeare, and Byron read his *Lectures on Dramatic Art and Literature*, which had been translated into English in 1815. In 1821 Byron read his brother Friedrich Schlegel's *Lectures on the History of Literature*, which had been translated into English in 1818. The Schlegels rejected classical drama, with its fixed formal rules, as a model for the modern poet. Instead they embraced 'Romantic drama' like Shakespeare's, in which disparate comic and romance elements enriched the main tragic action. Though Byron went further than any other British Romantic poet in theoretically rejecting the Schlegels' views, and in his determination to eschew 'bardolatry', his best plays did in fact combine neoclassical structure with Romantic elements.

Manfred

In August 1816 Byron was visited by the Gothic novelist Matthew Gregory Lewis, who recited for him his own translation of portions of the German dramatist Johann Wolfgang Goethe's Romantic drama, *Faust*. Inspired by this, that autumn Byron wrote the first two acts of a 'dramatic poem', *Manfred*, his most Romantic and German work, yet also demonstrating the compressed, static quality of his later neoclassical plays. Goethe later admired the play and in *Faust II* created a character, Euphorion, based on Byron, and representing the marriage between Greek and German art. In *Manfred* Byron adopted a traditional Christian form, the Faustian morality play – though only in order to subvert it. A decadent aristocrat is the embodiment of revolutionary energy. This Byronic hero defies moral law (it is hinted by committing incest with his sister and indirectly causing her death) and refuses either to be saved or to be damned by an external deity.

> *Spirit.* Mortal! Thine hour is come – Away! I say.
> *Manfred.* I knew, and know my hour is come, but not

To render up my soul to such as thee;
Away! I'll die as I have lived – alone.
...
Abbot. Cold – cold – even to the heart – But yet one prayer
Alas! How fares it with thee?
Manfred. Old man! 'Tis not so difficult to die. (MANFRED *expires.*)
(III, iv. 87–90; 149–50)

The original third act even incorporated anti-clerical humour in true medieval fashion, until Byron thought better of it. A philosophical play dramatizing man's existential dilemma would 'soar above the million' as Murray put it, yet, paradoxically it did utilize popular stage styles. Byron's protagonist was straight out of Gothic melodrama: a sinful aristocrat whose powers verged on the supernatural. We could compare Samuel Beckett's *avant garde* twentieth-century play, *Waiting for Godot,* which features characters borrowed from popular culture: Chaplinesque tramps with a music-hall double-act.

The form was a modified monodrama.[30] This solo piece for one actor had been popularized in Germany in the late eighteenth century, as a short element in the triple bill then expected. A chorus could incorporate a lyrical element, and a monodrama was usually accompanied by music. Byron used spirits and the Destinies to symbolize Nature:

> *The* SEVEN SPIRITS
> Earth, ocean, air, night, mountains, winds, thy star,
> Are at thy beck and bidding, Child of Clay!
> Before thee at thy quest their spirits are –
> What wouldst thou with us, son of mortals, say?
> (I, i. 132–5)

On 15 February 1817, Byron described *Manfred* as a play 'of a very wild, metaphysical, and inexplicable kind...but I have at least rendered it *quite impossible* for the stage, for which my intercourse with D[rury] Lane has given me the greatest contempt' (*L&J,* v. 170). Little did he know.

Manfred was in fact successfully performed long after the poet's death as a musical witch-drama in Alfred Bunn's production at Covent Garden 1834–5. The scenery was the main attraction, complete with mechanical waterfall and a Hall of Arimanes copied from John Martin's Byronic version of the Miltonic sublime: *Satan presiding at the Infernal Council.* The references to incest were cut, but Byron's rejected third act

as a palimpsest. The story of the failure to reform the Renaissance Venetian republic prompts Faliero's prophecy of its future degradation (when it would be invaded by Napoleon). The play was intended to generate British support for the nationalist Italian uprising against Austrian rule, which Byron hoped would soon break out, and which would in turn inspire British radicals to achieve Reform at home.

These plays also allude to their own censorship, highlighting the difficulty of communicating and interpreting the nation's history to its people in a metatheatricality, or discourse pointing to the work's status as art and specifically as historical art. For example, *Marino Faliero* concludes with the citizens vainly straining their ears to catch the Doge's words:

> *First Citizen.* His words are inarticulate, but the voice
> Swells up like mutter'd thunder; would we could
> But gather a sole sentence!
>
> (V, iv. 12–14)

A line to raise a laugh in Drury Lane's fourth and highest tier of galleries, if heard!

The production of *Marino Faliero*

This brings us to the vexed question of whether or not Byron wrote *Marino Faliero*, *The Two Foscari* and *Sardanapalus* with an eye to the stage, despite his frequent and fiery protestations to the contrary (*L&J*, viii. 68; viii. 186). His adherence to neoclassical form and conformity to the unities, like that which would be employed by Samuel Beckett, was certainly designed to concentrate the mind of a theatre audience solely on poetic language expressing the existential dilemma of action in a fallen world. When he heard a Drury Lane production was planned, his response was plainly equivocal: 'I hope and trust that Elliston *won't* be permitted to act the drama? – Surely *he* might have the grace to wait for Kean's return [from America] before he attempted it – though *even then* I should be as much against the attempt as ever' (10 May 1821. *L&J*, viii. 112).

Marino Faliero was acted at Drury Lane, 25 April 1821, only four days after publication. Murray had delayed publishing both the play and *The Prophecy of Dante* because of their revolutionary politics. He did try to get an injunction against the production at Byron's insistence but Lord Eldon deemed the play too seditious to be worthy of the law's protection, though he left the way open for Murray to bring an action before the King's bench.[33] Byron urged: '[L]et it by all means be brought to a plea – I am determined to try the right' (*L&J*, viii. 90). The production was meanwhile allowed to proceed.

Elliston had bought two copies on the day of publication and all 'objectionable' lines were carefully censored before being shown to the Examiner of Plays, John Larpent. This meant the rhetorical denunciations of aristocratic corruption were cut so the personal affront to his wife Angiolina now became the Doge's main motivation. The final scene in which the people support the Doge was entirely omitted and Act II, ii featuring the plebeian conspirators was the scene next most heavily excised. Many references to blood and revolutionary violence and to state torture were also removed. This amounted to over 1500 lines removed or 44 per cent of the whole play. *The Times* on April 26 commented that '*Procrustes-like*, they [the censors] have irreverently lopped and disfigured the body of the *Doge of Venice*, to fit him for the narrow bed of torture at Drury Lane'.

Though the actors worked round the clock, unsurprisingly they were not at first word perfect after only four days' rehearsal. The play had seven performances, and received mixed reviews. This was neither an absolute disaster nor an outright success by the standard of the times. Elliston had calculated it would be 'a sure £400 receipt for the Tuesday; it will not cost £20 to produce, & it might be performed three or 4 nights'.[34] In Italy, Byron had first read that the play was damned, then he received conflicting accounts. On 29 June, he wrote agitatedly to Murray to find out the truth, for: 'It is proper you should apprize me of this – because I am in the *third* act of a *third* drama – & if I have nothing to expect but coldness from the public & hesitation from yourself – it were better to break off in time' (*L&J*, viii. 144). David Erdman deduces from this that not just *Marino Faliero* but all the Venetian tragedies were written as possible stage plays, before Byron realized Elliston's production had not been a great success.[35]

Accounts of the play's reception give a clue to the way that lower class audiences were attuned to the slightest nuance, capable of political interpretation, left by the censor. The *European Magazine and London Review* noted disapprovingly of the Drury Lane performance that: 'The anti-patriotic sentiments scattered throughout the play seemed to constitute its strongest, and almost only, hold upon public attention' (Jan.–June 1821, p. 453). The *John Bull* (29 April 1821) reported that an 'uproar' by Queen Caroline's supporters greeted Angiolina's apparently innocuous speech on Virtue.[36] Marino Faliero is so excessively protective of his wife's honour that he plans to assassinate those who excused a young man who had written a libellous graffito on her. This excessive chivalry ironizes George IV who, despite his own promiscuity, was currently exposing his wife to prurient scandalmongering and public humiliation in a trial for adultery to secure a divorce. On 14 May Queen Caroline, currently a Whig heroine, attended the performance, thus capitalizing on the political subtext – such as it was – of the mangled play. The audience shouted for 'God save the Queen to be played'.[37] Though Elliston did not comply, at the close of the performance the audience substituted 'Queen' for 'King' in singing the national anthem.

Sardanapalus would follow up this critique of George IV in its portrayal of a degenerate Assyrian monarch who neglects his kingdom to spend all his time with his harem in a newly-built 'pavilion'. The opening words of the play were: 'He hath wrong'd his queen'. The Wagnerian conclusion has Sardanapalus voluntarily immolating himself on a flaming funeral pyre (symbolizing revolution), rather than be captured in a coup. He speaks prophetically and directly to George IV:

> ... and the light of this
> Most royal of funeral pyres shall be
> Not a mere pillar form'd of cloud and flame
> A beacon in the horizon for a day,
> And then a mount of ashes, but a light
> To lesson ages, rebel nations, and
> Voluptuous princes.
>
> (V, i. 436–42)

Byron blamed the production, not the play, for the relative failure of *Marino Faliero*. He said to Medwin: 'But the manner in which it was got up was shameful! All the declamatory parts were left, all the dramatic ones struck out; and [John] Cooper, the new actor, was the murderer of the whole. ... If he [Kemble] had acted 'Marino Faliero', its fate would have been very different'. After all this, he bragged: 'I hope, notwithstanding all that has been said, to write eight more plays this year, and to live long enough to rival Lope de Vega, or Calderon'![38]

Sceptical mystery plays

When a cool critical reception of the published texts of the Venetian tragedies followed the lukewarm reception of Drury Lane's production of *Marino Faliero*, Byron abandoned historical tragedy. He now turned back to the Christian literary tradition for material (the republican Milton) for two boldly revisionist dramas celebrating satanic intellectual rebels who risk damnation when challenging the shackles of moral law. The fact he was now unequivocal that *Cain* and *Heaven and Earth* were examples of 'mental theatre' or closet drama released the poet from the self-imposed straitjacket of realist neoclassicism, sufficiently to allow such Dantesque episodes as Cain's flight through the abyss of space in Act II.

> Why, I have seen the fire-flies and fire-worms
> Sprinkle the dusky groves and the green banks
> In the dim twilight, brighter than yon world
> Which bears them.
>
> (*Cain* II. i. 123–6)

It also allowed him to indulge in more philosophical discussion between the characters at the expense of the action. This is not to say that *Cain* could not have been produced for the stage, or that Byron may not have hoped it would be staged in the future. However, no one dared during the nineteenth century, for Murray's edition was denied protection of its copyright by Lord Eldon on account of its 'blasphemy'. It became a notorious text which was peddled by radical publishers alongside the works of Thomas Paine. *Cain* awaited an *avant garde* producer and found one after a hundred years in Konstantin Stanislavsky who staged it in revolutionary Moscow, in 1920, as a symbolic protest against the fratricide of civil war. Like *Marino Faliero*, *Cain* makes tragedy of revolution. The protagonist's recourse to violence and revolt fails and ends by merely justifying the *raison d'être* of the ruling order.

Heaven and Earth was formally even more experimental, being an apocalyptic play set at the time of the Deluge (another symbol of revolution). Byron confessed to Medwin that: 'I talked of writing a second part to it; but it was only as Coleridge promised a second part to 'Christabel'.[39] The promised second part was probably supposed to placate protesters by implying that the female protagonists would eventually be condemned and punished. For *Heaven and Earth* was even more daring than *Cain* as it celebrated the profane love of angels for mortal women. This proclamation of defiant humanism was inspired by an episode mentioned in Genesis but elaborated in the apocryphal text of the *Book of Enoch*. This play was never acted, but Gaetano Donizetti wrote a three act opera based on Byron's play and on Padre

Ringhieri's *Il Diluvio Universale* which was performed in Naples in 1830, six years after the poet's death.

William Charles Macready

Ultimately, Byron's plays would achieve a measure of success on the London stage. Long after his death they were adapted to become star vehicles for a powerful actor. Macready became Actor-Manager of Covent Garden in 1837. A friend of Charles Dickens, John Forster and Robert Browning, he was keen to reintroduce 'legitimate' plays of literary quality. *Werner* became one of the most successful plays in his repertoire, as we have seen. He also starred in *Sardanapalus* on 10 April 1834 with Ellen Tree as Myrrha, which was successful enough to warrant twenty-three performances. The spectacle of the final act was enhanced by sublime scenery based on John Martin's painting *The Fall of Nineveh* (1829), which had been inspired by Byron's play. He staged a well-received production of *The Two Foscari* on 7 April 1838, and though the text was not much longer than a normal stage play, he ruthlessly trimmed parts other than the protagonist. He also had a qualified success with a revival of *Marino Faliero* in 1842, much-cut and simplified as a star vehicle for himself.

Sardanapalus in the theatre

Sardanapalus, with its Eastern setting and final conflagration, of all Byron's plays would be the most susceptible to the lavish treatment in which the late nineteenth century theatre indulged. Charles Kean, son of Edmund, would stage it in the fashionable Princess's Theatre in 1853, featuring a chariot drawn by live horses, and a stage set by Thomas Grieve based on the latest archaeological research into ancient Assyrian architecture. The play was shortened and simplified but well acted, and was a popular success with ninety-three performances. An even more gorgeous musical version produced by Charles Calvert in 1875, received more than two thousand performances in the provinces and transferred to New York and London. *Sardanapalus* was also performed in Belgium, Sweden and Germany and inspired various operas.

Opera

Byron's Venetian plays also inspired nineteenth-century opera. In 1829, four years after the poet's death, *Marino Faliero* was adapted by

Casimir Delavigne, who made sexual jealousy the Doge's motivation. It was subsequently combined with Byron's original by Emanuele Bidera, the librettist of Donizetti's *Marino Faliero*. Mercadante and Verdi also wrote operas based on Delavigne. Donizetti's opera received its premiere in Paris on 12 March 1835, and was performed two months later in London (*CPW,* viii. 583). In 1867, W. Bayle Bernard also combined the play with Delavigne's version, and created a melodrama which used music from all three composers. Opulent sets recreated the atmosphere of Venice and a ballet of the carnival was choreographed. Though this lavish production was popular, it made a large loss because of its huge overheads. Byron would certainly not have relished the irony of seeing his austere neoclassical play turned into popular spectacle, melodrama and opera.

It can be seen that very specific historical circumstances of literary production – the split between the 'legitimate' and 'illegitimate' drama and between the stage and the page; repressive government censorship; the attempt of exiled aristocratic radicals to influence lower-class reformists – had helped to shape these *avant garde* dramatic poems. The result – their equivocal generic status of 'closet drama' – itself challenged contemporary readers to bring them to life through political action if not performance.

4
From Pilgrim to Patriot: Byron as Poet of Exile

Oh,
How beautiful is sunset, when the glow
Of Heaven descends upon a land like thee,
Thou Paradise of exiles, Italy!
('Julian and Maddalo', P.B. Shelley)

Mr. Cypress: Sir, I have quarrelled with my wife; and a man who has quarrelled with his wife is absolved from all duty to his country. I have written an ode to tell the people as much, and they may take it as they list.

(Thomas Love Peacock, *Nightmare Abbey*)

When the disgraced Byron left England in 1816 he created for himself the romantic role of the poet of exile, most misunderstood in his own country. The end of the Napoleonic Wars now allowed him to travel through Belgium, Germany and Italy, those usual destinations of the Grand Tour previously closed to the British. He settled in Italy for six years, residing first in Venice, then Ravenna, and finally Pisa. Much of his greatest poetry was produced from the heart of expatriate circles he gathered around him there. For the rediscovery and reinscribing of Italy, its countryside, literature, history, and political situation were central in bringing British Romantic writing into being. From the Della Cruscans in the late eighteenth century until the Brownings in the middle of the nineteenth we find many groups of expatriate English travellers and literati escaping scandal or bankruptcy to live cheaply in Italy.

In the 1780s the handsome aristocrat Robert Merry strangely prefigured Byron. Having squandered his fortune, losing as much as twenty thousand pounds a night in the London gambling hells, he escaped to Florence and became the charismatic leader of an early group of Italophiles, Bertie Greatheed, William Parsons and Hester Thrale Piozzi. The 'Della Cruscans' made common cause with aristocratic patriot poets like the Marquis Ippolito Pindemonte, Lorenzo Pignotti, Marco Lastri and Count Angiolo D'Elci in protesting against Austrian rule.

In 1817 Ippolito Pindemonte called upon Byron in Venice: 'He enquired after his old Cruscan friends – Parsons – Greathead – Mrs. Piozzi – and Merry – all of whom he had known in his youth'. Byron told Pindemonte, whom he described to Murray as 'one of their best going', that the English Della Cruscans had been extinguished by the satires of Gifford more than twenty years ago (*L&J*, v. 233–4). Pindemonte's quasi-Romantic verse was influenced by English poetry such as that of Gray and Young. There was much interaction between England and Italy, as circles of expatriate Italian writers also formed in Britain. Often political refugees, they satisfied the great demand for Italian lessons and fostered enthusiasm for Italian culture and political liberty.

Writing is often portrayed as an intensely solitary profession, especially for Romantic poets. But for coteries of expatriate writers it was also a social activity, deriving from their common attempt to saturate themselves in Italian culture. The Della Cruscans had modelled their reciprocal verse-making on the literary circle of the sonneteers Dante, Cavalcanti, Guido Orlandi, Cino da Pistoia, as Dante Gabriel Rossetti (nephew of Byron's doctor and travelling companion, John Polidori) would do later in the century.[1] The original *Accademia Della Crusca* of Florence was created to preserve the purity of the Tuscan tongue and its literature. It was swept away as redundant by Grand Duke Leopold in 1783 who instituted in its place a new 'Royal Academy of Florence' dedicated instead to promoting 'useful, enlightened sciences'. Resentment simmered among the literati. Though Merry and some of his Italian/British coterie became members of the new royal academy, nevertheless they produced their second book of poetry, *The Florence Miscellany* (1785), as an act of defiance. It has been described by Marshall as 'probably the most important book of poetry on Italian themes to appear in the eighteenth century'.[2] Though Hester Thrale Piozzi's disarming preface declared these were merely the occasional verses of dilettantes, the purpose of its imitations and translations of Dante, Petrarch and others, was ostentatiously to defend the transmission of the medieval Italian cultural heritage as a gesture against this Austrian interference. To avoid the censor, the tendentious bits had to be obtained separately from the printer and stuck into gaps specially left in the text.

In fact, the so-called 'tyrant' Leopold was actually a modernizer, sweeping away feudalism, abolishing the inquisition, and reforming the church and penal code. So the nature of Italian political and nationalist protest was framed in conservative terms. The Italian dissidents of this group who influenced the outlook of their English friends were reflecting aristocratic self-interest.[3] The study of medieval writers like Dante thus had an especially ambivalent significance for the Della Cruscans as later for the Romantics. Like Shakespeare in Britain, Dante could be converted into an icon of patriotism for the Italian nationalist movement, whilst also functioning as a medieval symbol of protest against modernity.

The Della Cruscans prefigured later developments in Romantic poetry to an uncanny degree. Jerome McGann has argued that, far from disappearing after being satirized by Gifford, the Della Cruscan style survived well into the 1830s, influencing the second generation of Romantic poets: Thomas Moore, Byron, P.B. Shelley, Felicia Hemans and Keats.[4] Other than Hemans, all those poets visited Italy themselves, of course. In both the Della Cruscans before Napoleon, and the Shelley–Byron group after Waterloo, we see the inspiration of Italy fomenting both a stylistic revolution in poetry and an enthusiasm for the cause of Italian liberation which Byron described as 'the poetry of politics'.

The second generation of Romantics rekindled political liberalism in literature but they addressed a more elite readership than those former English Jacobins of the 1790s, Wordsworth, Southey, and Coleridge.[5] After the crushing of the ideals of the French revolution and the final defeat of Napoleon, the cause of Italian nationalism allowed disaffected liberals the opportunity to criticize the British government's part in the Congress of Vienna (1815), which restored power to the Bourbon and Hapsburg dynasties. But those living in Italy could also make alliance with the disgruntled Italian aristocracy ousted by Austrian rule, and nostalgic for the feudal past. Italy therefore offered a meaningful, even prophetic, subject position from which to speak, for aristocratic yet Whig poets like Shelley and Byron, whose class was losing power to the bourgeoisie back in Britain, and whose party had been out of power for their entire lifetimes, with the exception of a few months' coalition government. As the cradle of European civilization, Italy gave them an international and transhistorical stage, even if they had to visualize posterity as their audience. For even Byron's popularity began to wane and Shelley anticipated that *The Prophecy of Dante* (1820) would 'only be *fully* appreciated by the select readers of many generations'.[6]

Every one of the canonical Romantic poets except Blake visited Italy. This is not surprising for when the frontiers of Italy were open again in 1815 after the Napoleonic Wars, our Shelley–Byron group were among a flood of Britons making their belated Grand Tour. Large British enclaves appeared in all the Italian cities. Alienated from their own past by political and industrial modernity, the British sought to appropriate Italian culture. Scott, Wordsworth, Byron and Shelley had all learned Italian before ever visiting the country, in order to read Italian poetry in the original. But this was no more than any educated person of the time. The semi-feudal society and rural landscape of Italy represented the past to a Britain leading the world in industrialization, and fearing the onset of democracy. Rome represented the religious past to Europe's leading Protestant power, and the ancient imperial past to the new British empire. Romanticism is deeply concerned with history; and this focus on Italy by Romantic writers was an attempt to revisit the Middle Ages and thus to assess their own fall into modernity.

* * *

On 23 April 1816 Byron left England forever. The momentous crisis of his personal life had coincided with that of Europe itself. To the egotism of Byron that did not seem surprising. Byron consciously compared his exile with that of Napoleon in St Helena. He travelled in a immense coach costing the enormous sum of £500, and containing its own bed, library and dining facilities, which had been specially constructed by Baxter as a copy of Napoleon's. When an inheritance later obliged him to adopt the forename Noel, he took a childish delight in using his initials.[7] His first destination was the field of Waterloo which he visited on 4 May, prompting the resumption of *Childe Harold's Pilgrimage*. In the third and fourth cantos of *Childe Harold*, the sufferings of the poet mirror those of war-torn Europe, much of it again in thrall to dynastic power after the failure of the French Revolution. On 10–16 May he journeyed up the Rhine, visiting Bonn, Coblenz, the Castle of Drachenfels and Mannheim before crossing into Switzerland at Basel. Here he visited the 'patriot field' of Morat, where the 'proud, brotherly, and civic band' of Swiss had defended their homeland in 1476 against the Burgundians, in a nobler battle than the 'king-making Victory' of the British and their allies at Waterloo.

Napoleon was the giant figure who had hitherto dominated Byron's poetical career, inspiring his creation of a series of magnetic but fallen men of action in his verse tales – the 'Giaour', Selim, Conrad, Lara and Alp. Bonaparte's abdication in 1814 had produced the disillusioned 'Ode to Napoleon Buonaparte', and a series of lyrics followed ventriloquizing the responses of his French followers to their hero's escape from Elba, his hundred days' return to France and eventual defeat. Some were published anonymously in the *Morning Chronicle*.

By placing Harold and his moralizing narrator on the battlefield of Waterloo, Byron is declaring himself 'The grand Napoleon of the realms of rhyme' (*Don Juan*, XI. 440). Canto III is self-consciously presented as a meditation on one ruined Titan by another. The origin, triumph and subsequent defeat of the French republic in the sickening revolution of the great wheel of history is the cataclysmic event with which the liberal Romantic poet also must come to terms. The Byronic narrator meditates on those flawed but great men presented as having changed the course of history by impressing their individuality on events: Napoleon and Rousseau. It is the implicit comparison with the disgraced poet himself, which endows the analysis of Napoleon with pathos:

> There sunk the greatest, nor the worst of men,
> Whose spirit antithetically mixt
> One moment of the mightiest, and again
> On little objects with like firmness fixt,
> Extreme in all things! hadst thou been betwixt,
> Thy throne had still been thine, or never been;
> For daring made thy rise as fall: thou seek'st
> Even now to re-assume the imperial mien,
> And shake again the world, the Thunderer of the scene!
>
> (III, 36)

Switzerland was an apt site for moralizing on the bitter paradoxes of the revolution. Its rural republics, some of which had pioneered adult male suffrage, had long been admired by Liberals as producing sturdily independent peasant-citizens as well as thinkers like Jean-Jacques Rousseau and Germaine de Staël. The young Wordsworth, echoed in the second half of the canto, had imagined Cumbria as a miniature British Switzerland. But in 1798 Napoleon had shocked even those British supporters of the revolution who had stomached the Terror, when he annexed Switzerland. This theme would be resumed in the fourth canto, where Napoleon is denigrated even more bitterly for his invasion of Italy as 'a kind/ Of bastard Caesar' (IV, 90), when ' ... France got drunk with blood to vomit crime' (IV, 97).

The third canto goes on to present various examples of exiled writers, from Rousseau whose 'life was one long war with self-sought foes' (III, 80) to Gibbon and Voltaire (III, 105) who had found Switzerland a refuge. All were banished by monarchical countries for challenging received religious beliefs in the Enlightenment, when intellectual revolt unmasked political tyranny.

> They made themselves a fearful monument!
> The wreck of old opinions –
>
> (III, 82)

Harold's loco-descriptive tour thus builds up an underlying case for the necessity of exile for the artist. An intellectual rebel (like Byron) whose 'thought seeks refuge in lone caves' (III, 5), the poet's lonely role will outlast that of the military genius (like Napoleon) in keeping alive the flame of revolutionary ideology through the long night of conservative reaction ahead:

> 'Tis to create, and in creating live
> A being more intense, that we endow
> With form our fancy, gaining as we give
> The life we image, even as I do now.
> What am I? Nothing; but not so art thou,
> Soul of my thought!
>
> (III, 6)

His pessimism is mitigated by a hope rather than belief in the capacity of words to communicate thoughts which may in turn inspire material change:

> I do believe,
> Though I have found them not, that there may be
> Words which are things...
>
> (III, 114)

The poet's personal agony parallels his political pessimism. What was startling to contemporary readers in *Childe Harold* was the way the narrator switched between his 'public' voice and the personal, confessional tone of the most intimate lyric. The canto opens and closes with his words to 'Ada! sole daughter of my house and heart', the baby daughter he will never see again.

> I see thee not, – I hear thee not, – but none
> Can be so wrapt in thee; thou art the friend
> To whom the shadows of far years extend:
> Albeit my brow thou never should'st behold,
> My voice shall with thy future visions blend,
> And reach into thy heart, – when mine is cold,–
> A token and a tone, even from thy father's mould.
>
> (III, 115)

This introduces a seductive appeal to Ada (and all the poet's young female readers of the future) to repudiate society's hatred and disapproval of the disgraced poet and his works which will be henceforth taught them:

> I know that thou wilt love me: though my name
> Should be shut from thee...
>
> (III, 117)

The notion of a fallen Lear-like father nourished and redeemed by a daughter-mother is an image which recurs throughout Cantos III and IV, counterpointing the main theme, the exploration of revolutionary but self-defeating masculinities of Napoleon (III, 36–45), Rousseau (III, 77–84), Cromwell and others. There is Julia Alpinula who died after a vain attempt to save her father's life when he was condemned to death as a traitor (III, 66). Most tellingly, there is the story in Canto IV of the Roman daughter who sustained her aged father, condemned to death as a traitor, by breastfeeding him in his dungeon (IV, 150). The generative power of woman had been repudiated in the ostentatious farewells of Harold to his mother, sister and mistresses (I, 10), and feared and condemned in the misogyny of the early cantos (II, 30–5). But now it is celebrated, 'Oh, holiest nurse!' (IV, 151), but only when drained of any connotations of autonomous sexuality, and put to the use of sustaining the republic, here embodied by the venerable patriot, her father. There could be no clearer indication that Byron's republicanism was patriarchal in nature, assuming a leadership from the top down, determined by right of birth, in class and gender, as had appertained in the classical republics he idealized.

The Shelleys

Byron had written about half of the third canto when he met Percy Bysshe Shelley on May 27 at Sécheron, near Geneva. He had already met Shelley's eighteen-year-old mistress, Mary Wollstonecraft Godwin, the bluestocking daughter of the feminist Mary Wollstonecraft and the philosophical anarchist William Godwin. She had been introduced to him by her stepsister of the same age, Claire Clairmont, in England. Claire's ambition was to be the mistress of a great poet too. She offered herself to Byron just before he went abroad and would bear him a daughter, Allegra, in January 1817. The eventual meeting between the two poets was the result of Claire's machinations, for when Percy and Mary set off for Italy, Claire persuaded them to stop in Geneva and wait there for Byron. They were willing enough, for Mary had already felt the power of the noble poet's personal charisma and Percy Shelley had been 'Byron mad' the year previously. He had already read Byron's *Poems: Original and Translated, English Bards and Scotch Reviewers*, and *Lara*, and almost certainly *Childe Harold's Pilgrimage* I and II and the tales.[8] He had also sent Byron a copy of *Queen Mab*.

Claire was delighted when, at last, she spotted Byron's name in the hotel guest book in Geneva, though he must have been tired after his journey, for he had put his age down as a hundred! The meeting between Percy Shelley and Byron was the beginning of one of the most fruitful friendships in literary history. On June 10 Byron took the Villa Diodati, with a magnificent view of the lake, to be only a few hundred yards from the Shelleys' house at Montalègre. Apart from one week when the Shelley group visited the valley of Chamouni, the two men were together daily from 27 May until 29 August when the Shelley group returned to England to arrange Claire's confinement. Byron's doctor, John Polidori, noted in his diary that they 'talked till the ladies' brains whizzed with giddiness, about idealism'.[9] No-one else in Byron's life was such a stimulating literary and intellectual companion. Shelley and Byron spent hours talking far into the night whenever they were together. Although Byron was the natural leader of this group at Geneva in 1816 and was so (in)famous as to be a tourist attraction in his own right in Italy, Shelley was more than an intellectual match for him. The group met again briefly at Venice in 1818, then reconvened at Pisa from October 1821 to July 1822. The handsome adventurer Edward Trelawny introduced himself to Byron in 1822 (the poet wrote that it was like coming face to face with his own Corsair) and Trelawny's account of first meeting the two poets illustrates the relationship between them. Byron called over Shelley, who seemed to the disappointed Trelawny merely a tongue-tied stripling in a schoolboy's jacket, and asked him to read over and comment on what he had written the night before. Then a magical transformation occurred: '[H]e [Shelley] waved his wand, and Byron, after a faint show of defiance, stood mute; his quick perception of the truth of Shelley's comments on his poem transfixed him, and Shelley's earnestness and just criticism held him captive. I was however struck with Byron's mental vivacity and wonderful memory; he defended himself with a variety of illustrations, precedents, and apt quotations from modern authorities, disputing Shelley's propositions, not by denying their truth as a whole, but in parts...'[10]

Shelley and Byron were both reformers in politics, both aristocrats who were short of money, both had been condemned by English society for their sexual behaviour (the Lord Chancellor would deprive Shelley of parental rights over his children by his first wife Harriet because of the radical views expressed in *Queen Mab*). But their philosophical tempers were completely opposed, for while Shelley was an idealist and a meliorist, Byron was sceptical and pessimistic. Though both protested against conventional sexual mores, Shelley believed in Wollstonecraftian feminism and free love, whereas Byron led the life of an aristocratic libertine in Venice. Shelley's intellectual and political daring encouraged Byron to leave mere fashionable verse behind him, while Byron's pragmatic concern with the literary market acted as a corrective to Shelley's elitism.

Frankenstein engendered

Each evening from June 14–18, while the Villa Diodati resounded to the rumble of summer thunderstorms and the crack of lightning, the group, who had spent their days sailing on the lake, entertained each other by telling ghost stories from *Fantasmagoriana*, a collection of German tales translated into French. According to Mary's account from the preface of *Frankenstein* (1831), Byron was the instigator of a contest in which all except Claire participated: 'We will each write a ghost story,' said Lord Byron. 'The noble author began a tale, a fragment of which he printed at the end of his poem of Mazeppa. Shelley, more apt to embody ideas and sentiments in the radiance of brilliant imagery, and in the music of the most melodious verse that adorns our language, than to invent the machinery of a story, commenced one founded on the experiences of his early life. Poor Polidori had some terrible idea about a skull-headed lady, who was so punished for peeping through a key-hole – what to see I forget – something very shocking and wrong of course ... '[11] At midnight on the 18th, after an evening of Gothic stories, Byron began declaiming the section of Coleridge's *Christabel* describing the witch's breast, 'Hideous, deformed, and pale of hue ... ' so effectively that Shelley ran shrieking from the room. When he had recovered, he explained that, when looking at Mary, he had suddenly visualized a woman with eyes for nipples.

The only successful story produced by the ghost-story competition was Mary Godwin's *Frankenstein*. Inspired by Percy Shelley's and Byron's nightly philosophical discussions on 'the nature of the principle of life', accounts of recent scientific experiments which used electricity in attempts to galvanize the limbs of dead animals, and a nightmare prompted by her recent fears and experiences of childbirth and child death, Mary came up with the basic idea of *Frankenstein*. It would be completed and published in 1818, when it was a sensational success. Byron thought it 'a wonderful work for a Girl of nineteen – *not* nineteen indeed at that time' (*L&J*, vi. 125–7). It would set Gothic fiction on a new course for the nineteenth century, as well as acting as prototype for a whole new genre of science fiction. It is also a philosophical novel of ideas. Subtitled 'The Modern Prometheus', it is today recognized to be an important feminist critique of the Romantic Prometheanism which was currently inspiring the poetry of her male companions.

Polidori, years later, after he had been dismissed by the poet, developed some ideas from Byron's fragment into a Gothic production of his own: *The Vampyre: a Tale* (1819). This was also published in the *New Monthly Magazine* 11: 63 (1 April 1819) and *Galignani's Messenger*, together with a spurious 'Account of Lord Byron's Residence in the Island of Mityline' and attributed to Byron. Byron was incensed and wrote to the editor of Galignani's insisting a contradiction be published. Polidori publicly acknowledged his authorship in a letter to the *Courier* on 5 May 1819. Despite this, the text was associated with Byron in the public mind and attained great success on the continent. It would become one of the inspirations behind Bram Stoker's *Dracula* (1897).

Rousseau

On 22 June the two poets went on a tour of Lake Geneva, visiting Meillerie, Clarens and Vevey and other spots associated with Rousseau's sentimental novel, *La Nouvelle Héloïse*. They also visited the Chateau de

Chillon and Gibbon's house. The influence of Rousseau and Shelley can be traced in the strong note of idealism sounded in the second half of the third canto of *Childe Harold*, counterpointing Haroldian fatalism. The wanderer, 'Whose bark drives on and on' (III, 70), seeks escape from human society and from his own consciousness by mystically merging with Nature:

> I live not in myself, but I become
> Portion of that around me;
>
> (III, 72)

There is a tone of uncertainty, however, in the adoption of a quasi-Wordsworthian pantheism:

> Are not the mountains, waves, and skies, a part
> Of me and of my soul, as I of them?
>
> (III, 75)

Shelley had persuaded Byron to take Wordsworth seriously. After reading the most recent version of Leigh Hunt's *Feast of the Poets* (1815) Byron had been stung to realize that the best critics now rated the Lake poet more highly than himself. He later admitted to Medwin, that 'Shelley, when I was in Switzerland, used to dose me with Wordsworth physic even to nausea; and I do remember then reading some things of his with pleasure'.[12] The aggrieved Wordsworth, when he read the third canto, described Byron as 'poaching on his manor'.[13] However, in the passage describing the contrast between complete calm followed by tempest at Lake Leman by night, and the poet's delight in the power of the elements, (III, 85–97), we can see Byron has absorbed the Wordsworthian influence and reshaped it in his own passionate image:

> ... Most glorious night!
> Thou wert not sent for slumber! let me be
> A sharer in thy fierce and far delight,–
> A portion of the tempest and of thee!
> How the lit lake shines, a phosphoric sea,
> And the big rain comes dancing to the earth!
> And now again 'tis black, – and now, the glee
> Of the loud hills shakes with its mountain-mirth,
> As if they did rejoice o'er a young earthquake's birth.
>
> (III, 93)

In the days following the tour with Shelley on Lake Geneva, Byron wrote the six Clarens stanzas on the ideal of Love manifest within the beauty of nature (III, 99–104), and the strongly Shelleyan note on them. Shelley was at this time beginning the composition of his 'Hymn to Intellectual Beauty' on the same theme. Both poets were inspired by Rousseau, and Byron was influenced by Shelley, who was developing his concept of the imagination as an intuitive power achieving the synthesis of reason and emotion, capable of effecting the regeneration of the individual and of society. Byron, too, expressed a Romantic view of poetic creativity as the quintessence of individual personality:

> Could I embody and unbosom now
> That which is most within me, – could I wreak
> My thoughts upon expression, and thus throw
> Soul, heart, mind, passions, feelings, strong or weak,
> All that I would have sought, and all I seek,
> Bear, know, feel, and yet breathe – into *one* word,
> And that one word were Lightning, I would speak;
>
> (III, 97)

By the end of the month Byron had composed 'The Prisoner of Chillon' and completed Canto III of *Childe Harold*. He realized later that the third canto was exploratory in its thought rather than synthesized. He mordantly described it as 'a fine indistinct piece of poetical desolation, and my favourite. I was half mad during the time of its composition, between metaphysics, mountains, lakes, love inextinguishable, thoughts unutterable, and the nightmare of my own delinquencies. I should, many a good day, have blown my brains out, but for the recollection that it would have given pleasure to my mother-in-law ... ' (*L&J*, v. 165).

To Shelley's disappointment, Byron soon reverted to his original inability to apprehend nature as a restorative power. Following the Shelleys' departure to England, from 17–29 September Byron toured the Bernese Oberland with Hobhouse, keeping a confessional Alpine Journal for his half-sister Augusta, whom he was never to see again. Afterwards he wrote his considered view: 'I am a lover of nature and an admirer of beauty. I can bear fatigue and welcome privation, and have seen some of the noblest views in the world. But in all this the recollections of bitterness, and more especially of recent and more home desolation, which must accompany me through life, have preyed upon me here; and neither the music of the shepherd, the crashing of the avalanche, nor the torrent, the mountain, the glacier, the forest, nor the cloud, have for one moment lightened the weight upon my heart, nor enabled me to lose my own wretched identity in the majesty, and the power, and the glory, around, above, and beneath me'.[14] In September and October he wrote the first two acts of *Manfred*, a poetical expression of this theme. In fact, even 'The Dream', 'Darkness', 'The Prisoner of Chillon' and 'Prometheus', which were all written in June and July 1816, when Shelley was present, deal with the inevitable extinguishing of the light of the human mind imprisoned in clay, rather than affirming Shelleyan hope. Nevertheless, Byron's humanist celebration of man's endurance and defiance of his metaphysical limitations had been heightened by his respect for his friend's beliefs. Shelley, for his part, responded to Byron's cosmic pessimism in *Manfred* and *Cain*, for he was driven to question but reaffirm his idealism in poems like 'Julian and Maddalo' and *Prometheus Unbound*.

Friends for six years, Shelley and Byron read and reacted to all each other's major works. Shelley incorporated references to or portraits of Byron in 'Julian and Maddalo', 'Lines Written Among the Euganean Hills', 'The Two Spirits: an Allegory', 'Epipsychidion', *Adonais*, 'Hellas' and 'Sonnet to Byron'. Mary Shelley represented a Shelleyan and a contrasting Byronic character in her novel *The Last Man* (1826), written when both men were dead and she felt herself to be the last survivor of their group. On his part, Byron's *Manfred*, whose protagonist is on a self-destructive quest to be reunited with his idealized epipsyche, is obviously influenced by *Alastor*. Percy enthused both Mary and Byron with his fascination for this trope. In *Frankenstein*, *The Revolt of Islam*, 'Epipsychidion', *Manfred*, *Cain* and *Heaven and Earth*, the Platonic idea of the bifurcation of the soul into differently sexed halves is combined with the Gothic preoccupation with sibling incest, resulting in the Narcissistic Romantic theme of twins, doubles or divided selves needing completion.

Another preoccupation of the group that summer was the myth of Prometheus, who could be appropriated as a Romantic humanist hero. Percy Shelley read Aeschylus's *Prometheus Bound* to Byron. As well as *Manfred*, this inspired Byron's ode 'Prometheus'. Mary subtitled *Frankenstein* 'The Modern Prometheus', and Shelley himself went on in 1819 to write *Prometheus Unbound*. Each writer's rewriting of the myth shows a different perspective: Byron's dark preoccupation with the Gods' torture of the hero; Mary's ironic deconstruction of the male egotistical delusion that his quest is philanthropic; and Percy's hero's ability to subdue hate and tyranny through forgiveness and love.

When he returned to England Percy Shelley wrote Byron a long letter on 29 September 1816 urging him to devote his powers to a political end. He had already suggested that Byron write an epic on the French Revolution:

> You have already given evidence of very uncommon powers. Having produced thus much, with effort, as you are aware, very disproportionate to the result; what are you not further capable of effecting? What would the human race have been if Homer, or Shakespeare, had never written? or if any false modesty, or mistake of their own powers, had witheld them from consummating those unequalled achievements of mind by which we are so deeply benefited? I do not compare you with these. I do not know how great an intellectual compass you are destined to fill. I only know that your powers are astonishingly great, and that they ought to be exerted to their full extent.
>
> (*LPBS*, i. 507)

Whilst Byron was not permanently converted to Shelleyan idealism, the philosophical dialectic between the two poets challenged and developed his own scepticism. It would soon be necessary for him to develop an entirely original poetic form in order to express the resulting Romantic irony, peculiar to him. This would eventually produce his greatest poem, *Don Juan*. Shelley must have recognized this, for despite regret at Byron's 'bitter mockery of our common nature' (*LPBS*, ii. 198) he immediately apprehended the philosophical stature of that poem, as perhaps no other contemporary of the poet did. It may well have been Shelley's encouragement which was responsible for Byron's persistence with it in the teeth of universal condemnation. Though a sexual satire was not the sort of epic on the French Revolution Shelley had hoped for, he pronounced the poem 'astonishingly fine', commenting 'I think I see the trace of my earnest exhortations to him to create something wholly new' (*LPBS*, ii. 323).

When he left Switzerland on 28 August, Shelley had taken the manuscript of Byron's third canto of *Childe Harold* with him. He wrote as soon as he docked on 8 September to assure Byron that the Childe was safe: 'His only adventure since he quitted the paternal roof has been inglorious. He was taken for a smuggler, and turned over and over by a greasy Custom-house officer, to see if lace, &c., were hidden within'.[15] Thereafter he reported delivering the manuscript to Murray three days later, then conscientiously wrote again on 29 September that a price of 2000 guineas had been agreed, and he anticipated soon receiving the proofs. But on 2 October Shelley had to write to Murray requesting they should be sent to him. Having still not received them, Shelley wrote again on 30 October protesting that he was authorized to correct the proofs of the poem. But the Murray circle were determined to repudiate the influence of Shelley, whose politics they abhorred. Murray assiduously flattered Byron with Gifford's praises ('...the whole volume beams with genius. I am sure he loves you in his heart...') and successfully persuaded Byron to retain him as editor, to Shelley's morti-fication.[16] The *Quarterly* editor excised all the more radical political content from the notes, and even made textual changes. Though Byron protested over these, he eventually acquiesced and even expressed his gratitude to Gifford for his loyalty during this period of his disgrace 'despite of difference of years – morals – habits – & even *politics...*' (*L&J*, v. 154; 169).

Hobhouse was also jealous of Byron's new friend's influence, com-menting on the new canto: 'It is very fine in parts, but I don't know whether I like it so much as his first cantos. There is an air of mystery and metaphysics about it...'.[17] Walter Scott, however, in his review of the poem for the *Quarterly*, praised Byron's incursion into the Words-worthian territory of the moral associations of nature, as a more 'immortal' subject than his usual ruminations on history and culture. But Scott was dismayed by the fact that, though the younger poet gave a most poignant and 'beautiful description of the evening which pre-ceded the battle of Quatre Bras' (III, 21–8), Byron could describe the scenes at Waterloo 'without dropping even one leaf of laurel on the head of Wellington'. Scott probably spoke for many in a Britain busily engaged in creating a cult of military heroism incarnated in the public art and architecture of London. The staunchly Evangelical Countess Spencer was organizing a ladies-only public subscription, which com-missioned from Richard Westmacott a colossal nude statue of Achilles for Hyde Park, as a tribute to Wellington (rapidly nicknamed 'the ladies' fancy' and soon garnished with a fig leaf). Trafalgar Square, Nelson's column and Waterloo Bridge would follow in due course.

Scott was also horrified by the stanzas regretting the demise of the ideals which inspired the French revolution (III, 83–4), but he reas-sured the reader that he believed Byron only affected such political opinions for 'the sport of whim and singularity'.[18] The literary qual-ity of the new canto was enthusiastically acknowledged back in Britain, but for many upper-class and Evangelical readers the dawning realization of Byron's radicalism following on the sexual scandal would soon put him beyond the pale.

Italy

On 5 October Byron travelled to Italy with Hobhouse, crossing the Alps by the Simplon road. Perhaps they had been reading Ann Radcliffe's *The Italian* on the way, for they certainly prepared for brigands. Hobhouse recalled, 'We had four brace of pistols in our carriage, two swords, two sword-sticks, and Byron's dagger. We furnished Springhetti [their Italian guide] with a brace of pistols, and my postilion'. They were sure that as soon as they crossed the border into Milanese territory 'that the breeze was softer, the clouds thrown farther back than in the north, the sky more blue, the houses more white, the groves more green ... '.[19] Of course, 'Italy' was a mere geographical expression at this time. As when Byron and Hobhouse had arrived in 'Greece' six years earlier, the travellers themselves conferred a mythical unity, quite at odds with current political reality, on these territories, through their knowledge of classical Greek or Latin respectively. Each Italian region had its own distinct dialect, culture and traditions. Napoleon's regime had imposed a superficial unity on these regions through conquest which inspired in its turn a patriotic reaction which was not yet truly nationalist. This patriotic feeling was further increased when most of Italy was given to the hated Austrians after Napoleon's defeat in 1815. But the concept of a nation-state was at odds with strongly localized affiliations for much of the nineteenth century.

That October the friends stayed at Milan. They frequented the theatre and opera, and also visited the Teatro Re, the common people's theatre. They were soon befriended by members of the Italian literati such as the charming Abate Ludovico Di Breme, aristocratic leader of the Romantic school and a liberal in politics; Vincenzo Monti, the most famous poet of the day; the writer Pietro Borsieri; Silvio Pellico, the dramatist; and the novelist Henri Beyle (Stendhal). Stendhal wrote that Byron's presence inspired 'the finest conversation which I have ever known in my life; a volcano of new ideas and generous sentiments'.[20] Both Di Breme and Monti told Byron that contemporary Italian poetry would not bear comparison with that of the past. The living poets they most highly esteemed were Monti, Pindemonte and the patriot poet and novelist Ugo Foscolo, who was a refugee in Britain. In the preface to the fourth canto of *Childe Harold*, Byron paid tribute to these poets as

selects & reduces them to order – like distance in the landscape' (*L&J*, v. 221). The analogy with picturesque landscape painting is telling.[22] The first draft was completed in the summer nights following days spent swimming in the Adriatic and reading Boccaccio with Marianna.

On 31 July he was visited by Hobhouse and M.G. Lewis. From August to December Byron assiduously revised and added to this ambitious poem. Byron and Hobhouse also collaborated on the extensive prose notes, which would frame the poetry, providing not just a reference guide for tourists ('After a walk of twenty minutes across a flat well wooded meadow, you come to a little blue lake ... ' [*CPW*, ii. 230]) but a republican point of view on Italy's present subjugation both to the Austrian authorities and to Romish 'superstition'. Hobhouse's antiquarian prose commentary became so voluminous that it eventually had to be published separately as *Historical Illustrations to the Fourth Canto of Childe Harold*. Byron's comments on Tasso, Petrarch, Dante and Boccaccio pick up and exemplify his preoccupation in the canto with the role of the poet as necessarily oppositional: a prophet unhallowed in his own country.

Byron's Romantic poem represents the end of the tradition of the European aristocrat's Grand Tour, which had begun in the late seventeenth century. The set-pieces in *Childe Harold*, the Rhine journey, contemplation of the Alps, meditation on the ruins at Rome, were the familiar territory of eighteenth-century topographical poetry and travel literature. But Byron's fluency and flexible handling of the Spenserian stanza allowed him to infuse the genre with the varying moods of personal response rather than an Augustan assumption of shared standards. So his fourth canto and its notes would bridge the gap between the classically-educated nobleman and his middle-class readership, who were now beginning to travel to Europe, especially as the verse provided the finer feelings experienced by the traveller at each cultural landmark. Quotations from the poem would lace Murray's guidebooks, which led the field along with those of Thomas Cook and Baedeker later in the century.

The fourth canto was dedicated to Hobhouse, befitting its emphasis on art and antiquities, in contrast to the Shelleyan concern with nature in the third. In his prefatory letter, Byron draws attention to the date on which it was written, the anniversary of 'the most unfortunate day of my past existence', his marriage. His tribute to Hobhouse's loyalty and friendship, therefore, is contextualized by this reminder of the obloquy heaped on Byron's head in England. It introduces the subject of his exile, 'I've taught me other tongues'; but also his admission that he still loves 'the inviolate island of the sage and the free'; and his determination to write for Britain:

> I twine
> My hopes of being remembered in my line
> With my land's language ...
>
> (IV, 9)

But the prefatory letter also strongly condemns the jingoism of 'songs of exultation still yelled from the London taverns, over the carnage of Mont St Jean' and British 'betrayal of Genoa, of Italy, of France, and of the world' in the parcelling-up of Europe during the Congress of Vienna. Byron insists on his and Hobhouse's patriotism, which is redefined as continuing the tradition of British liberalism, including the independence necessary to criticize the government. He commends his friend's radical commentary, *The Substance of some Letters Written by an Englishman Resident at Paris During the Last Reign of the Emperor Napoleon* (1816).[23] His own poem would inculcate the opposite of jingoism: cosmopolitanism. This was the Enlightenment virtue promulgated by travel. The European Grand Tour tradition had, moreover, been an important contributory factor in engendering the whole concept of Italian nationalism, in the same way that a classical education had led to Philhellenism. It was European tourists who conceptualized the peninsula as a whole, rather than in terms of separate cities or regions. '[I]ndeed, the idea of Italy as a single nation in the modern sense was one of the tourists' most important contributions. "Las Italias", wonderfully described by Cervantes in the sixteenth century, had been glimpsed as a single Italy, one in mind and spirit, born of the creative imagination of the entire Continent'.[24]

The first twenty-nine stanzas celebrated the traditional British love for Venice, as another mercantile, maritime empire based on trade with which the British, more than other European nations, identified. Antonio Canaletto had catered almost exclusively for British tourists with his views of the city.

> I lov'd her from my boyhood – she to me
> Was as a fairy city of the heart ...
> And Otway, Radcliffe, Schiller, Shakespeare's art,
> Had stamp'd her image in me ...
>
> (IV, 18)

She is bound up with the British national consciousness, embedded in our literature:

> Shylock and the Moor,
> And Pierre, cannot be swept or worn away
> (IV, 4)

The fall, first to Napoleon and then to the Austrians, of the Venetian republic which had been seen as an ideal combination of the classical republican tradition with a Christian culture, is a warning most of all to her successor in greatness:

> ... and thy lot
> Is shameful to the nations, – most of all,
> Albion! to thee: the Ocean queen should not
> Abandon Ocean's children; in the fall
> Of Venice think of thine, despite thy watery wall.
> (IV, 17)

Byron's pilgrim then follows the usual tourist route to Rome, via Arqua, Ferrara, Florence, Lake Trasimene, and Terni. In the Preface, Byron had explained that in this last canto 'there will be found less of the pilgrim than in any of the preceding, and that little slightly, if at all, separated from the author speaking in his own person. The fact is, that I had become weary of drawing a line which every one seemed determined not to perceive...' (*CPW*, ii. 122). For the rather two-dimensional persona of the worldweary cynic, Harold, could not adequately express the more complex moods of the later cantos. Also as Byron became more adept at constructing a palimpsest of historical exemplae, he preferred to locate changing responses within one psyche, in a first-person narrative. His fame meant he could now rely on readers' familiarity with the Byronic melancholic personality he dramatized as his public image, and could thus dismiss the apparatus of a fictional character. He describes himself ironically as 'a ruin amidst ruins' (IV, 25). By visiting the graves and places associated with Petrarch, Dante, Tasso, Ariosto, Alfieri, and Boccaccio, and meditating on their imprisonment or banishment by the civil authorities or their neglect, he implies a connection between himself and the Titans of Italian literature. When contemplating the decay of former grandeur in Venice and the overgrown ruins of Rome, he questions how far Art transcends the limitations of mortality, the destructive power of nature. Stanzas 42 and 43 incorporate a translation of Vincenzo da Filicaja's sonnet 'Italia, Italia, O tu coi feo la sorte' (also translated by Robert Southey and Felicia Hemans), in which Italy's natural beauty itself seems to invite the rapine of spoilers.

At last the pilgrim reaches his shrine: 'Oh Rome! my country! city of the soul!' (IV, 78). The noble traveller recognizes her through his knowledge of classical texts and responds appropriately to her past grandeur and present powerlessness in allusions to her mythology:

> The Niobe of nations! there she stands,
> Childless and crownless, in her voiceless woe;
> An empty urn within her withered hands,
> Where holy dust was scatter'd long ago;
>
> (IV, 79)

Contemplation of Rome had traditionally provided the visiting ruling class of Britain with what James Buzard has termed 'pseudo-historical legitimization...by imagining their nation as heir to the great but fallen Roman Imperial tradition' in spreading the rule of the British Empire.[25] But Byron, revisiting Europe after the final defeat of Napoleon, calls upon such associations only to emphasize his difference of view. Here imagery of the Roman republic is applied to celebrate Simon Bolivar's revolution against imperial Spain in South America and George Washington throwing off the British colonial yoke in the North, in contrast to stagnation in Europe itself:

> Can tyrants but by tyrants conquered be,
> And Freedom find no champion and no child
> Such as Columbia saw arise when she
> Sprung forth a Pallas, armed and undefiled?
> Deep in the unpruned forest, 'midst the roar
> Of cataracts, where nursing Nature smiled
> On infant Washington? Has Earth no more
> Such seeds within her breast, or Europe no such shore?
>
> (IV, 96)

Byron's status as a classically-educated aristocrat, which the contemporary reader might initially have supposed would underpin endorsement of the hegemony of the ruling class, is actually called upon to validate instead the proud independence of his oppositional discourse.

The vision of democracy which had briefly blazed in the French Revolution could be said to have inspired Byron's passionate rhetoric of freedom ('Yet, Freedom! yet thy banner, torn, but flying,/ Streams like the thunder-storm *against* the wind' [IV, 98]) while paradoxically also necessitating his self-conscious questioning of his own role of noble spokesman ('It is not that I may not have incurr'd/ For my ancestral faults or mine the wound/ I bleed withal ... ' [IV, 133]). A Romantic discourse is thus produced in which the poet dramatizes himself as lone wanderer in Europe, speaking out of his solitude for and to the individual common man at home. The narrator's authority is deemed to lie not in his rank *per se* but in his ability to free himself from social constraints and in his superior capacity for heightened sensibility.

Hobhouse and Foscolo

On 8 January 1818 Hobhouse left for England with the MS of Canto IV. On 23 March, he happened to meet and befriend the exiled Italian patriot poet, Ugo Foscolo, at a London dinner party. The story of the secret collaboration of these two on an essay on Italian literature appended to the *Historical Illustrations*, has been pieced together by E.R. Vincent.[26] Hobhouse had dined so well that night, that at 3 a.m. he had to get up to take rhubarb pills, but felt worse and tried calomel pills while soaking his feet in hot water. These treatments proving ineffective, he decided he was dying and wrote a memorandum on the disposition of his papers. When he decided he would, after all, live, 'Byron's bulldog' characteristically sat up reading Livy until dawn. Back to his sober self the next day, he wrote to Foscolo explaining that in their collaboration on the expository notes to *Childe Harold,* he and Byron felt they needed to provide a survey of contemporary Italian literature, but, as Byron had admitted in his preface, neither felt adequate to the delicate task; 'The state of literary as well as political party appears to run, or to *have* run, so high, that for a stranger to steer impartially between them is next to impossible' (*CPW*, ii. 123). Never was spoken a truer word! But Hobhouse rushed in where angels feared to tread. The poem and notes were already set up in the press but there was just time to add the essay. Would Foscolo help? Foscolo promised 'a few pages', but in fact the published *Essay on the Present Literature of Italy* totalled 138 pages, of which the central biographical-critical sketches of Cesarotti, Parini, Pindemonte, Monti and Foscolo himself were almost certainly entirely provided by the Italian writer. Both agreed that the essay would appear under Hobhouse's name and no money changed hands at first, though Hobhouse promised and later paid the impecunious Foscolo regularly for materials to be included in the account of recent Italian history he planned as a further appendix to *Childe Harold*.

On 28 April 1818 the fourth canto of *Childe Harold's Pilgrimage* was published, as well as the *Historical Illustrations* including the essay. To Hobhouse's chagrin, the literati, including Byron, were as one in hailing the brilliant essay on Italian literature and finding the rest of the notes tedious (*L&J*, vi. 72). Murray, who had been very reluctant to publish them because of their radicalism, wrote to Byron: 'I am anxious to know if you are satisfied with Mr. Hobhouse's notes. The parts he thinks best are those upon the Antiquities; but we feel very little interest for them, and much prefer the "essay on Italian Literature".' Worse, when the essay was read in Italy it caused a storm of controversy. The Countess of Albany was highly offended at the reference to herself. Ippolito Pindemonte was still so enraged at the way he had been described that he refused to contribute to a memorial to Byron on the poet's death. Foscolo's views on the literary scene were partisan and he had given himself great prominence, prompting a fierce sixteen-page rejoinder from Di Breme which the mischievous Byron passed on with glee: '[Di Breme] has brought all Italy into a squabble about his damned doctrines ... Row him – I say he gives *you* devilish bitter words' (*L&J*, vi. 63). It was hardly surprising that Di Breme would be annoyed that his friend Hobhouse had left him out of the account altogether! He also rightly suspected the true authorship of the essay. Foscolo and Hobhouse concocted an open letter in reply to Di Breme, in which, Hobhouse told Byron, 'I have quoted De Breme's own words against Monti so I am in hopes of a squabble ... '. Whereas Hobhouse was evasive on the question of authorship, Foscolo categorically denied to Silvio Pellico that he had taken any part whatever in the essay.

Byron and Isaac Nathan

Hobhouse's discomfiture during this episode may be imagined. It is ironic, in view of his knowing deception of Byron and his readership, that he himself was always the first to dissuade Byron from collaborations with anyone other than himself. Back in London early in 1815, Byron had dismayed Hobhouse by agreeing to the request of the Jewish musician Isaac Nathan, to provide him with lyrics for traditional airs and music of the synagogue. Collections of folksongs and national airs were all the vogue, and music publishers like George Thomson, Thomas Preston and James Power specialized in providing highly-priced editions complete with music. *A Selection of Irish Melodies* (1808–34), with lyrics by Thomas Moore was particularly popular. Byron was determined to rival these. Moreover, his Calvinist upbringing had steeped him in the Old Testament, and in the Dissenting tradition of using the bondage of the Jews as a metaphor for contemporary tyranny. In his reminiscences Nathan remembers how Byron enjoyed the challenge of improvising or adapting his verse to the constraints of the music.[27]

The music and lyrics were to be published together with Nathan receiving all the profits. Murray resented this arrangement and pressed Byron to let him publish the lyrics in the fourth volume of a *Collected Works*, which would eventually come out in June. Byron agreed, but then was put into an awkward position when Nathan (naturally enough) objected, in case music publishers pirated the lyrics before his own edition came out. Douglas Kinnaird encouraged the project with Nathan but Hobhouse strongly supported Murray in the wrangle that followed. The publisher wrote to Byron on 17 February 1815, to persuade him he was demeaning himself and advise him to listen to: ' ... Mr Hobhouse who still thinks it is not precisely the same thing to have music made to one's poems, and to write poetry for music, and I advise you most conscientiously to abide by the determination of Mr. Hobhouse's good sense'. The anti-Semitism of Byron's friends and Moore's fear of competition was used to good account to protect Murray's business interest in the poet. However, Byron refused to terminate his arrangement with Nathan entirely, as Hobhouse, Moore and Murray urged. The first number of *A Selection of Hebrew Melodies* was published in April, as a lavish and ornamented quarto edition, featuring Nathan's musical arrangements to twelve of the poems, and priced at one guinea. Nevertheless, Murray succeeded in undercutting Nathan's success, by obtaining Byron's permission to publish the whole twenty-five lyrics without music as a separate edition in May, probably without paying any fee for copyright either to Nathan or Byron.[28] This was in demi-octavo and cost only 4s.6d. Nathan brought out his second number of *A Selection of Hebrew Melodies*, with settings to a further twelve lyrics, on April 1816. Despite all the opposition of Byron's friends and the anti-Semitic reviews, Nathan's editions had proved a great success, his profit being estimated at five thousand pounds, in comparison with Murray's £836. 5s.

Beppo

Even while he was revising and adding to the fourth canto of *Childe Harold*, Byron's fertile imagination was at work on another project.

Having already depicted his beloved Venice as a tragic but Romantic heroine, 'a sea Cybele, fresh from ocean, / Rising with her tiara of proud towers' (IV, 2), he now wanted to portray her resilience, humour and adaptability to changing political circumstances through giving a realistic portrait of a feisty contemporary Venetian woman. In her extravagant sentimental novel/ picturesque tour, *Corinne, ou L'Italie* (1807), the late Madame de Staël had symbolized Italy as a proudly independent Romantic heroine, an improvisatory woman poet, insufficiently valued by her conventional English lover. This was an attempt to characterize the culture of the South, a counterpart to her account of Northern art in *De l'Allemagne,* as well as to portray Italy under Napoleon's dominion as a doomed heroine. Byron's stanzas on the Coliseum by moonlight and on the sublimity of St Peter's in his fourth canto had been influenced by *Corinne.* Indeed, his poem may have been originally conceived as a masculine response to the Romantic feminism of the novel, for Harold bears some resemblance to De Staël's British hero, the oddly-named Nelvil. Now Byron took the familiar trope of creating a heroine representing her land, and gave it a new comic twist. The modern Laura, unlike the saintly object of Petrarch's admiration, does not exemplify ideal courtly love. She comforts herself with a lover when her husband disappears. But when he unexpectedly returns years later, dressed as a Turk, she is not discomposed and is soon ordering him to shave off his beard. Byron plays on the puritanism of his English readership in a beautifully understated ending, in which it is clear that none of the characters in this Italian eternal triangle has any thoughts of punishment for an erring wife, duels or divorce ('I've heard the Count and he were always friends' [99]). It is only the British reader who doesn't assume they will form an amicable *ménage à trois.*

Byron had heard the story which forms the basis of *Beppo* from Pietro Segati as a piece of Venetian gossip. It satisfied his liking for 'fact' as the basis of his poetry, and the central character being a Venetian merchant turned Turk provided a wonderful opportunity to satirize his own earlier material in the romantic Oriental tales. He had written lyrics, narrative poems, a dramatic poem, topographical poems and satires. Now he was to attempt comedy. On 19 January 1818 Byron sent the MS of *Beppo* to Murray, who brought it out as quickly as 28 February. *Beppo* was published anonymously, because Byron was nervous that the experiment would not succeed. But also he wanted to enjoy the fun of the readers' puzzlement. For hitherto he had encouraged them to see his verse as the product of the proud, melancholic persona he had created. But, as Byron said with reference to Francis Jeffrey: 'I was not, and, indeed, am not even *now*, the misanthropical and gloomy gentleman he takes me for, but a facetious companion, well to do with those with whom I am intimate, and as loquacious and laughing as if I were a much cleverer fellow. I suppose now I shall never be able to shake off my sables in public imagination' (*L&J*, v. 186).

Beppo was also an experiment in transmuting into English the flavour of Italian burlesque poetry. The intricate *ottava rima* stanza itself, though introduced into English literature in the sixteenth century by Sir Thomas Wyatt, had attracted few poets before. In September Byron was visited by Douglas Kinnaird, his brother, Lord Kinnaird, and William Stewart Rose, a member of the *Quarterly* coterie. Rose gave Byron a copy of *Whistlecraft*, by his friend John Hookham Frere, which Hobhouse pronounced 'excellent and quizzical – no better since the days of Swift'.[29] This was a mock-heroic poem, combining the burlesque style of Francesco Berni with that of Luigi Pulci's *Morgante Maggiore,* a sprawling digressive fifteenth-century anti-romance in *ottava rima*, but which made satiric allusions to contemporary England. This was the catalyst Byron needed. The verse form was a better vehicle than the Spenserian stanza for expressing both sides of the Byronic persona: swelling idealism (in the first six lines) and undercutting humour (in the concluding couplet).

> Her glossy hair was cluster'd o'er a brow
> Bright with intelligence, and fair, and smooth;
> Her eyebrow's shape was like the aerial bow,
> Her cheek all purple with the beam of youth,
> Mounting at times, to a transparent glow,
> As if her veins ran lightning; she, in sooth,
> Possess'd an air and grace by no means common:
> Her stature tall – I hate a dumpy woman.
>
> (*Don Juan*, I, 61)

Byron saw too that Pulci's device of a garrulous narrator and improvisatory style would suit his own 'mobility' of temperament. What was more, and was his own flash of genius, he realized this narrative style could be adapted to relating fabliau material. When he had been in Brussels, his relative Pryse Gordon had given him the *Novelle Galanti* of the Abate Giambattista Casti, and Byron wrote back to tell him, 'I cannot tell you what a treat your gift of Casti has been to me; I have almost got him by heart. I had read his 'Animali Parlanti', but I think these 'Novelle' much better. I long to go to Venice to see the manners so admirably described' (*L&J*, v. 80). Though the example of *Whistlecraft* showed him the way, it was the Voltairean Casti's unmasking of the sexual hypocrisy of the *ancien régime* which provided the real inspiration behind *Beppo* and *Don Juan*.[30]

In *Beppo* Byron ventriloquised the improvisatory panache he associated with Italy.[31] The digressive cosmopolitan narrator hints suggestively at the usefulness of gondolas, communicates the unique atmosphere of the Venetian carnival, discourses on the custom of the *cavalier servente*, and sardonically implies that the English reader may actually learn something from the example of Italian passion and Mediterranean tolerance and sophistication. In this stanza, the content – a celebration of the sensual sound of the Italian language – is cleverly underlined by the poet's obvious difficulty in finding enough rhymes for *ottava rima* metre in English, which he turns to comic account:

> I love the language, that soft bastard Latin,
> Which melts like kisses from a female mouth,
> And sounds as if it should be writ on satin,
> With syllables which breathe of the sweet South,
> And gentle liquids gliding all so pat in,
> That not a single accent seems uncouth,
> Like our harsh northern whistling, grunting, guttural,
> Which we're obliged to hiss, and spit, and splutter all.
>
> (*Beppo*, stanza 44)

Ravenna

In 1819, Byron became the *cavalier servente* of the nineteen-year-old Countess Teresa Guiccioli, announcing to Hobhouse, 'I am in love, and tired of promiscuous concubinage, and have now an opportunity of settling for life' (*L&J*, vi. 108). Though she was no bluestocking, Teresa was well-read and had first attracted Byron through her passionate enthusiasm for Dante and Petrarch. Teresa's fifty-year-old husband was the richest man in the Romagna, had been a friend of Alfieri's, and was the principal patron of the theatre in its ancient capital city, Ravenna. He was a sinister figure, and one of his previous wives had died in suspicious circumstances. Teresa's father, Count Ruggero Gamba Ghiselli and younger brother Pietro were the leaders of the Romagnan Carbonari, a secret society led by aristocrats, plotting to overthrow the government.[32] Byron visited Teresa at Ravenna and eventually settled there in 1820. At first he shared the Palazzo Guiccioli at the invitation of the Count, then he took a house romantically situated opposite the tomb of Dante. 'I was never tired of my rides in the pine forest: it breathes of the Decameron; it is poetical ground. Francesca lived, and Dante was exiled and died at Ravenna. There is something inspiring in such an air'.[33] The Romagna was an area seldom visited by foreign tourists and here Byron thoroughly integrated himself into Italian life and literature. He became a popular figure in the city because of his charity to the poor and sympathy with the working class. It was at Ravenna that he composed *The Prophecy of Dante* at Teresa's suggestion. Dante had found a haven at Ravenna when exiled by his enemies at Florence, and Byron could identify with him. The poet told Medwin, 'The place of Dante's fifteen years' exile, where he so pathetically prayed for his country, and deprecated the thought of being buried out of it; and the sight of his tomb, which I passed in my almost daily rides, – inspired me'.[34] That summer he was initiated into the Carbonari, as honorary leader of the *Turba* or section of working men. He allowed his house to be used as their arsenal. He was watched closely by spies; his letters were opened. Poems considered subversive, like the fourth canto of *Childe Harold* and *The Prophecy of Dante* were proscribed by the authorities. Byron wanted *Marino Faliero* and *The Prophecy of Dante* published together to inspire support in England for the revolution, and the latter to be translated into Italian and circulated there. But Murray, despite repeated appeals, made sure publication was delayed until 21 April – safely after the rising.

Byron's letters to England in 1820 were full of allusions to the prospective revolution. But in the end all came to nothing. The leaders of the uprising were betrayed and the plot failed on 24 February 1821. All Byron's hopes for a free Italy were blasted. In despair he thereafter threw himself into composition, following up *Marino Faliero* with four more plays and the satire *The Vision of Judgment* in an incredibly productive year. But in July the Gambas were ordered to leave the Romagnan state in twenty-four hours, and departed for Florence. Teresa by now was formally separated from her husband, but was required to reside with her father. Byron was reluctant to leave Ravenna, where he had put down roots, but he, too, would have to move to Tuscany to join her. On 6 August 1821 Shelley visited Byron at Ravenna for two weeks and Byron read him the fifth canto of *Don Juan*. Shelley wrote to Mary that he had stayed up all night talking to Byron, and had differed with him even more than ever. The pair decided that Byron, the Gambas and Teresa would settle at Pisa, near the Shelleys, who were now married.

Shelley found the Casa Lanfranchi for him. This was a sixteenth-century palace on the main road along the right bank of the Arno, built by the family mentioned as the persecutors of Ugolino in Dante's *Inferno*. Following the failure of the Italian uprisings, the Shelley-Byron group was plunged even further into political pessimism. Shelley expressed to Mary a wish 'to form for ourselves a society of our own class, as much as possible, in intellect or in feelings'.[35] Such a group formed, including Shelley's friends Edward and Jane Williams, his cousin Thomas Medwin, the Irishman John Taafe, and Edward Trelawny, which Byron joined by 1 November 1821. Mary described them as 'a little nest of singing birds'.[36]

Pisa

At this time Shelley and Byron were both defining their views on poetry, Shelley writing *A Defence of Poetry* (1821) in response to Peacock's *Four Ages of Poetry* while Byron had in February composed a letter to Revd William Lisle Bowles in defence of Pope, published as a pamphlet on 31 March and afterwards extended. This robust assertion of his belief in the classical tradition of literature, coming from the leading Romantic poet of the day, appeared quixotic to contemporary readers. In poetry as in religion, politics and sexuality Byron upheld in principle the very standards he challenged in practice. What was more he felt no compunction in lambasting his rival Romantic poets: '[T]here have sprung up two Sects of Naturals – the Lakers – who whine about Nature because they live in Cumberland – and their *under-Sect* – (which some one has maliciously called the "Cockney School") – who are enthusiastical for the country because they live in London' (*CMP*, p. 156). In an exchange of letters, Shelley persuaded Byron to reconsider his contempt for the poetry of John Keats (lampooned in the letter to Bowles as 'Mr John Ketch', *CMP*, p. 157). Shelley consolidated his victory by writing an elegy for Keats, *Adonais* (1821), where Byron is portrayed as chief mourner. Byron responded by instructing Murray to omit his castigation of Keats from all future publications, and by describing *Hyperion* as 'a fine monument'.

By now, Shelley himself had begun to be disillusioned with his earlier utopian belief in social progress. The two friends were therefore philosophically less at odds than previously, and united in their support of political freedom for Italy and Greece. Shelley was encouraging about *Don Juan*, and, though he did not agree with Byron's experimentation with neo-classical drama, such was his enthusiasm for *Cain* that on 12 January 1822, he wrote to John Gisborne, 'Space wondered less at the swift and fair creations of God, when he grew weary of vacancy, than I at the late works of this spirit of an angel in the mortal paradise of a decaying body'. On 26 January he wrote, 'Cain is apocalyptic – it is a revelation not before communicated to man'.[37]

In 1822 Shelley and Byron decided to launch a periodical to be published in England but specializing in Italian literature, and invited Shelley's friend, the journalist Leigh Hunt, to join them. Byron sent Hunt money for his travel expenses. Nevertheless, relations became strained between the poets, partly because of Shelley's frustrated sense of rivalry with his friend. He told Horace Smith dispiritedly, 'I do not write – I have lived too long near Lord Byron & the sun has extinguished the glowworm'.[38] There was bad feeling, too, over Byron's implacable hostility to Claire's wishes over the care of Allegra. At this juncture Allegra died from fever in the convent in which he had insisted on placing her. Their friendship was at a low ebb, but Shelley was determined to make a success of *The Liberal* for Hunt's sake, and effected a reconciliation. But the dazzling prospect of a collaboration between Shelley and Byron was never to materialize for on 8 July Percy Shelley and Edward Williams were drowned in a sailing accident.

Dante

The Byron–Shelley circle, dubbed 'the Satanic school' by Southey, were initiators of the early nineteenth-century championing of Dante as a Promethean model of the poet, prophet of the Reformation and herald of modernity. Byron said, 'He is the poet of liberty. Persecution, exile, the dread of a foreign grave, could not shake his principles'. Shelley described Dante as 'the first awakener of an entranced Europe'.[39] This theme would be taken up later in the century by Walter Pater and John Addington Symonds. It was important for the Romantics to identify past artists who rebelled against authority as their forbears, and this tendency would eventually result in the concept of the Italian Renaissance as a period differentiated from the Middle Ages. It was finally defined as such by Jacob Burckhardt in 1860.[40] Like Shakespeare, Dante had been condemned as a primitive or 'Gothic' writer by the Augustans. He attracted the Romantics for the same reason. Whereas Shakespeare was being coopted into the reactionary nationalist canon of English Literature, Dante's influence on Chaucer and especially the republican Milton could suggest an alternative Whiggish canon in which British contemporary expatriate liberal poets guarded and handed on the torch of liberty, supposedly kept alight since classical times by the Italian republics of the Middle Ages. However, Dante could also be appropriated by conservative Romantics as a Catholic mystic, warning against the abandonment of the concept of divine retribution, which would lead to the moral relativism of the Enlightenment and from thence to the anarchy of the French Revolution. A conservative Christian Dante would be celebrated in Arthur Hallam's prize-winning oration in 1831.

The fascination of the British Romantics with Dante's poetry was fuelled by August Wilhelm Schlegel's 1791 essay on the *Commedia*, Friedrich Schlegel's *Lectures on the History of Literature*, translated by J.G. Lockhart (1818), Coleridge's 1818 lecture on Dante, Henry Hallam's *Europe in the Middle Ages* (1818), J.C.L. Sismondi's *Histoire des républiques italiennes au moyen âge*, sixteen vols (1809–18) and *De la littérature du midi de l'Europe*, four vols (1813), and by the Rev. H.F. Cary's 1814 translation of the *Commedia*. The Pisan group studied Dante together, and John Taafe produced the first English commentary on the *Commedia*, which Byron persuaded Murray to publish in 1822.[41] Both Byron and Shelley wrote English poems in *terza rima*; both experimented with translations of passages from the *Commedia*. It was difficult for English radicals emancipating themselves from Protestant predestination to come to terms with Dante's grim account of divine justice, however. In argument with Shelley, Byron exasperatedly described the *Commedia* as 'a scientific treatise of some theological student...obscure, tiresome and insupportable'.[42] Yet he also took issue with Friedrich Schlegel's view that the *Commedia* lacked 'gentle feelings': 'Why, there is gentleness in Dante beyond all gentleness, when he is tender. It is true that, treating of the Christian Hades, or Hell, there is not much scope or site for gentleness – but who *but* Dante could have introduced any 'gentleness' at all into *hell*?' (*L&J*, viii. 39–40). Dante's humanity in the characterization of sinners like the incestuous adulterers Francesca and Paolo seemed to Byron to transcend the oppressive theology ostensibly governing the religious epic, presumably in the same way that Michelangelo's celebration of the human body in *The Last Judgment* in the Sistine chapel creates a tension with its ostensible didactic purpose.

To Byron, Dante's poetry proves the existence in the thirteenth century of a unifying Italian culture, the precondition of a nation-state. Dante's conservative vision of restoring a Holy Roman Empire ruled by Rome as the centre of Christendom is reinterpreted by Byron's *The Prophecy of Dante* as a newly relevant call to unity: 'and we/ her sons, may do this with one deed- /Unite' (II, 145). In this act of poetic ventriloquism, Byron speaks through Dante in a dramatic monologue which creates a palimpsest of historical moments: that of Dante look-ing back to the classical time of Virgil and forward to that of Byron, when he appeals to modern Italy on the brink of revolution:

> We can have but one country, and even yet
> Thou'rt mine – my bones shall be within thy breast,
> My soul within thy language ...
>
> (II, 19–21)

It was Dante as an individual and his place in history which primarily interested Byron, exemplifying the crucial role of the poet. The shade of Dante is resurrected to speak in person reluctantly to the modern reader:

> A spirit forces me to see and speak
> And for my guerdon grants *not* to survive
>
> (III, 32–3)

Speech of the historical personage, Dante, not merely his text, is thus supposedly guaranteed to be unliterary and therefore free from artifice. This ventriloquism attempts to obscure both the fictionality of Dante's epic and Byron's actual poem and endows both poets with mystical knowledge and the ability to transcend the particular times and cir-cumstances of their speech acts, 'I am not of this people, not this age' (I, 143). The poet of the past speaks to the present. Dante is the Gothic, the Other repressed by the Enlightenment, back fresh from the infernal regions, cursing the city who exiled him for his moral criticism of its rulers:

> Oh Florence! Florence! Unto me thou wast
> Like that Jerusalem which the Almighty he
> Wept over.
>
> (I, 60–3)

And in the poem's future, our present, the voice will be overlaid by that of Byron's own from the grave, now revealed as a true patriot reproaching Britain for not appreciating him when alive:

> Alas! How bitter is his country's curse
> To him who *for* that country would expire.
>
> (I, 69–70)

The poem seeks to demonstrate that the individual poet's voice can be detached from the historical conditions which produced it; may be conserved and preserved for the future, its flavour unimpaired. Though the prophecy of Dante is ostensibly presented to goad the contemporary reader to revolutionary action, its proud detachment of poets' identities from their own time and society nevertheless reveals its inherent cultural pessimism and alienation.

Byron's most important poems were inspired by Italy: the tourist's tribute in *Childe Harold's Pilgrimage* Canto IV; a gossipy account of the Venetian carnival in *Beppo;* the historical plays set in Renaissance Venice, *Marino Faliero* and *The Two Foscari;* poems ventriloquising Italian poets, *The Lament of Tasso* and *The Prophecy of Dante*, the latter in *terza rima;* and the greatest transpositions of the *ottava rima* metre and the Italian burlesque style into English, in *Don Juan* and *The Vision of Judgement.* As with Chaucer, Shakespeare and Milton before him, Italy shaped Byron's vision and prompted technical experimentation. 'I have always thought the Italians the *only* poetical *moderns*; our Milton and Spenser and Shakespeare (the last through translations of their tales) are very Tuscan, and surely it is far superior to the French School' (*L&J*, iv. 50).

5
The Bookseller to the Admiralty and the Board of Longitude Beset by Pirates: Byron, *Don Juan* and the Freedom of the Press

> Some have accused me of a strange design
> Against the creed and morals of the land,
> And trace it in this poem every line:
> (*Don Juan*, IV, 5)

> Why Man the Soul of such writing is it's licence? – at least the *liberty*
> of that *licence* if one likes – *not* that one should abuse it – it is like
> trial by Jury and Peerage – and the Habeas Corpus – a very fine
> thing – but chiefly in the *reversion* – because no one wishes to be
> tried for the mere pleasure of proving his possession of the privilege.
> (Byron to John Murray, 12 August, 1819)

The demand for political reform in England resurfaced with a vengeance
with the end of the Napoleonic threat. Byron's friends John Cam
Hobhouse, Scrope Davies, Douglas Kinnaird, and Sir Francis Burdett
were gentlemen radicals who by 1818 cast their lot with the lower-class
reformers in defiance of the aristocratic Whigs they judged incapable
of effective opposition. They (and Byron *in absentia*) were members of
the Benthamite Rota debating club, and in spring 1819 first Douglas
Kinnaird and later Hobhouse were selected as parliamentary candidates
by the Westminster Committee in attempts to unite the various radical
and Whiggish groups. All reforming factions could at least unite nega-
tively, in attacking the corruption of the court, the unreformed parliament and in rejecting the Burkean ideal of stability achieved by the
dialectic of the traditional two parties.

Meanwhile, the revolutionary artisans, the Spenceans, had instigated
a popular uprising, the Spa Fields riots (1816), and an unsuccessful

attempt to overthrow the government, the Cato Street conspiracy (1820). It was generally believed that a working-class revolution was imminent. In the aftermath of the 'Peterloo massacre' (1819), when a peaceful reformists' meeting was brutally attacked by the yeomanry, and in the hullabaloo over the trial of Queen Caroline in 1820, there was an eruption of popular feeling against a government which seemed to have turned its attack from the French to its own lower classes and who re-affirmed the hereditary privilege of rank and sex. Both events gained a symbolic significance through their representation in street politics, prints, ballads and newspapers. In this climate, the phenomenal growth in the dissemination of radical print culture was demonized for inflaming the working class, of whom about 75 per cent were now literate. The Tory government's response was to increase those repressive measures which had since the mid 1790s curbed the radical press. Even before these additional powers, in 1811, publishers John and Leigh Hunt had each been jailed for two years for seditious libel, for an *Examiner* article denying an ecstatic assertion in the *Morning Post* that the Prince Regent was an 'Adonis of loveliness'! But in 1817 Habeas Corpus was suspended, after 103 Whigs voted with the government majority, and the Seditious Meetings Act of 1795 was renewed.[1] Sidmouth wrote to all the Lords-Lieutenants pointing out that that JPs could demand bail for those charged with seditious libel and that unlicensed sellers of tracts could be prosecuted under the Hawkers and Pedlars Act. Immediately scores of provincial and metropolitan radical leaders were arrested, fined and imprisoned, and Cobbett fled to America. The radical propagandists launched their counter-offensive with W.T. Sherwin's *Weekly Political Register,* T. J. Wooler's *Black Dwarf,* which sold 12,000 copies an issue, and Richard Carlile's the *Republican* which reached 15,000 in 1819. They also sought to bring the walls crashing down which had enclosed the publication of polite literature through prices kept artificially high by 'the Trade'. The so-called republic of letters was set to become a democracy. Works of Enlightenment radicalism and even Romantic poetry suddenly became dangerously subversive in the eyes of the Establishment when produced cheaply enough to be read by the working classes. Peacock's Mr Flosky in *Nightmare Abbey* (a caricature of Coleridge) bewailed, 'How can we be cheerful when we are surrounded by a *reading public,* that is growing too wise for its betters?'

The government had no answer but repression. After Peterloo parliament was specially recalled to pass the infamous Six Acts. These included measures against the circulation of political literature, and further increases in paper tax and stamp tax aimed to wipe out radical newspapers. Now priced at 6d, sales of the *Republican* were reduced to 1000 copies a week. The penalty of banishment for seven years was introduced for a second offence under the existing laws against seditious and blasphemous libel.

The freedom of the press now itself became a radical cause. Propagandist publishers like William Hone and Richard Carlile turned their own libel trials into publicity for the Paineite texts they peddled, which had to be quoted and discussed in detail, and thus sold more copies. Furthermore the trials themselves were showcases for the right to what Hazlitt termed a 'fourth estate', and the radicals published transcripts of them in pamphlet form. Censorship thus paradoxically engendered a spawning of more and more radical print culture. Philosophical radicals also took up the question of the freedom of the press in works such as Samuel Bailey's *Essay on the publication of opinions* (1821), James Mill's essay on the 'Liberty of the press' in the *Encyclopaedia Britannica* (1821), and Jeremy Bentham's *On the Liberty of the Press and Public Discussion*, published by Hone.[2]

* * *

The world of radical propaganda has traditionally been assumed to be quite divorced from that of the high art of Romantic poetry. In fact the dialogue between the two cultural communities produced a public debate on the question of free access to print culture. The most celebrated example of this was provoked by the self-exiled Lord Byron's tendentious decision in 1819 to publish a sexual satire, *Don Juan*, which was 'as free as La Fontaine – & bitter in politics' (*L&J*, vi. 76). In revenge for his disgrace of 1816, his new satire aimed a personally-motivated blow at the Evangelical Christianity utilized by the Church and King party as a tool of social control over subalterns such as the working classes, women and colonial subjects. Despite its aristocratic narrator, the new satire was seized upon with alacrity by radical publishers who both pirated and parodied it. For the rest of his writing life, Byron's poetry was to be used in the propaganda campaigns of the radicals. When he eventually broke with Murray over *Don Juan*, he chose the most respectable of the radical publishers, John and Leigh Hunt, to publish the remainder of his writing.

This is not to deny that Byron was personally equivocal about working-class political mobilization. He confessed to Augusta, ' ... I am not democrat enough to like a tyranny of blackguards ... ', though he prophesied that when the revolution came: 'I will be one ... "I love a row"'(*L&J*, vi. 229). When Hobhouse himself was committed to Newgate without trial on 13 December 1819 for inflammatory language in an anti-Whig pamphlet, Byron's malicious response was to pen a ballad 'My boy Hobbie O' mocking Hobhouse's alliance with the 'blackguard' radicals, and to send it to Murray. Inevitably it was passed to the Tory newspapers, which leapt at the opportunity of casting scorn on Hobhouse's pride in his friendship with the noble poet. While Hobhouse's martyrdom in gaol earned him the Westminster seat in March 1820, Byron, who preferred revolution to constitutionalism, joined the Italian secret society of the Carbonari that summer. In Ravenna, not votes but his aristocratic status and money to buy arms ensured his appointment as 'Capo' or chief of the 'Turba' (Mob), the working-class section of the movement plotting to overthrow Austrian rule (*Life,* ii. 866–7). In February 1821, however, the Neapolitan revolution collapsed, and the planned Romagna uprising failed, its leaders betrayed.

Byron was aware that because of his European reputation, his financial independence, and his residence in Italy, he was well-placed to voice the call for liberty both home and abroad.[3] He consciously sought to increase his power to influence men's minds in three ways. Firstly, he extended the range of his writing to 'repel the charge of monotony and mannerism' (*L&J,* vi. 25): embarking on comedy and burlesque in *Beppo* and *Don Juan* as well as disciplined tragedy in the neoclassical Venetian dramas. He wanted to be the greatest poet of the age not merely the most popular: 'They made me without my search a species of popular Idol – they – without reason or judgement beyond the caprice of their Good pleasure – threw down the Image from it's pedestal – it was not broken with the fall – and they would it seems again replace it – but they shall not,' (*L&J,* vi. 106). He recognized that the critical disfavour into which he had fallen, and his distance from London, had helped him find greater artistic independence.

Secondly, Byron tried to by-pass the oppressive censorship of the day: by writing from abroad, by tactically adopting anonymity, and eventually by setting up his own periodical to publish his and Shelley's verse, a tactic which would also enable him to retain his copyrights. Thirdly, he made up for his physical absence by providing an intimate relationship with his readers in textual form: encouraging the private circulation in literary London of confessional 'unofficial' prose writings in MS: his letters, journals, and his memoirs (*L&J,* viii. 176). In 1819 he arranged that these would be read by posterity by commissioning Thomas Moore to publish them after his death.[4] He colluded in the posthumous reportage of his conversations with would-be Boswells like Shelley's cousin, Captain Medwin, even enjoying 'quizzing' posterity by teasing and deliberately misleading note-taking acquaintances like Lady Blessington.

Byron and Murray

Murray could madden Byron by not providing instant information on the critical and popular reaction to recently-published works. For example, in June 1818 the poet was on tenterhooks to ascertain the response to *Beppo*, which had come out anonymously on 28 February and to *Childe Harold's Pilgrimage* Canto IV, which appeared on 28 April. He was itching to follow up *Beppo* with a more ambitious *ottava rima* burlesque. Letters usually took a little more than two weeks to arrive. He wrote to rebuke the publisher for his silence on 16, 18, 25, 28 and 30 June. In the penultimate letter he talked of transferring his allegiance to Longman's and in the last threatened never to write to Murray again. His letters to Hobhouse and Kinnaird bewail the financial embarrassment he was experiencing, whilst the sale of Newstead was being completed, through Murray's sloth in sending '*ready* money – I am sure I always give him ready poetry' (*L&J*, vi. 56). Hobhouse had encouraged him to break with the publisher in his letter of 5 June: 'That Gentle [Murray] flourishes exceedingly and the Canto sells prodigiously. The Illustrations go on & off so he tells me very well, 1000 about of the sec. edit gone already – Beppo a fifth edition. I give you these items to calm your conscience. Don't be afraid, draw away – you have made the man's fortune'.[5] Murray wrote at last on the 16th to inform Byron of the favourable reaction to both poems and to forward 1000 guineas on account, and he wrote again on 7 July, apologizing and thanking the poet for his 'several kind as well as entertaining letters' (*Smiles*, i. 395). Byron was immediately appeased, reassured by the news that 3000 copies of the experimental *Beppo* had been sold before the poem was generally known to be his. This pattern was to be often repeated in the next few years. The poet was frequently unreasonably impatient. However, Murray could be very slow both in correspondence and in publishing manuscripts. He blamed his 'constitutional indolence' and the pressure of business, but the savage attacks on Byron in the press had alarmed him, and he undoubtedly made use of the distance between them to facilitate blatant procrastination in publishing a controversial work like *Don Juan* or a poem overtly fomenting revolution in Italy like *The Prophecy of Dante*.

Byron's prose: letters and memoirs

Yet, ironically, it was Murray himself who had first encouraged Byron to experiment with prose and with comedy. The difficult situation of writing from abroad for a British readership was initially intensely stimulating for both poet and publisher, despite the vagaries of the postal system. Byron's letters were a revelation, and Murray was the recipient of the liveliest of them. Murray wanted to capitalize on Byron's versatile autobiographical prose. Copies of his 'Swiss journal', written for Augusta when her brother left England for ever in 1816 were shown to Albemarle Street acquaintances (*Smiles*, i. 381). When the poet explored Italy, Murray wrote: 'Pray keep an exact Journal of all you see, and write me faithful accounts of sights, curiosities, shows, and manners', (*Smiles*, i. 371). The staid publisher was also titillated by risqué anecdotes of the poet's Venetian mistresses when Byron revelled in his libertinism in 1817–18. Both writer and recipient knew perfectly well that these the wittiest letters of the age would be shown to the inner circle in literary London, would be copied and sedulously collected and eventually published for posterity.[6] Adopting the genre of the apparently private letter also allowed Byron to give full rein to the ribald style permissible in male intimates. Murray spotted Byron's potential for sexual comedy and urged him to transpose it into verse: 'Give me a poem – a good Venetian tale describing manners formerly from the story itself and now from your own observations, and call it 'Marianna' (*Smiles*, i. 372). The suggestion had borne fruit in the poet's first experimental comic tale, *Beppo*. Murray then asked for 'another lively tale like 'Beppo' or will you not give me some prose in three volumes?' (*Smiles, i. 396).* In January 1818 Byron was trying his hand at a novel with a hero named Don Julian, then fixed upon a novel in rhyme, *Don Juan*, again in *ottava rima* (Broughton, *Recollections,* ii. 88). As early as 22 January 1817, the publisher had also urged: '…unbeknown even to your bosom friend Hobhouse…attempt some work in prose which I will engage to keep sacredly secret and publish anonymously' (*Smiles*, i. 371). This was the spur which produced the infamous *Memoirs*. Murray's words show he intuitively divined that the faithful Hobhouse would oppose his exploitation of Byron's frankness, in encouraging confessional revelations which would destroy what was left of his reputation. Sure enough, it was Hobhouse's opposition which eventually triumphed when the manuscript was ceremoniously consigned to the flames in Murray's drawing-room after Byron's death.

Don Juan

Obviously there was a continuum in Byron's use of the autobiographical impulse in letters, memoirs and fictional poetic narrative. He began *Don Juan* on 3 July 1818, and first mentioned it to Murray on 10 July in the same letter in which he announces his intention of writing 'a memoir of my life', which he originally intended as a preface to a projected Collected Works (*L&J*, vi. 59). By the end of August he decided that the *Memoirs* could only be published posthumously, and concentrated on *Don Juan* I and II through the autumn and the spring of 1819. For the next two years he wrote sections of the poem and the memoirs sporadically and coterminously. So autumn 1819 would see him working on the episode which would become Cantos III and IV, while he gave Moore the MS of the *Memoirs* on 11 October 1819. In 1820 he embarked on another section of *Don Juan*, again in October, and we find him sending Moore a continuation of the *Memoirs* in November.[7] It seems likely that shaping a posthumous narrative of self in the *Memoirs* was a useful exercise preparatory to the staging of the contingent contemporary self in the narrator/persona of the serialized poem, and helped Byron achieve that separation of narrator and protagonist in *Don Juan* which had broken down in *Childe Harold's Pilgrimage*. But it would be naive to imagine that these parallel narratives were simply divided by genre into 'fiction' and 'truth'. Both were self-justificatory narratives shaped by the poet's desire for revenge against the society which condemned his treatment of his wife. Even if the *Memoirs* were to be published posthumously, Byron was still constrained by the necessity of avoiding too great a breach of protocol in revealing embarrassing details about the living or their descendants, for he had given Murray *carte blanche* to show them to whoever he wished. 'The life is *Memoranda* – and not *Confessions* – I have left out all my *loves* (except in a general way) and many other of the most important things – (because I must not compromise other people) so that it is like the play of Hamlet – "the part of Hamlet omitted by particular desire"' (*L&J*, vi. 236). But in *Don Juan*, as in Rousseau's *Confessions*, it is assumed that psychosexual experience represents the authentic self. Moreover, the poem teased its readers by the implicit promise that it could be read as a *roman á clef*. They could study the origin of the Byronic psyche in the fictional childhood of the hero, and observe the splitting of the author's character into the innocence and experience of the fictional protagonist and his narrator.

The brilliance of the poem's unique colloquial yet aristocratic style, seesawing from idealism to scepticism, owes much to the letters.

Compare Byron's passionate love letters written in Italian to the Countess Guiccoli, his mistress from 1819 until his death: ('Let me go – it is better to die from the pain of separation, than from that of betrayal – my life now is a constant agony. I have enjoyed a unique and final happiness in your arms – but – oh God! How much more those moments are costing me!' *L&J* vi. 170) with those sardonically confiding his humiliation to male friends in London: 'I like women – God he knows – but the more their system here developes upon me – the worse it seems – after Turkey too – here the *polygamy* is all on the female side. – – I have been an intriguer, a husband, and now I am a Cavalier Servente. – by the holy! – it is a strange sensation' (*L&J,* vi. 226). The poem's narrator switches from one register to the other, sometimes within a stanza:

> I hate inconstancy – I loathe, detest,
> Abhor, condemn, abjure the mortal made
> Of such quicksilver clay that in his breast
> No permanent foundation can be laid;
> Love, constant love, has been my constant guest,
> And yet last night, being at a masquerade,
> I saw the prettiest creature, fresh from Milan,
> Which gave me some sensations like a villain.
>   (*Don Juan,* II, 209)

The 'mobility' of letters, each appropriate to a designated readership – feminine/ masculine, Italian/ English, romantic/ satirical – is the origin of the janus-faced narrator of *Don Juan* to whose 'scorching and drenching at the same time' Murray's friend Francis Cohen objected. (Byron replied exasperatedly: 'Did he never play at Cricket or walk a mile in hot weather? – Did he never spill a dish of tea over his testicles in handing the cup to his charmer...' [*L&J,* vi. 207]!)

The first draft of *Don Juan* Canto I and the mock Dedication of the poem to the Tory poet laureate, Robert Southey, was finished by 6 September, and revised by the 19th. On 11 November, a fair copy, swelled with additions, was posted to Murray. As usual, Byron sent on afterthoughts while the poem was being set up in press, such as Julia's letter and the opening passage on heroes. Despite its carefully contrived impression of spontaneity, there were so many alterations on the manuscript of Canto I that Byron was compelled to make the fair copy himself. Truman Guy Steffan has commented that many stanzas are as heavily worked over as those of Keats's densely-textured 'The Eve of St. Agnes'.[8] On 11 November he gave the final version to Lord Lauderdale who was returning to London, together with two poems copied by Mary Shelley: *Mazeppa*, a tale in his old romantic style, and 'Ode on Venice'.

Disapproval of the Murray circle

His friends later tried to excuse the ribaldry of the satire by saying that his exile meant Byron was out of touch with the adoption of bourgeois values by the ruling class. But of course Byron was perfectly aware that revulsion against the profligacy of the Regency was producing a mood of moralism: that was the point of the poem. He instructed Hobhouse to offer the poem to another publisher 'if the damned Cant and Toryism of the day … make Murray pause' (*L&J*, vi. 76–7). What he didn't guess, though, was that Hobhouse himself would be more scandalized than the publisher and, through a misguided sense of protectiveness, would be instrumental in organizing the opposition of the 'Utican senate' to publication. Hobhouse admitted to Byron: 'Murray, I believe, would publish a Fanny Hill or an Age of Reason of your's [*sic*] – The Hitch will not come thence so be tranquil – '.[9] Hobhouse's rhetoric here already situates the poem alongside two favourite texts of the radical underground. He confided to his diary on 26 December: 'I have my doubts about 'Don Juan'; the blasphemy and bawdry and the domestic facts overpower even the great genius it displays. … Murray called and wanted to advertise at once. I told him I was not sure about the publication' (Broughton, *Recollections*, ii. 107). Hobhouse arranged to meet Hookham Frere on 29 December who came down 'decisively against publication' because 'a friend of freedom should be a friend to morality' particularly at a time of religious revival. Hobhouse realized that Frere, whose own *ottava rima* burlesque *Whistlecraft* had already been eclipsed by Byron's *Beppo*, was hardly an impartial commentator. But he was rattled. On 5 January Hobhouse wrote a long letter to Byron to which he had obtained the agreement of Murray, Douglas Kinnaird, Scrope Davies, Hookham Frere, and Thomas Moore. Hobhouse argued that, though Byron had 'perhaps found [his] real forte in this singular style', the allusions to Lady Byron would only rekindle the glowing embers of the separation scandal; readers would assume Byron was associating himself with the protagonist and was indirectly boasting about his Venetian libertinism; that any respectable female reader would be forced to cram *Don Juan* into her pocket like Lydia Languish with *The Man of Feeling*, when surprised by visitors; that the parody of the ten commandments would give a handle to Tory assertions of the poet's atheism; that the Lake poets were 'grovellers' not worth stooping to satirize and that the attack on Castlereagh would result in a duel. The objectionable parts – especially the allusions to Annabella – were 'so mixed up with the whole work...that I know not how any amputation will save it: more particularly as [they]...are in point of wit and humour & poetry the very best beyond all doubt of the whole poem –'.[10] Hobhouse therefore urged Byron to suppress the poem altogether.

For expediency, Hobhouse stressed, it was necessary these days for all friends of Liberty to castigate the sexual immorality associated both with the Tory court of the Prince Regent and the ossified Whig aristocracy who made a mockery of an Opposition. The appearance of respectability was necessarily carefully cultivated by Regency wits turned reformers like Hobhouse, just as the working-class radicals at St Peter's Field would seize the moral high ground from the ruling class by their disciplined demonstration that *they* were no bloodthirsty mob though the yeomanry were. But *Don Juan,* set at the time of the French Revolution, associated the celebration of sexual freedom in the story with the freethinking and liberal politics of the aristocratic narrator.[11] This raised the spectre that moderate gentleman reformers, like Hobhouse, most wanted to exorcise: that of subversive Gallic libertine freethinkers and philosophers who had opened Pandora's box in 1789 and let loose republicanism, democracy and feminism upon the world.

Byron protested to Murray, 'If the poem has poetry – it would stand – if not – fall – the rest is "leather and prunella"...Dullness is the only annihilator in such cases –' (*L&J,* vi. 95). But he was severely shaken by Hobhouse's 'very clever letter'. For the moment he even acquiesced with the decision of Hobhouse's 'puritanical committee', though he hinted to the publisher 'we will circumvent them on that point in the end', and ordered Murray to print off fifty copies of the first canto for private distribution to intimates. But by 22 February, he was insisting on publication and thereafter brooked no opposition (*L&J,* vi. 100). Enraged by Murray's lack of response to his usual stream of additions and emendations, he wrote cuttingly to Kinnaird on 9 March: 'I have had no answer from him to any letter – for these three months – if the tradesman don't understand civility – change him – he is but a sort of intellectual tailor – & in taking measure of men's minds, would trust to his journeymen;– but if he or they don't make up my suit in time – we'll take another' (*L&J,* vi. 103). Murray's eventual would-be flattering reply suggesting Byron give up frivolity to occupy himself with a 'great work' produced indignation: '[Y]ou have so many *"divine"* poems, is it nothing to have written a *Human* one?' He also threatened: '[S]ince you want *length* you shall have enough of *Juan* for I'll make 50 cantos' (*L&J*, vi. 105). But his enthusiasm had been sufficiently dampened that the first draft of the second canto, begun on 13 December and completed by mid January 1819, was not revised, copied and sent to Murray until 3 April 1819. Ominously there was silence from London for two months.

Byron tried to appeal to Murray's entrepreneurial daring: 'Methinks I see you with a long face about "Don Juan" anticipating the outcry – and the Scalping reviews that will ensue ... Why – Man – it will be Nuts to all of them' (*L&J*, vi. 123). But Murray dragged his feet in agreeing a fee for the copyright, and passing on the second canto to Hobhouse. Gifford privately deplored 'so much beauty so wantonly and perversely disfigured' in the second canto (*Smiles*, i. 404). Though the poet would correct his tragedies according to Gifford's suggestions, *Don Juan* was never submitted to the *Quarterly* editor's judgement. Murray tried flattering the noble poet into toning down the suggestive passages: 'Think of the effects of such seductive poetry! It probably surpasses in talent anything you ever wrote.' He also encouraged the use of *double-entendre*: 'Pray use your most tasteful discretion so as to wrap up or leave out certain approximations to indelicacy' (*Smiles*, i. 401–2).

In return Byron peppered 'Murray's parlour boarders' with defences of the poem, sometimes asserting that it fulfilled a true moral purpose in unmasking cant, and sometimes strategically presenting the poem as a mere trifle not worth making a fuss about: 'Do you suppose that I could have any intention but to giggle and make giggle?' (*L&J*, vi. 208). Sometimes he affected avarice: ' "Regard for my fee" is the ruling passion' (*L&J*, vi. 100). This was merely a clumsy attempt to enact the role of professional writer.[12] At the time he wrote this letter he knew he had published his best work in Cantos III and IV of *Childe Harold's Pilgrimage*, despite the fact that the critical tide had turned against him after the separation scandal. It was also the phase in his literary life in which he was least in need of money.

Financial settlement

For, at the same time that Byron was sending the first cantos of *Don Juan* to his advisers in England, he was also writing to Hobhouse and Douglas Kinnaird concerning the settling of his financial affairs. Newstead Abbey had finally been sold for 90,000 guineas, but little of this was left when the poet's debts were paid and after £66,000 was put in trust for Lady Byron, according to their marriage settlement. However, for the first time in his adult life, Byron was released from the burden of guilt and debt of his aristocratic heritage. He was compelled to live on the interest of the £66,000, invested in the five per cent government funds, which amounted to £3300 p.a., together with £200 p.a. paid by Sir Ralph Milbanke. As a landless rentier, Byron could live in aristocratic style in Italy on this income which was only a third of that necessary to sustain the full London season. Because of his unearned income he was freed from the mercenary considerations which necessarily dominated the writing life of contemporaries like Leigh Hunt or Robert Southey who lived entirely by the pen.

The effect of this financial settlement may also have been psychologically quite profound. Byron's sense of self was rooted in an eighteenth-century belief in the political and personal independence of the landed aristocrat, who could supposedly rise above the vested interests of patronage and trade. The failure of his marriage before a male heir had been born, and the sale of Newstead, saw the fall of his 'house' in all senses of the word. The serialized writing of both the *Memoirs* and *Don Juan* can be seen as the reiterated attempt to prevent, by writing, the disintegration of a coherent stable self.

> The heart is like the sky, a part of heaven,
> But changes night and day too, like the sky;
> Now o'er it clouds and thunder must be driven...
>   *(Don Juan,* II, 214)

Anonymity

So convinced was he of its merit, and desperate for *Don Juan* to see the light of day, that by March Byron acquiesced in the humiliating procedure whereby his greatest poem would be brought out anonymously and without even the name of the publisher. This was to protect Murray from imprisonment if the poem was prosecuted for seditious libel, blasphemy or obscenity. Byron was unwilling to attack Robert Southey anonymously, so the satirical Dedication to the Poet Laureate was dropped on May 6. He substituted 'Difficile est propria communia dicere' ['Tis no slight task to write on common things'] from Horace's *Art of Poetry* for the tendentious original motto 'Domestica facta' ['domestic politics'].[13] He also agreed to cut stanzas attacking Castlereagh, and omitted lines 'which Ladies may not read' in Canto II.

But he flatly refused most suggested emendations ('You shan't make *Canticles* of my Cantos' 6 April 1819, *L&J*, vi. 105) and exploded in wrath when he discovered 'damned cutting and slashing' had occurred in the published version. Stanzas 15 and 131 of Canto I had been omitted, as were the concluding couplets of I, 129–30, and there were several other changes.[14] As well as this censorship, Murray made many errors through sheer incompetence, for he had the poem reset without using Byron's corrected proof as the printer's copy. Byron's laziness exacerbated this, for after he had corrected and returned the initial proof he had written: '... you had better proceed to the publication without boring me with more proofs' (*L&J*, vi. 125).

After an exciting advertising campaign in which mysterious notices appeared, 'In a few days – Don Juan', Cantos I and II came out on 15 July 1819, and Byron received £1525 for them. From 17 September to 30 November he wrote the first draft of another canto, which by 19 February 1820 he had lengthened, divided in two, revised, copied and sent to London. But Murray was reluctant to publish any more of *Don Juan*. Though he sent Byron proofs on about 23 April, he made no move to publish Cantos III and IV. There had been an extraordinarily hostile outcry against the poem, led by *Blackwood's Edinburgh Magazine*, who denounced the poem as 'filthy and impious' and 'the very suicide of genius'.[15] The *British Critic* thundered: 'Nor is it a history only, but a manual of profligacy... We should have the worst opinion indeed of any man, upon whose family table this volume were to lie exposed'.[16] But, instead of dropping it as a failed experiment, as he had promised, Byron was soon boasting about *Don Juan* as a seminal work in all senses. He crowed to Kinnaird: 'As to "Don Juan" – confess – confess – you dog – and be candid – that it is the sublime of *that there* sort of writing – it may be bawdy – but is it not good English? – it may be profligate – but is it not *life*, is it not *the thing*? – Could any man have written it – who has not lived in the world? – and tooled in a post-chaise? in a hackney coach? in a Gondola? against a wall? in a court carriage? in a vis a vis? – on a table? – and under it?' (*L&J*, vi. 232).

Deferred ending and serial publication

Murray saw that charges of immorality could be best be refuted by using the age-old escape-clause of other purveyors of the myth: that of the didactic morality-tale ending. He therefore urged Byron to send the Don to Hell, cleverly pointing out the comic potential of describing the other inhabitants of the infernal regions. But the poet merely taunted his adviser's enquiries about the ending. He had already struck fear into Murray's heart by announcing 'My poem's epic, and is meant to be/ Divided in twelve books…' (I, 200). Sometimes Byron threatened to write fifty (*L&J,* vi. 105) or a hundred cantos (*L&J,* x. 150) before he came to the finale. He never seriously contemplated using the traditional supernatural ending with the Don dragged to Hell when he shakes the hand of the stone statue of the father of one of his victims. Instead, the poet talked variously about substituting marriage for Hell, having Juan become a convert to Methodism or decapitated in the French Revolution (*L&J,* viii. 78).[17]

The strategy of an endlessly deferred ending was, of course, all part of the poem's refusal to make absolute moral judgements. It was also integral to its serial publication. It appeared in six parts and, giving a foretaste of serialized popular periodical fiction later in the century, Byron openly declared its continuation would last as long as his readers' approbation lasted:

> But for the present, gentle reader! and
> Still gentler purchaser! the bard – that's I –
> Must, with permission, shake you by the hand,
> … We meet again, if we should understand
> Each other…
>
> (*Don Juan,* I, 221)

Byron eventually declared he would continue *Don Juan* as long as he could write (*L&J,* x. 135) and described it as a 'poetical *Tristram Shandy*' (*L&J,* x. 150). The poem is thus an organically unfolding Romantic fragment, shaped both by the symbolic and the actual death of the author into an endless deferral of meaning.

Improvisation

Byron insisted on the poem as improvisatory: 'I *have* no plan – I *had* no plan – but I have or had materials'. Of course, the conventional features of the Don Juan myth dictated a basic outline, and the poet's claim 'My poem's epic' promises the stock episodes of 'love and war, a heavy gale at sea' (I, 200). Also, right from Canto I we are aware of a specific late eighteenth-century setting. But Byron indicates that his 'materials', both his life experience and perhaps his historical reading too, will be the matter which he will shape and improvise upon according to contemporary events. Shelley's advice to write an epic on the

French revolution had not been entirely ignored. For, as the modern editor of the poem has pointed out, the story of Juan takes place in a time scheme from the mid-1780s to about 1793, building towards the French Revolution, being counterpointed with the narrator's contemporary time from 1818–24, when the *ancien régime* was restored, together with his memories of 1808–16 when the outcome of Napoleon's career was to be decided (*CPW*, v. xxiii–xxiv).

The pirates

Although Murray can be criticized for vacillating between his genuine admiration of the poem and his timorousness in publishing it, it must be acknowledged that he was in a genuine dilemma. The first instalment, bearing only the name of the printer, had been an open invitation to radical publishers, such as William Benbow, William Hone, Richard Carlile, William Sherwin and William Dugdale, to produce pirated versions. Usually these propagandists provided political tracts and cheap editions of Thomas Paine and any contemporary or eighteenth-century texts of a sceptical or radical nature. They were now making common cause with Romantic poetry.

Wat Tyler

In 1817 they had scored a brilliant propaganda victory by procuring and printing the 1794 play, *Wat Tyler*, by the former revolutionary turned Tory, Robert Southey. To the Poet Laureate's discomfiture his injunction to prevent the infringement of copyright was not supported by Lord Eldon, who refused the law's protection to a work he judged a seditious libel. The Law was thus proved an Ass. As William H. Wickwar has pointed out, this precedent meant henceforth 'anyone was at liberty to pirate any work which he thought the Lord Chancellor might think criminal'.[18] Southey was publicly humiliated when 25,000 twopenny editions of his youthful work were sold in the street alongside the *Black Dwarf*. It was particularly galling since he was a prominent campaigner for the suppression of cheap inflammatory tracts sold by hawkers to the urban poor. Byron had commented at the time: 'I hate all intolerance, but most the intolerance of Apostacy ... It is no disgrace to Mr. Southey to have written *Wat Tyler*, and afterwards to have written his birthday odes ... but it is something, for which I have no words, for this man to have endeavoured to bring to the stake (for such he would do) men who think as he thought, and for no reason but because they

think so still, when he has found it convenient to think otherwise'
(*L&J*, vi. 220).

Lord Byron's Poems on his Domestic Circumstances

Byron himself had already attracted the attention of radical publishers
in 1816, when he rashly had Murray print and privately circulate to
intimates two poems on the separation: the sentimental 'Fare thee
well!' to his wife and the snobbish, vitriolic 'A sketch from private life'
attacking her female companion, Mrs Clermont, whom he suspected of
mischief-making. By 14 April 1816 they had found their way into the
Champion newspaper accompanied by a violent denunciation of the
poet's politics, evidenced in his recent poems on Napoleon, and shameful conduct to his wife. The radical publishers Richard Edwards and
William Hone exploited the controversy by publishing the poems in
pamphlets, which went into numerous editions, entitled *Lord Byron's
Poems on his Domestic Circumstances,* sometimes adding spurious poems
attributed to the poet. Several replies then appeared, either supposedly
by or addressed to Lady Byron.[19] Lady Caroline Lamb, Byron's erstwhile
mistress and Annabella's cousin, then threw fuel on the flames by publishing her novel, *Glenarvon,* on 9 May. In this *roman á clef,* a thinly
disguised Byron is portrayed as the Gothic villain: a murderer and the
debaucher of six innocent women who is finally sent to Hell by a
ghostly friar. So when Byron decided to publish his own version of the
Don Juan myth, he can be seen to be responding to an existent furore
in print over his libertinism, which had already attracted the attention
of the radicals.

Don Juan and William Hone

Within four days of publication of Cantos I and II, William Hone published *'Don John'; or, Don Juan unmasked, being a Key to the Mystery
attending that remarkable Publication, with a descriptive Review of the Poem
and Extracts.* Hone, infamous for his parodies of the creed, catechism
and litany, drew embarrassing attention to the double standard which
permitted 'the Publisher to the Board of Longitude, and of the Quarterly
Review – the Bookseller to the Admiralty, and a strenuous supporter of
orthodoxy and the Bible Society' to publish Byron's 'poetical commandments' ['Thou shalt believe in Milton, Dryden, Pope;/ Thou shalt
not set up Wordsworth, Coleridge, Southey…' (*Don Juan,* I. 205–6)],
while a Birmingham bookseller, Joseph Russell, was even now awaiting

trial for selling Hone's satirical *Political Litany*, over which the author had been unsuccessfully prosecuted three times for blasphemy in 1817. Hone wonders what the Tory critics at the *Quarterly Review* will have to say to this poem, when the editor himself 'has participated in its preparation for the press'. He helpfully provides for Gifford a suitably reactionary review for the *Quarterly*, execrating the poem's 'rank sedition and licentious profligacy of manners' (p. 36). This was a palpable hit, for the *Quarterly* did indeed remain uncomfortably silent on the subject of the poem, in deference to Murray. Hone points out that the poem has been published 'in direct contempt of Bills of Indictment and Crown Office prosecutions, and in utter defiance of Grand Juries and the King's Attorney-General' (p. 38), for only a publisher 'who has government support and Government writers to back him' would avoid the automatic prosecutions suffered by the radicals.

Hone followed this up with a spoof continuation of the poem, *Don Juan, Canto the Third* (1819), in which his ridicule of the aristocrat poet is tinged with a desire to claim common cause with this writer, who, it seems, would 'prop the pillars of a falling cause' (Stanza 24) [i.e. Reform]. So he imagines Juan/ Byron returning to London and becoming a radical newspaper-seller. For:

> As well with Dons with Sculls no atom fuller,
> Sherwin, or Watson, Hunt, Carlile, or Wooler...
> That if he flock with birds of such a feather,
> He can't complain if they get shot together.
>
> (Stanzas 18–19)

Juan/Byron's paper is called 'the Devilled biscuit', implying his poem was a spiced-up trifle, and he serenades the workers in the street to the sweet sounds of a guitar, rather than propagandizing. However, though he hopes to evade prosecution this way, he is hauled before the Bench as a street-musician. The magistrate accuses him of pouring 'your venom thro' our lower ranks' (p. 49). Hone reminds his working-class readers, in an incorporated account of a Westminster election meeting, that Byron's friend Hobhouse had spoken well for Reform and seconded Sir Francis Burdett (p. 28; p. 38). But Hone cannot resist mocking Byron's aristocratic classical allusions and learned notes. For himself, Hone relishes the use of street slang: 'The Dwarf [Wooler]'s a tightish little Bit of bantam' (p. 19), 'To queer a mob' (p. 15) or 'Jaw them' (p. 15). Byron knew about the existence of the many spoof cantos which had appeared, and it is difficult not to imagine he had read Hone's parody and was riposting when he did eventually bring Juan to London and revelled in concocting an elegy for a dead highwayman in Regency flash slang:

> Who in a row like Tom could lead the van,
> Booze in the ken, or at the spellken hustle?
> Who queer a flat? Who (spite of Bow-street's ban)
> On the high toby-spice so flash the muzzle?
> Who on a lark, with black-eyed Sal (his blowing)
> So prime, so swell, so nutty, and so knowing?
>
> (XI, 19)

As Kyle Grimes has observed, Hone's parody, in appropriating the Byronic narrator, 'ironically levels the ground between peer and commoner, between Murray and the respectable press and Hone and the radical press, and – perhaps most profoundly – between those "gentlemen in their closets" and the "common and ordinary people"'.[20]

Pirated editions

By October, J. Onwhyn brought out 'an exact copy from the quarto edition' at 4s without paper covers. William Sherwin, founder of the *Republican* and *Sherwin's Political Register,* followed suit with another exact copy dated 1820, though possibly issued earlier. The aristocratic poet's unmasking of the vice and hypocrisy of his class proved so useful to the cause of reform, that William Benbow later actually adopted Byron's head as his shop sign in Leicester Square.[21] He declared that Byron wrote without hypocrisy 'in the true spirit of an epicure and a libertine', while other pirates cashed in by printing spurious obscene memoirs like Jack Mitford's *Voluptuous Amours of Lord Byron.*[22]

With Murray's editions only bearing the name of his printer, Thomas Davison of Whitefriars, it seemed unlikely that he could bring a successful prosecution against the radicals for infringing the copyright.[23] Also, it was apparent that there was a new readership of working-class and lower middle-class readers avid for Byron's poetry at an affordable price.[24] The decision to produce a particularly sumptuous volume costing £1 11s 6d had been an attempt on Murray's part to avoid the attentions of the 'Society for suppressing the vices of persons whose income does not exceed £500 per annum'.[25] Byron was depressed when in

October Murray told him that he had only sold 1200 out of the 1500 quarto edition. But with the pirated editions selling for a few shillings, Murray had to bring out an octavo at 9s 6d to compete, and the last one hundred and fifty copies of the quarto edition of 1500 had to be sold as waste paper. This octavo was reprinted in 1820 and 1822. But it is a measure of the success of the pirated editions that by 1822 Murray needed to slash his price to 5s for two new editions in an even smaller octavo. The publishing history of Byron's *Don Juan*, by both the publisher to the Admiralty and his piratical foes, dramatically demonstrates the rapidity of the transition from upper-middle-class willingness to pay heavily for polite literature as an elitist commodity in the first quarter of the century to the belated provision of affordable reading-matter for the lower orders. Demand for *Don Juan* was fuelled by the mystery of anonymous authorship, and by controversy when Blackwood, Murray's Edinburgh agent, refused to sell it and the reviewers attacked it.

In October 1819 Byron offered to repay the money he had received for the copyright. He was nervous that if Murray sought an injunction against the pirates and lost the case, he might lose his paternal rights to guardianship of his daughter Ada on account of its immorality. This had happened to Percy Shelley over *Queen Mab*, another much-pirated Romantic poem. Murray's lawyer, Sharon Turner, sternly warned him that 'the evil' of cheap pirated copies would circulate, 'injuring society wherever it spreads', but he was pessimistic about the success of an injunction. He consulted a 'highly moral' colleague, Lancelot Shadwell, who thought a case could be made that Juan's story usefully demonstrated 'the ill effect of ... injudicious maternal education' upon a young boy (*Smiles*, i. 401–2)! But in the event the injunction was granted without question.

However, from now on Byron's works would feature prominently in the campaign of radical publishers to expose the nonsense of the Seditious and Blasphemous Libels Act of 1819. An injunction would be refused in 1823 against the pirate Dugdale for publishing later sections of *Don Juan*; as had happened with *Cain*, on the grounds of its supposed blasphemy; while John Hunt was indicted in December 1822 for libel against the late George III for publishing *The Vision of Judgement*. The *Black Dwarf* printed an account of the trial with copious extracts from the poem. Byron's poetry was merely used for propaganda purposes by some campaigners like Richard Carlile who really preferred propagating 'useful knowledge', and disapproved of aristocratic literature. Carlile pirated Byron's works even though he thought little of *Cain*, considered *Don Juan* was mere 'squibbery' and the *Vision* 'slip-slop'. Carlile procured and published Byron's letter of 8 February 1822 to John Murray protesting that *Cain* was not an argument but a drama, and therefore could not be deemed blasphemous, but offering to come to England to take the consequences of publication in person. Carlile took this as a challenge to the Society for the Suppression of Vice to prosecute the drama, and hoped to spur them on by publishing an edition of *Cain* at sixpence.[26] Wickwar has made the important point that 'any litigation about a poem was bound to affect the whole community of readers and writers much more than the prosecution of a publisher of political works, especially as political prosecutions were a long-established habit … Whenever a poem was brought into Court the injustice of the law of Criminal Libel was demonstrated. Whenever a poem that was undoubtedly a criminal libel was left unprosecuted it helped to make plain how partial was the administration of the law'.[27]

Moreover, despite Carlile's obtuseness, as Hone had immediately realized, *Don Juan* itself signals an affinity with the radicals in its very textual devices. As Marcus Wood has pointed out, 'Byron's poem is full of minor parodies of forms long established as favourites in radical political satire'.[28] Not only was there the literary parody of the ten commandments in the style of Hone; but the suppressed Dedication to Southey (which was pirated in the 1830s, if not earlier, as a broadsheet) included a parody of *Sing a Song of Sixpence*, which Wood reminds us was a favourite radical device. Byron also used references to popular advertising (I, 17), criminal argot (XI, 17, 19) and the jargon of a doctor's prescription (X, 41): all the sort of verbal tricks beloved by radical publicists. It is therefore naive to assume that publication by the pirates was fortuitous and that this distorted the contemporary reception of a fairly innocuous comic poem. Critics have also been misled by Byron's disarming claims that his satire was no fiercer or more bawdy than Fielding, Smollett, Prior, Swift and Pope, for these Augustan satirists had been reinforcing the agreed standards and ideology of a stable community of eighteenth century readers. The major satire of the Romantic age, however, presents itself as the deliberately provocative libertine text of an individual (the textually created Byronic persona) writing *against* social conformity.

The *Don Juan* legend

It was not only the anonymity of the poem which signalled to the pirates that its own publisher was afraid it could be judged seditious, but also its title which attracted their attention. Many radical publishers supplemented their political and philosophical tracts with libertine literature, for ideological reasons as well as to profit to the full from their roles as the purveyors of unofficial culture. Iain McCalman has commented that *Don Juan* and *Queen Mab* were pirated by some radicals specifically for their libertarian attitudes about sexuality.[29] Radical publishers circulated birth control information as well as translating anticlerical French writers like Voltaire and Rabelais; erotic classical verse by Ovid or Catullus; and reprinting the homegrown libertinism of Rochester, Cleland and John Wilkes.[30] The aristocratic tradition of freethinking, combining scepticism towards institutional religion with sexual libertarianism, had, after all, contributed to the Enlightenment critique of the *ancien régime* which had brought about the French Revolution. In 1822 Benbow brought out an English version of *Amours of the Chevalier de Faublas* (1787–9), a bawdy novel by the prominent revolutionary, Louvet de Couvray. *Blackwood's* juxtaposed Byron's poem with this tale which also treats the sexual initiation of a sixteen-year-old youth. But in Byron's hands the story of the making of a libertine turns not into pornography but sophisticated self-reflexive comedy. For Canto I makes (its own) literary censorship the issue. The Bowdlerization of classical poetry, the mystification of natural history and the suppression of the instinctual drives through religious education all ironically achieve the opposite of their aim, resulting in Juan's extraordinary libido.

> Juan was taught from out the best edition,
> Expurgated by learned men ...
> > (*Don Juan*, I, 44)

> But not a page of anything that's loose,
> Or hints at continuation of the species,
> Was ever suffer'd, lest he should grow vicious.
> > (*Don Juan*, I, 40)

> Arts, sciences, no branch was made a mystery
> To Juan's eyes, excepting natural history.
> > (*Don Juan*, I, 39)

The first stage version of the Don Juan legend had been Tirso de Molina's *El Burlador de Sevilla* (1630) which the narrator claims to have seen (I, 203). The history of the various versions of the Don Juan legend – some comic and some tragic – was well known to readers, and was summarized by a reviewer as follows:

> The beautiful opera of 'Don Giovanni' of the Italians, written and adapted to the music of Mozart for representation by Lorenzo da Ponte, is taken from it; – but its first appearance upon the stage was in Spanish, as a Comedy, under the title of '*El Burlador de Sevilla, y Combidada de Piedra,*' (the Joker of Seville and the Stone Guest,) by Gabriel Tellez of Madrid, an author of considerable merit, better known by the assumed name of Tyrso de Molina. It was three times translated into the Italian language before the one adapted for musical representation mentioned above, viz. by Cleognini, Giliberto, and Goldoni. Molière, being strongly solicited by his company of comedians to do so, produced a Comedy in five acts, called 'Le Festin de Pierre,' in imitation of it, which first appeared upon the stage in 1665. T. Corneille soon afterwards put this piece into verse … In 1676 Don Juan made his appearance in this country, in a tragedy, called 'The Libertine,' by Shadwell, the poet-laureate; who made his hero desperately wicked, and crowded so many extravagancies into his piece, that, although vigorously written, it was soon laid aside. Latterly he has appeared, and elicited a great deal of attention, in a pantomimic, or melodramatic form at most of the minor theatres in London, and, no doubt, also at most of their (by no means behind-hand) brethren in the country.
>
> (*Miniature Magazine* 3 [October 1819], 236–9)

The frame-device of a cautionary tale allowed the staging of the sexual corruption and freethinking of an aristocratic libertine before the scandalized bourgeois theatre audience. The myth could have a dangerously anti-clerical or salacious edge, in versions where the satiric wit of the protagonist outweighed the punitive ending.[31] The declaration right at the opening of Byron's poem that his hero is to be identified with – not the Renaissance morality play or the high art of Molière or Mozart – but the Drury Lane pantomime *Don Juan; or the Libertine Destroyed* could also be seen as provocatively populist. For – though the narrator of sexual innuendo must conventionally address a male upper-class readership – ('Ring for your valet – bid him quickly bring/ Some hock and soda-water, then you'll know/ A pleasure worthy Xerxes…' [II, 180]) – it might well be expected that both women and the working classes would also, covertly, enjoy the spectacle of the comic demise of the aristocratic male predator into a mere pantomime character, in poetry as they did upon the stage. As Moyra Haslett has pointed out, controversy was already rife over the cult of Don Juan which thrived in theatrical London from 1788–1824, and which culminated, after the first English production of Mozart's *Don Giovanni* in 1817, in a profusion of burlesques and parodies, six different versions of which were playing simultaneously early in 1818.[32] These included Thomas Dibdin's *Don Giovanni: or, A Spectre on Horseback!; Harlequin's Vision; or, The Feast of the Statue*; G. Smith's *Don Giovanni, Being an Accurate Account of his Peregrinations in Hell, Italy, Paris, London, and the Country; Giovanni in the Country; or, A Gallop to Gretna Green!; Giovanni the Vampire; or, How shall we get rid of him?; Don Giovanni in Ireland; Don Giovanni in Botany Bay; or The Libertine Transported; Giovanni in Paris*; and W.T. Montcrieff's notorious cross-dressed version, *Don Giovanni in London, or The Libertine Reclaimed*, starring Madame Vestris in tights. John Keats, Charles Lamb, and William Hazlitt had reviewed various productions. Byron's comments about his poem echo Leigh Hunt's in an enthusiastic *Examiner* review of 5 and 26 January 1817 that pantomime 'makes giggle all those who can afford to be made giggle', where Hunt also hails it as 'the best medium of dramatic satire'.[33] Byron was doubtless provoked to oppose Coleridge's view of the myth in chapter 23 of *Biographia Literaria* (1817), where the traditional morality tale ending of Shadwell's tragedy is praised compared with the modern glamorizing of the anti-hero in Byronic drama like Maturin's 'jacobinical' *Bertram* (see *L&J*, v. 267).

Byron's poem, with its Italian stanza form, burlesque style and high romantic idealism striated with fabliau farce, does have an appeal comparable with highly fashionable Italian opera or the *Don Giovanni* of Mozart. It has its share of operatic tragedy, for example in the death of the Greek maiden Haidée:

> Twelve days and nights she wither'd thus; at last,
> Without a groan, or sigh, or glance, to show
> A parting pang, the spirit from her past:
> And they who watch'd her nearest could not know
> The very instant, till the change that cast
> Her sweet face into shadow, dull and slow,
> Glazed o'er her eyes – the beautiful, the black –
> Oh! To possess such lustre – and then lack!
> (*Don Juan*, IV, 69)

But this is followed by the sort of puncturing deflation that the London pantomime applied to reduce high European art to bawdy cynicism.

> But let me change this theme, which grows too sad,
> And lay this sheet of sorrows on the shelf;
> I don't much like describing people mad,
> For fear of seeming rather touch'd myself...
>
> (*Don Juan,* IV, 74)

Though Byron had failed, as either a member of the Drury Lane sub-committee or as a tragedian himself, to fuse the fracture in early nine-teenth-century theatre audiences, he succeeded in his poem in mixing registers and speaking dialogically to box and gallery. He was accused by moralist contemporaries, and in the twentieth century by T. S. Eliot, of pandering to popular taste. His resistance to the triumph of bour-geois moral values united elements of high and low art as few poets have since (including Eliot).

The representation of women

The poem's attack on Victorian bourgeois moralism, however, specifi-cally targeted women. The poem opens with a misogynist caricature of a female pedant: the character combining portraits of the poet's wife and his mother. Inez and her favourite female authors, Maria Edgeworth, Sarah Trimmer and Hannah More, it is suggested, have sublimated their desire for a more powerful role in society into an evangelical zeal which society sanctions as it conforms with their conventional feminine role. As 'Morality's prim personification' (I, 16), the wife colludes with advo-cates, judges and physicians to police her husband's sexuality. As a wid-owed mother she converts the gaze of desire into the inquisitorial repressive conditioning of her son:

> But that which Donna Inez most desired,
> And saw into herself each day before all
> The learned tutors whom for him she hired,
> Was, that his breeding should be strictly moral;
>
> (*Don Juan,* I, 39)

This demystification of the new nineteenth-century ideal of pious motherhood was followed up by the portrayal throughout the poem of women of all countries and climes (including the hypocritical Inez) as actually libido-driven. Byron boasted to Medwin, 'You see I am true to Nature in making the advances come from the females' (*Medwin*, p. 165). Women initiate the sexual encounters, sometimes reducing the famous libertine, Don Juan to exhaustion. This is a reversion to an older patriarchal ideology, emanating from the Judeao-Christian tradition, blaming the daughters of Eve for sexual temptation. It is the basis of traditional misogynistic mockery of the sexuality of older, powerful women, like Inez, Gulbeyaz, Catherine, and the Duchess Fitz-Fulke. But this alternates with the Byronic romanticization of the young passionate woman who suffers or dies for love. The constant images of the Fall which permeate the poem only reinforce her role as a sexual rebel:

> '...a headlong, headstrong, downright she,
> Young, beautiful, and daring – who would risk
> A throne, the world, the universe, to be
> Beloved in her own way...
>
> (VI, 3)

I have argued elsewhere that this Byronic sexual libertarianism exposed the sexual double standard, and can even be seen as contributing to the development of nineteenth-century feminism.[34] We see it warring with Wollstonecraftian rationalist feminism in the psyche of Jane Eyre.

Women readers

However, the women readers, who had formed a large part of Byron's readership when he was known as the melancholic poet of lost love, were not enthusiastic about the new satiric poem. The poem was judged too risqué for respectable women. Byron commented that 'There has been an eleventh commandment to the women not to read it – and what is still more extraordinary they seem not to have broken it' (*L&J*, vi. 237). Augusta herself refused to read it. The travel writer, Miss Jane Waldie, complained to Murray: 'Why will Lord Byron write what we may not read?' though Lady Caroline Lamb confessed, 'You cannot think how clever I think "Don Juan" is, in my heart' (*Smiles*, i. 405). She published two anonymous parodic 'continuations' of the poem, *A New Canto* (1819) and *Gordon, A Tale. A Poetical Review of Don Juan* (1821). The narrator of the latter praises the poet's mastery and genius, but castigates his scepticism and immorality in a discussion with a ghostly visitor from Italy. Both parodies envision the hellfire and final judgement which traditionally await the libertine and, it is implied, his author.[35] Another ex-mistress, Claire Clairmont, also made notes in her diary for a satire on the poem, which she considered merely self-justificatory: 'a soliloquy upon his own ill-luck – ungraceful & selfish – like a beggar hawking his own sores about and which create disgust instead of pity' (*Life,* ii. 840). Annabella took Byron's satiric portrait of her in surprisingly good part, showing she was not such a prig that she had no sense of humour:

> The impression was not so disagreeable as I expected. In the first place I am very much relieved to find that there is not anything which I can be expected to notice. As for myself, I do not think that my sins are in the pharisaical or pedantic line, and I am very sure that he does not think they are, but avails himself of the prejudices which some may entertain against me, to give a plausible colouring to his accusations. I must confess that the quizzing in one or two passages was so good as to make me smile at myself – therefore others are heartily welcome to laugh ...[36]

Byron made clear he was throwing down the gauntlet to women by repudiating the sentimental depiction of sexual relationships of his earlier poetry: 'Neither will I make "Ladies' books" "al dilettar le femine e la plebe" – I have written from the fullness of my mind, from passion – from impulse – from many motives – but not for their "sweet voices"'(*L&J*, vi. 105–6). He reported that Theresa Guiccioli, after reading a bad translation in French, 'paid me some compliments with due *drawbacks*' on *Don Juan.* He said he suspected that it would live longer than *Childe Harold,* but she retorted, 'I would rather have the fame of Childe Harold for three years than an Immortality of Don Juan'. The poet commented: 'The truth is that *it is too true* – and the women hate every thing which strips off the tinsel of *Sentiment* & they are right – for it would rob them of their weapons. – I never knew a woman who did not hate *De Grammont's memoirs* – for the same reason' (*L&J*, vii. 202). When Teresa persuaded him to discontinue the poem in July 1821, he made similar comments (*L&J*, viii. 148).

The Queen Caroline affair

A specifically political context for the poem's exposure of the sexual double standard was the Queen Caroline affair. Whigs, radicals and 'Female Reformers' had long united in making capital out of the Prince

Regent's persecution of Caroline after their separation, his failed attempt in 1805 to prove she had given birth to an illegitimate child, and his accusations of her adultery with her Italian courier when she went abroad in 1814.[37] But the propaganda on her behalf reached its height in 1820, when, on the death of George III, she returned to claim her rights as Queen and was actually put on trial for immorality by the monarch who was himself a by-word for libertinism, profligacy and excess. Queen Caroline thus became a heroine for the Whigs and radicals for her cause united anti-government opposition, paradoxically by drawing on both monarchist and republican sentiments, male chivalry and feminism simultaneously. Caroline even died as a tragic heroine. She was refused entrance at Westminster Abbey for the coronation in 1821. She was taken ill and died only a few days later.

As might be expected, the trial, with its parade of servant witnesses and sordid hunt for 'evidence' of the Queen's sexual proclivities, and endlessly multiplying web of gossip, offered the radical publishers undreamed-of possibilities for pamphlets combining sexual scandal and political propaganda. An outburst of pamphlets and posters appeared, as well as verse satires, including Hone and Cruikshank's *The Queen's Matrimonial Ladder* and *Non mi Ricordo*, Dolby's *The Queen and Magna Carta; or, The Thing that John Signed*, and Benbow's *Kouli Khan, Or the Progress of Error*.

It was at the time of Caroline's trial, when Hobhouse was continually sending him messages from the Queen and asking him to find Italian witnesses to vouch for her morality, or himself to return to England to testify on her behalf, that Byron wrote Canto V. Hobhouse protested at Byron's coarse joke about the Queen in stanza 61 and it was removed. More important is his portrayal of the Turkish Sultana Gulbeyaz. She is first seen as an arrogant aristocrat and sexually predatory for procuring a young man for her pleasure, but this lapse is then juxtaposed to the wholesale sexual tyranny of her husband whose harem comprised 'Four wives and twice five hundred maids unseen' (V, 148). An allusion to the Queen Caroline affair is likely, especially as readers might remember Cruikshank's print 'Royal condescension' (1817) where Caroline is dressed in Turkish fashion, having just returned from Tunis.

Cantos III, IV and V

Byron did not urge on the publication of the second section of the poem so enthusiastically as the first. He complained, 'the outcry has not frightened but it has *hurt* me', pretending that Cantos III and IV were 'very decent' and 'dull' (*L&J*, vii. 35). Canto V had been begun on 10 October 1820, this draft being revised and copied by 26 December. But significantly this time he sent the MS off to Douglas Kinnaird on 28 December, saying firmly: 'Tell Mr. M[urray] that he must settle something yes or no – if no – go to another' (*L&J*, vii. 255).

The end of the Murray-Byron partnership was in sight. Murray had made it abundantly clear he wanted to publish no more of *Don Juan*. The poet wrote stoically to the publisher on 4 January, 'I have written to you at least ten letters' (*L&J*, viii. 56). By February Byron was brought to agree to Murray's request that the question of payment be deferred until the level of sales could be ascertained. But Murray wanted to be sure it would be the last canto. Byron replied: 'The 5th is so far from being the last of D.J. that it is hardly the beginning. – I mean to take him the tour of Europe – with a proper mixture of siege – battle – and adventure – and to make him finish as *Anarcharsis Cloots* – in the French Revolution' (*L&J*, viii. 78). In March he received and declined an offer from a publisher named Fearman to publish the poem, whose continuation was presumably eagerly awaited (*L&J*, viii. 91). On 29 June, the author tried to put Murray in his (tradesman's) place: 'You must permit me to choose my *own* seasons of publication. All that you have a right to on such occasions is the mere matter of barter – If you think you are likely to lose by such or such a statement. – It is now two years nearly that MSS of mine have been in yr. hands in Status quo' (*L&J*, viii. 144). On 6 July, Byron caved in and announced that he was not continuing *Don Juan* – but on the order of his Italian mistress, not Murray's advisers. This promise presumably broke the impasse, for it resulted in Murray's publication of Cantos III, IV and V on 8 August 1821, still without the names of the author or publisher. Byron reproached Murray with the printer's errors, although he had refused to receive or correct the proofs. He wickedly parodied the excuses he anticipated Murray making for the low price of one thousand guineas proffered for Cantos III, IV and V: ' " "heavy season" ["]flat public" "don't go off" – ["]Lordship writes too much – Won't take advice – declining popularity – deductions for the trade – make very little – generally lose by him – pirated edition – foreign edition – severe criticisms &c.' (*L&J*, viii. 187). He eventually accepted £1525. Byron told Murray on 4 September the new cantos were 'excellent...I regret that I do not go on with it – for I had all the plan for several cantos – and different countries & climes' (*L&J*, viii. 198).[38]

Although Byron was no longer the darling of the quarto-buying aristocracy, the booksellers' messengers still crowded Albemarle Street to an extent that the parcels of books had to be thrown out of the windows to satisfy their cries (*Smiles*, i. 413). It seems that Byron had found a new public and Leigh Hunt commented that the 'new popularity' *Beppo* and *Don Juan* brought him surprised the poet (Leigh Hunt, *LBC*, p. 125). Murray did not even offer a quarto, but even so within days the pirates were producing copies at less than half Murray's price of 9s 6d for the octavo.[39] William Sherwin sold his edition for 4s. Even he was undercut when early in 1822 William Benbow brought out a 'whitey-brown' duodecimo of all five cantos for half-a-crown, and was followed by Hodgson and Company in 1822, Peter Griffin in 1823 and G. Smeeton in 1826.[40] Murray himself brought out two editions in the smaller format in 1821, priced at 5s.

Murray's memoirs suggest his aversion to publishing *Don Juan* had been increased by a letter he had received from the acidic reviewer of the *Quarterly*, John Wilson Croker, on receipt of the MS of Cantos III and IV on 26 March 1820. Croker astutely blamed Murray for not having had the courage to publish the earlier cantos openly, for – had his name and title been emblazoned on the cover – Byron would have been more amenable to revisions suggested by the Murray circle. 'Why smuggle it into the world and, as it were, pronounce it illegitimate in its birth?' (*Smiles*, i. 414). This shamefacedness was asking for critics to denounce the poem's immorality. The ensuing denunciations only goaded the poet into further excesses. Croker thought that the poem's sexual suggestiveness was 'nothing to make such a terrible rout about'. However he was shocked by the political satire denouncing British self-satisfaction over Waterloo, criticizing the British Government and berating the poet laureate, Robert Southey. But he put these excesses down to an immature desire to shock, for he could not believe that anyone of Byron's birth and talents could really have 'anything in common with the miserable creatures called radicals – as Hobhouse and Leigh Hunt would like to appear' (*Smiles*, i. 413). He saw the poet as an opportunist, a maverick like Brougham. Croker was really disturbed that radical publishers were using Byron's name and that the poet connived at attracting such 'jackal followers' by writing letters, which he knew would be circulated by Murray in London, threatening to return to England to lead them on horseback in their fight for reform. He concludes in a Southeyan strain: '…for your own sake as a tradesman, for Lord Byron's as a poet, for the sake of good literature and good principles, which ought to be united,…take such measures as you may be able to venture upon to get Lord Byron to revise these two cantos and not to take another step in the odious path which Hobhouse beckons him to pursue'.

It is ironic that Hobhouse was seen in this light by Croker because he had just been elected a radical MP, when in fact he had strenuously opposed the publication of *Don Juan.* Moreover, on 23 November 1821 Byron was devastated to receive a letter, which he described to Kinnaird as 'one of the grossest ever written in style and manner', from Hobhouse urging him not to publish *Cain,* which he judged ' a complete failure'. Their friendship never really recovered, and from henceforth his London friends were consulted less and less about his work in progress. What Byron needed now were advisers who were both sympathetic to his liberalism and to innovation in literature. He turned to Percy Shelley and Leigh Hunt.

6
The Eagle, the Wren, and the Snake: Byron and *The Liberal*

...Byron, Shelley, Moore, Leigh Hunt...are to lay their heads together in some Town of Italy, for the purpose of conducting a Journal to be directed against everything in religion, in morals and probably in government and literature, which our Forefathers have been accustomed to reverence.

> (Letter from William Wordsworth to
> Walter Savage Landor, 20 April 1822)

Lord Byron being a somewhat whimsical nobleman, has lately hired two or three Cockneys as menial servants. They are to do his dirty work, for which they are to receive his cast-off clothes, and, we believe, twenty pounds per annum. They look about after the manner of pimps and purveyors; and as it is according to human nature to feel uppish on preferment, these flunkies occasionally enact high life below stairs, and waltz away with washer-women and bar-maids and used-up kept-mistresses.

> ('On the Scotch Character – by a Flunky',
> *Blackwood's Edinburgh Magazine*, 13 [1823], 365–67)

When Byron and his friend Percy Shelley invited Leigh Hunt in 1822 to join them in producing a quarterly periodical from Pisa, Shelley (whom Byron nicknamed 'the snake') was privately not overly optimistic: '...how long the alliance between the wren and the eagle may continue, I will not prophesy' (*LPBS*, ii. 719). There is evidence that both the snake and the eagle had dreamt of challenging the sway of the *Edinburgh* and *Quarterly* for some years. During 1814–15 Shelley had been immersed in radical networks, and liaised with the freethinker George Cannon in launching a philosophical journal the *Theological*

Inquirer; or, Polemical Magazine. He contributed 'A Refutation of Deism' and extracts from 'Queen Mab'.[1] In 1819 he tried to persuade Peacock that a new periodical could succeed 'if a band of staunch reformers, resolute yet skilful infidels, were united in so close and constant a league as that in which interest and fanaticism have bound the members of that [*Quarterly Review's*] literary coalition!'[2]

By the 1820s, when the libel laws were used to enforce ever more stringent censorship on literature, founding a journal seemed less a political crusade and more a desperate attempt to enable his poetry to be published at all. Even Byron, the eagle of verse, whose popularity Shelley envied so much, struggled to make his voice heard. His unpublished manuscripts were mounting up at Albemarle Street. The eagle had himself been limed, for the more he struggled against the control of the *Quarterly* coterie over the publication process of his poetry the more he exposed himself to the vitriolic attacks in the press from which he had previously been protected.

So Byron, too, considered founding a journal to break the stranglehold the quarterlies held over the literary public sphere. Trelawny stated: 'Byron thought it indispensable to the preservation of his popularity that he should keep continually before the public; and thought an alliance with an able and friendly newspaper would be an easy way of doing so. Not that he would or could submit to the methodical drudgery of continually writing for one, but that he might occasionally use it for criticizing and attacking those who offended him, as a vent for his splenetic humours' (Trelawny, *Records,* p. 205). Ironically, Murray himself unsuccessfully tried to recruit Byron to write for a periodical, as early as 29 September 1816: 'I am thinking more seriously than ever of publishing a monthly literary journal...If I succeed, I will venture to solicit the favour of your powerful assistance in the shape of letters, essays, characters, facts, travels, epigrams, and other – to you – small shot' (*Smiles,* i. 367). This publication would materialize as *Blackwood's Edinburgh Magazine,* set up as a livelier Tory rival to the *Edinburgh Review* than the staid *Quarterly,* which was lampooned by Peacock in *Melincourt* as the 'The Legitimate Review'. Murray sought anonymous contributions from Byron again on 22 September 1818. This was a blatant attempt to tempt him away from the influence of radicals like Shelley and Hobhouse, and enlist him amongst the young Tory wits of *Blackwood's.* John Wilson, John Gibson Lockhart and William Maginn were engaged in a wholesale onslaught on the Leigh Hunt circle, which they snobbishly derided as suburban or 'Cockney'. The *Quarterly* also lashed out at Shelley and Keats, and Hunt reciprocated with a satire against Gifford: *Ultra-Crepidarius* (1823). It soon seemed necessary that a new quarterly be founded, representing a more radical outlook than the Whiggish *Edinburgh*. An Aberdonian schoolfellow of Byron's, John Scott, visited him in Venice before becoming editor in 1820 of the new (*Baldwin's*) *London Magazine* which crusaded against the scurrility of *Blackwood's Magazine*. The journal probably took the name of the capital to defy the appellation 'Cockney'. Scott, a discerning critic, recruited a galaxy of star writers, which included De Quincey, William Hazlitt and Charles Lamb. But such was the deadly seriousness of Regency literary warfare that on 27 February 1821 Scott was tragically killed in a duel with Lockhart's friend, Jonathan Christie.

On Christmas day 1820 Byron proposed to Moore that they collaborate in setting up a periodical: 'I have been thinking of a project for you and me, in case we both get to London again, which (if a Neapolitan war don't susticate) may be calculated as possible for one of us about the spring of 1821. . . . The project, then is for you and me to set up jointly a *newspaper* – nothing more or less – weekly, or so, with some improvement or modifications upon the plan of the present scoundrels, who degrade that department; – but a *newspaper*, which we will edite [sic] in due form, and nevertheless with some attention. There must always be in it a piece of poesy from one or other of us *two* . . . ' (*L&J*, vii. 254). He wrote again on 2 January 1821: 'I wish you to think seriously of the Journal scheme – for I am as serious as one can be, in this world, about any thing,' (*L&J*, viii. 55). On 22 June 1821 he tried again but without success (*L&J*, viii. 140), again in July (*L&J*, viii. 147) and again plaintively in August: 'Is there no chance of your returning to England, and of our Journal?' (*L&J*, viii. 166).

Leigh Hunt

It was doubtless Shelley who proposed instead 'the wren', his chirpy friend Leigh Hunt, as a possible factotum for the new journal. As editor of the *Examiner* and poet, Hunt represented an interface between the world of Radical publishing and avant garde poetry. He was also almost destitute, having fecklessly frittered away the immense sum of £1400 which Shelley insured his own life to borrow for him in 1818, and was therefore open to the prospect of further aristocratic patronage.

Byron had met Leigh Hunt through Thomas Moore. In May 1813 he visited him in prison where he held court as the latest martyr for Reform, serving a two-year sentence for libel on the Prince Regent. The journalist, who propagated the cultivation of cheerfulness in all circumstances, had painted a sunny sky on the ceiling and roses climbing the walls of his cell. Leigh Hunt dedicated *The Story of Rimini* (1816), his experimental Dantean poem, to Byron, who had commented on it in MS, and subsequently recommended publication to Murray. However, Hunt's importance was greater as a cultural critic than a poet. The Hunt brothers had for fourteen years published the brilliant Sunday newspaper, the *Examiner*, whose declared object was 'to assist in producing Reform in Parliament, Liberality of opinion in general (especially freedom from superstition) and a fusion of literary taste into all subjects whatsoever. It began with being of no party; but Reform soon gave it one'. Hazlitt wrote in the *Edinburgh Review* in May 1823: 'the *Examiner* stands next to Cobbett in talent, and is much before him in moderation and steadiness of principle'. Hunt did not concern himself with the practical minutiae of a programme for Reform. His rhetoric attacked the whole spectrum of abuses – political corruption, packed juries, gross sinecures, the slave trade, corporal punishment, and the Draconian penal code – as products of the same unreformed governmental system.[3] His distinctiveness lay in his linking of the political with the cultural life of the individual. He advocated a love of reading with moral earnestness as one of the rights of man enabling everyone to take an active role in the public sphere.

The first critic to acknowledge the true stature of Wordsworth, in December 1816 Hunt went on to hail a new school of poetry in his groundbreaking 'Young Poets' article. This celebrated Byron's third canto of *Childe Harold* as his best poem yet, and introduced to his readers the new poets Percy Shelley, John Keats and John Hamilton Reynolds. He associated the new school with progressive politics. By the time Byron left England, he and Hunt had become close literary acquaintances rather than personal friends. But Byron never forgot Hunt's loyalty during the separation scandal: 'When party feelings ran highest against me, Hunt was the only editor of a paper, the only literary man, who dared say a word in my justification' (*Medwin*, pp. 253–4). Before he left for Italy to help start up the new journal, Leigh Hunt published a profile of Byron's literary career in the *Examiner* 29 (1821). He was certainly not sycophantic, characterizing Byron's poetry as 'the poetry, not of imagination, but of passion and humour'. He perceptively pronounced, 'His *Don Juan* is perhaps his best work, and the one by which he will stand or fall with readers'.

It was Shelley who had urged the journal scheme forward. He wrote to Leigh Hunt on 20 December 1818 telling him that Byron invited him to come to Italy and edit a literary periodical in which they all would join. 'He talked a good deal about you, & among other things he said that he wished you would come to Italy, & bade me tell you that he would lend you the money for the journey (4 or £500) if you were prevented by that consideration' (*LPBS*, ii. 67). But the survival of the *Examiner* depended on Leigh's journalism. In 1821 John Hunt, now sole proprietor and printer of the *Examiner*, was fined and condemned to serve a year in Coldbath-fields prison for libellous comments on the House of Commons. Leigh suffered a nervous collapse and his literary journal the *Indicator* failed the same year. But when his nephew Henry Leigh Hunt took over editorship of the *Examiner,* Leigh decided he could try to send the *Examiner* articles, and edit the new journal from Italy. On 26 August 1821 Shelley wrote again that Byron '...proposes that you should come out and go shares with him and me in a periodical work, to be conducted here; in which each of the contracting parties should publish all their original compositions, and share the profits. He proposed it to Moore, but for some reason it was never brought to bear. There can be no doubt that the *profits* of any scheme in which you and Lord Byron engage, must from various, yet cooperating reasons, be very great'.[4] Leigh Hunt agreed that Byron would doubtless be able to set up both himself and his brother John in their finances, and predicted with his customary optimism: 'We will divide the world between us, like the Triumvirate'.[5] He thus attempted to accept Byron frankly as both an aristocratic patron of the project and a fellow republican.

Hunt (whom Byron described as 'the vainest man on earth', *L&J*, x. 105) boasted of his professional expertise: 'I have a good deal of experience in periodical writing, and know what the getting up of the *machine* requires, as well as the soul of it'. It was true that Leigh's journalistic talents were the source of the *Examiner's* success. But what Byron initially did not realize, and Shelley was too loyal to admit to, was that Leigh Hunt had a virtually pathological inability to manage money. Byron later described the attempt to extricate him from his debts as 'like pulling a man out of a river who directly throws himself in again' (*L&J*, x. 138). He was a perpetual leech on his long-suffering brother John, who had taken on sole proprietorship of the *Examiner,* while continuing to pay Leigh his share of the profits. This protected his delicate younger brother from sharing prison sentences for libel, but also enabled John's son to take over management of the paper. Leigh, like William Godwin (another sponger on Shelley), believed that it was the duty of wealthy liberals to support poverty-stricken intellectuals without expecting any demeaning gratitude in return. 'I must trouble you for another "cool hundred" of your crowns, & shall speedily, I fear, come upon you for one more,' he would cheerily write to Byron.[6] He cultivated an irritating childlike persona, later cruelly caricatured by Dickens in *Bleak House*'s Harold Skimpole, whose determined irresponsibility functioned as a strategy for extorting patronage while refuting the commercial values of the age. Byron, on the other hand, having abandoned his spendthrift youth, worried constantly about 'the funds', and fancied himself a sharp negotiator in the business side of his writing. The eventual collapse of the periodical was the result not so much of a clash of personalities, as lack of clarity on both sides as to whether Byron's role was aristocratic patron or literary and business partner. For Byron's straightforward business relationship with John Hunt as the publisher of *Don Juan* Cantos VI–XV, not only survived the wreckage of *The Liberal* but succeeded in implementing a successful new marketing strategy.

* * *

Byron had furnished apartments in his own house, the Palazzo Lanfranchi at Pisa, for the Hunt family. But there could be no easy amalgamation between the aristocratic bohemianism of Byron's way of life and the Hunts' bourgeois cult of the fireside. Byron was offended by Marianne Hunt, who felt her respectability compromised by meeting his mistress. Marianne, on the other hand, thought Byron was being ridiculously severe on her progressively-reared six children (whom he privately termed 'Yahoos' and 'Hottentots'), for 'disfiguring the walls of a few rooms'. Byron had his own menagerie, as reported by Shelley to Thomas Love Peacock: 'Lord B.'s establishment consists besides servants, of ten horses, eight enormous dogs, three monkeys, five cats, an eagle, a crow, and a falcon; and all these, except the horses, walk about the house, which every now and then resounds with their unarbitrated quarrels, as if they were masters of it'. He then added: 'I have just met on the grand staircase five peacocks, two guinea hens, and an Egyptian crane. I wonder who all those animals were before they were changed into these shapes'! (*LPBS*, ii. 330–1).

Two such egoists as the wren and the eagle could never be soulmates. Nevertheless, Hunt and Byron respected and stimulated each other as literary colleagues. They fell into a pleasant routine, which the Poet of Cheer later recalled:

> Lord Byron, who used to sit up at night, writing Don Juan (which he did under the influence of gin and water), rose late in the morning. He breakfasted; read; lounged about, singing an air, generally out of Rossini, and in a swaggering style, though in a voice at once small and veiled; then took a bath, and was dressed; and coming downstairs, was heard, still singing, in the court-yard, out of which

the garden ascended at the back of the house. ... I was generally at my writing when he came down, and either acknowledged his presence by getting up and saying something from the window, or he called out 'Leontius!' and came halting up to the window with some joke, or other challenge to conversation. ... When the heat of day declined, we rode out, either on horseback or in a barouche, generally towards the forest. ... Trelawny sometimes went with us, on a great horse, smoking a cigar. We had blue frockcoats, white waistcoats and trowsers, and velvet caps *A la Raphael*; and cut a gallant figure.[7]

The death of Shelley

Upon Shelley's shoulders had fallen the task of maintaining harmony between Hunt, Mary and Byron, all of whom were linked by their close relationships to him rather than to each other. So when he was tragically drowned in a sailing accident on 8 July, only five days after the Hunts' arrival at Pisa, the periodical was predestined to a short life even before it was launched. Byron and Hunt fruitlessly searched the coast until they were informed, on the 18 July, that Shelley's decomposed body had been washed ashore and temporarily interred on the beach. Hunt's copy of Keats's *Lamia* was still in his pocket. Edward Trelawny obtained permission to have the bodies of Shelley and his friend Edward Williams cremated, so that their ashes could be buried in the Protestant cemetery in Rome. Byron wrote to Moore: 'You can have no idea what an extraordinary effect such a funeral pile has, on a desolate shore, with mountains in the back-ground and the sea before, and the singular appearance the salt and frankincense gave to the flame. All of Shelley was consumed, except his *heart*, which would not take the flame, and is now preserved in spirits of wine' (*L&J*, ix. 197). The distressed Hunt sat in the carriage, while Byron made himself watch. After seeing the brains seethe in the fire, he threw himself in the water and swam so far out to sea that he became badly sunburned. Both poets got drunk on the way back in the carriage and found themselves laughing hysterically. Hunt had to be forced to give up Shelley's heart to Mary, such was his possessive grief. He preserved a fragment of jawbone like a relic for the rest of his life.[8]

Resumption of *Don Juan*

Byron, though less overtly emotional, was very deeply affected. Byron's grief for his friend had literary repercussions. He wrote bitterly to Murray's *Quarterly* coterie: 'You are all brutally mistaken about Shelley who was without exception – the *best* and least selfish man I ever knew. – I never knew one who was not a beast in comparison' (*L&J*, ix. 189–90). Even before Shelley's death, Byron seemed to rededicate his energies as a poet in the first week in July, when, as its modern editor has noted, *Don Juan* took a new crusading direction as an anti-war anti-epic, whose ideological commitment was to be plainly declared in a new Preface (*CPW*, v. 717). Though Shelley never dreamt of the extent of his influence on his more successful friend, Byron's confidence in himself as a Liberal poet had surged as a direct result of his friend's presence. He was especially inspired by the prospect of the literary collaboration with both snake and wren. On 8 July, Hunt wrote to his sister-in-law of Byron's 'great ardour' for the periodical, which the noble poet had first suggested should be called the *Hesperides* before his inspired second choice of *The Liberal* was adopted. That same day (ironically the very day of Shelley's death, though he did not know it), Byron defiantly announced to Murray his resumption of *Don Juan*. He solemnly told Murray he had 'obtained a permission from my Dictatress to continue it – *provided always* it was to be more guarded and decorous ... How far these conditions have been fulfilled may be seen perhaps by and bye ... ' (*L&J*, ix. 182). He was mischievously referring to the transvestite harem episodes which Murray would later describe as 'so outrageously shocking that I would not publish them if you were to give me your Estate – Title and Genius'. Moreover, scientific examination of the original dating of the manuscripts has shown Byron had actually resumed *Don Juan* in January! On 8 July Byron was really preparing to write Canto VIII, a fierce denunciation of imperial warfare. By 12 July he was already looking forward to Canto IX, for he wrote to Moore asking for the return of some previously excised stanzas satirizing Wellington, for its opening.

The death of Shelley and the gloating treatment of it in the Tory press crystallized this determination of Byron's to devote the rest of his writing life to an ideological war against the Tory administration, the Lake poets, and the imperialism they supported.[9] Despite the failure of *The Liberal* itself, the attempted collaboration inaugurated one of the most intense periods of inspiration of Byron's life. Canto after canto of *Don Juan* poured continuously from his pen from April 1822 to May 1823, so that all eleven were written before any were published. No longer was the Murray coterie consulted. The slight emendations suggested by Mary Shelley, in the course of making the fair copies, were the only reader's comments made before publication. Not only were these cantos composed very quickly, but there was little sign on the manuscripts of revision and accretion. Walter Scott thought these last cantos of *Don Juan* the most powerful things Byron ever wrote.[10]

Hostility to the collaboration

But without Shelley's constant encouragement, Byron was always liable
to be swayed by the universal hostility to *The Liberal* of all his old friends,
especially Douglas Kinnaird, Thomas Moore and John Cam Hobhouse.[11]
He invited Moore to contribute on 12 July: 'Do send Hunt any thing in
prose or verse of yours, to start him handsomely – any lyrical, *ir*ical, or
what you please' (*L&J*, ix. 183). He tried again on 27 August 1822: 'Leigh
Hunt is sweating articles for his new Journal; and both he and I think it
somewhat shabby in *you* not to contribute. Will you become one of the
properrioters?' (*L&J*, ix. 197).[12] But Moore had been suspicious of Shelley,
and was too much a denizen of Holland House, the headquarters of the
Whigs, to risk his reputation with a radical publication. Hazlitt later
recalled: 'Mr Moore darted backwards and forwards from Cold-bath-
Fields Prison [where John Hunt was serving his sentence] to the Examiner office, from Mr. Longman's to Mr. Murray's shop in a state of
ridiculous trepidation, to see what was to be done to prevent this
degradation of the aristocracy of letters, this indecent encroachment of
plebeian pretensions, this undue extension of patronage and compromise of privilege. The Tories were shocked that Lord Byron should grace
the popular side by his direct countenance and assistance; the Whigs
were shocked that he should share his confidence and counsels with
any one who did not unite the double recommendations of birth
and genius – but themselves!' (*LBC*, pp. 54–5). Hazlitt comments that
Moore had been invited to assist in the undertaking, 'but he professed
an utter aversion to, and warned Lord Byron against, having any concern with *joint publications*, as of a very neutralizing and levelling
description'. Both Moore and Hobhouse thought it particularly
demeaning for Byron to collaborate in a mere 'pot au feu', especially
when all contributions were anonymous, as was the convention of periodical publication. Then, in September 1822, 'Mr. Hobhouse rushed
over the Alps, not knowing which was more awful, the mountains, or
the Magazine,' commented Hunt drily (*LBC*, p. 48). Hobhouse persuaded Byron to pull out of *The Liberal* and to write for the *Examiner*
instead, but John Hunt successfully opposed the idea (Broughton,
Recollections, iii. 2; *L&J*, x. 66).

The break with Murray

Byron hoped the journal would enable him to get his controversial work
into print, control the publication process, and retain his copyrights.

Back in February 1822, the same month he had sent Hunt his expenses, Byron had been so exasperated with Murray that he had told Kinnaird to retrieve his manuscripts and find another publisher for the *Vision*. Kinnaird failed utterly, and Byron admitted to Moore that it 'has appalled the Row' (*L&J*, ix. 118). The experience would be repeated the following year with the later cantos of *Don Juan*. It was apparent that none but the Radical publishers would now risk gaol for the sake of publishing such controversial works. However, on 6 March Byron was 'melted' by a flattering epistle from Murray and tried to come to an accommodation with him. He asked Moore to send Murray a drama written in a popular style, *Werner*, proposing it be published in one volume with *Cain*'s sequel, *Heaven and Earth*, together with some shorter poems. As well as this sweetening of the pill, he declared himself willing to 'soften' *Heaven and Earth* (*L&J*, ix. 136). He suggested that Murray publish the *Vision* under another imprint or as a foreign edition, and cheaply enough to outwit the pirates (9 April 1822). But an ominous silence from Albemarle Street ensued. On 26 May Byron even suggested reverting to having these dramas printed at his own risk, with 'published by the Author' to be printed on the title page as a sign he would bear all the loss (*L&J*, ix. 163).

But all was stasis. Murray would publish no more cantos of *Don Juan; The Vision of Judgment* had remained in MS since October 1821 and the projected volume of *Werner* and *Heaven and Earth* had been set up in print but the publisher could not bring himself to print the latter Biblical 'mystery play' after the storm with *Cain*. Murray was paralysed by his reluctance to countenance the inevitable break with the poet who had made his fortune. Byron began to think posterity would from now on constitute his chief readership: '*My* object is not *immediate* popularity in my present productions...But *mark what I now say* – that the time will come – when *these* will be preferred to any I have before written' (*L&J*, ix. 92–3). At other times he was tempted to by-pass the respectable republic of letters and go straight to the masses. He had contemplated distributing copies of the *Vision* to friends in order that it would be pirated (6 Feb. 1822, *L&J*, ix. 100).

The reality of Byron's association with the Hunt brothers hit the appalled Murray for six, in the shape of a blunt demand for some of Byron's manuscripts from John Hunt, whom Byron described as 'a steady, bold fellow, such as *Prynne*, for example, and full of moral, and, I hear physical courage' (*L&J*, x. 105). On 3 July, Byron had written a note to be delivered by John Hunt to request Murray to give him the corrected and 'softened' proofs of *The Vision of Judgment*, for publication in *The Liberal*. This poem was a brilliant parody of the Laureate's eulogy commemorating the late George III's triumphant entry into paradise. He made a point of asking Murray to be sure to give Hunt the preface, which attempted to evade prosecution by emphasizing that the poem was an attack on Robert Southey rather than the late King. He repeated these instructions in a second letter on 6 July, explaining that John Hunt was willing to publish this controversial work at his own risk, and that this would relieve Murray of his 'dilemma'. Byron's enthusiasm for the periodical generated another letter on July 8 asking that the Pulci translation ('the best thing I ever did in my life') and 'any prose tracts of mine' be also handed over to John Hunt, 'for Mr Leigh Hunt is arrived here and thinks of commencing a periodical work – to which I shall contribute – I do not propose to you to be the publisher – because I know that you are unfriends – but all things in your care except the volume now in the press [i.e. *Werner, Heaven and Earth,* etc.] – and the MSS purchased of Mr Moore [i.e. *Memoirs*] – can be given for this purpose' (*L&J*, ix. 182).

The 'Emperor of the West' did not care for the bluff manners of the newly-released jail-bird, John Hunt, and an altercation ensued. Unbeknown to either John or the Pisan circle, Murray revenged himself by handing over the original manuscript instead of the revised proof, minus the explanatory preface, and thus helped to ensure that Hunt was prosecuted by his namesake Charles Murray, of the Constitutional Association. Byron did not realize what had happened until the first number of *The Liberal* was published on 15 October 1822. On 24 October he wrote in cold anger to Murray threatening, if the correct manuscripts were not forthcoming, to make the matter public and accused Murray of allowing himself to be manipulated as a tool by Southey and his employers. A statement accordingly appeared in the *Examiner* on November 3 announcing that Murray 'contrived to evade sending the preface to the present publisher'. On 31 October Byron wrote again quite calmly, requesting all unpublished corrected manuscripts to be sent to Douglas Kinnaird. Murray was devastated. Leigh Hunt wrote gleefully to his brother,

> Poor Murray is indeed in a deplorable state, and one should pity him, as you are inclined to do, if he were not so profoundly servile. What do you think? He writes to Lord B. how delighted he should be, if his Lordship would but be 'so nobly generous' as to let him publish works of 'his former glorious description' (admire the invincible impudence lurking at bottom of this adulation); and he adds,

in another letter, *that he sits of a morning, for hours, looking at his Lordship's picture!* Imagine the languishing bookseller![13]

Byron now offered John Hunt the six unpublished cantos of *Don Juan*, but proposed to publish at his own risk, retain his copyright and settle for a proportion of the profits. He also offered both dramas to *The Liberal*. Byron wrote to Kinnaird on 2 November: 'I am not at all sorry to be rid of him [Murray] for he was a sad shuffler' (*L&J*, x. 26). He continued to write to Murray as a friend, but warned the Hunt brothers that Murray's coterie would do all they could to sabotage their joint enterprise.

This was all too true. First Murray retained the innocuous *Werner* and published it without permission on 23 November. Byron let this go without protest. Next Murray deliberately publicized a previous ingratiating letter of Byron's, conceding the journal was 'a bad business' and describing his relationship to Hunt as merely charitable. He also circulated gossip that Byron had referred to Hunt as 'an old proser' and to his children as unmanageable. This was picked up by the Tory press, delighted with more ammunition to sink *The Liberal* and humiliate 'The King of Cockayne'. The Hunt family in London wrote to Leigh in puzzled anger. Leigh behaved with great dignity, telling his family and Byron, 'We give importance to nonsense of this kind by attending to it'.[14] Byron was genuinely remorseful, but Hunt felt that: 'He ought to have cut the matter short by saying as much now in public'.[15] Even Mary Shelley, herself on bad terms with Leigh Hunt, rebuked Byron for betraying his friend. Byron commented ruefully to Hobhouse, 'I have offended everybody like the old man and his Ass' (*L&J*, x. 57).

Byron, disgusted by Murray's exploitation of his private letters, gave him his dismissal on 6 November: 'As a publisher I bid you a final farewell' (*L&J*, x. 28). Murray's reply was almost incoherent between rage at the Hunts and self-justification: 'Never since I have been a publisher did I ever observe such a universal outcry as this work [i.e. *The Liberal*] has occasioned and it is deemed to be no less dull than wickedly intended – finding all this attributed to you and moreover that you were accused of mercenary motives I felt it a duty that I owed to you to read that part of your letter in which you communicate the cause of – and your motives for contributing to this work to every gentleman who is in the habit of visiting at my house ... You see the result of being forced into contact w[it]h wretches who take for granted that every one must be as infamous as themselves – Really Lord Byron – it is dreadful to think of yr. association with such outcasts from Society ...' (*Life*, iii. 1040). Byron replied calmly, accepting that Murray meant well towards him personally, but maintaining that as he had treated the Hunts so unfairly: 'I shall withdraw from you as a publisher, on every account, even on your own, and I wish you good luck elsewhere' (*L&J*, x. 36). When Murray sent him the *Quarterly* (which contained Bishop Heber's remarks on his 'degradation'), he returned it uncut and unread.

The Liberal

When the scheme looked certain to founder, Byron would try to pass off *The Liberal* as a mere charitable enterprise to help the Hunts. Macaulay, looking back at Byron's career from 1831 claimed that in fact he had suffered from delusions of grandeur:

> A new dream of ambition arose before him – to be the centre of a literary party; the great mover of an intellectual revolution; – to guide the public mind of England from his Italian retreat, as Voltaire had guided the public mind of France from the villa of Ferney. With this hope, as it should seem, he established *The Liberal....* The plan failed and failed ignominiously: Angry with himself, angry with his coadjutors, he relinquished it; and turned to another project, the last and noblest of his life.[16]

Byron probably did hope to take the lead amongst the liberal writers in exile. He turned for cultural authority to cosmopolitan literary models as an alternative to the nationalist canon undergoing construction, in which Shakespeare, Milton and Wordsworth sanctified the monarchy, the Protestant religion and the English countryside, and together formed a distinctively British sensibility. But he was a polemicist rather than a critic (infamously denigrating Keats's 'p-ss a bed poetry' and 'Turdsworth') and was as impatient with Hunt's literary theorizing as with Southey's experimental hexameters. Neither Percy Shelley nor Leigh Hunt were much in sympathy with Byron's attack on 'Bardolatry', his quixotic defence of Pope in letters contesting Bowles's *Strictures on the Life and Writings of Pope* or his revisionist attempt to return to Augustan genres which resulted in the failed satires *The Blues* and *The Age of Bronze* and the neo-classical Venetian plays, written in strict accordance with the unities.

Nevertheless, Byron had some common ground with Leigh Hunt. For both were searching to legitimize anti-Establishment writing. Hunt also looked backward; he claimed that the so-called new school of poetry were not innovators but were restoring the true tradition of

British poetry – that of Chaucer, Shakespeare and Milton – which had been merely interrupted at the Restoration of the monarchy by a sterile French formalism. The anti-clericalism of Chaucer, Shakespeare's tragedies of tyrannical or usurping monarchs, Milton's republicanism all demonstrated to Hunt an alternative British tradition of fierce independence and progress towards liberty.

The first number

The first number of *The Liberal: Verse and Prose from the South* opened with Leigh Hunt's Preface, which declared: 'The object of our work is not political...' yet insisted nevertheless on the necessarily ideological nature of literature (a claim to be strenuously opposed by Victorian assimilators of Romanticism, like Arnold), '...inasmuch as all writing now-a-days must involve something to that effect, the connexion between politics and all other subjects of interest to mankind having been discovered, never again to be done away' (p. vii). Hunt launched a full-scale attack on the Coleridgean notion that a 'clerisy' should educate the lower classes into loyalty, through literature validating the values of the Establishment, upholding the Monarchy and national Church (p.vi):

> But when we know, – and know too from our intimacy with various classes of people, – that there is not a greater set of hypocrites in the world than these pretended teachers of the honest and inexperienced part of our countrymen; – when we know that their religion, even when it is in earnest on any point (which is very seldom) means the most ridiculous and untenable notions of the DIVINE BEING, and in all other cases means nothing but the Bench of Bishops;- when we know that their morals consist for the most part in a secret and practical contempt of their own professions, and for the least and best part, of a few dull examples of something a little more honest, clapped in front to make a show and a screen, and weak enough to be made tools against all mankind;- and when we know, to crown all, that their 'legitimacy,' as they call it, is the most unlawful of all lawless and impudent things, tending, under pretence that the whole world are as corrupt and ignorant as themselves, to put it at the mercy of the most brute understandings among them, – men by their very education in these pretensions, rendered the least fit to sympathize with their fellow men, and as unhappy, after all, as the lowest of their slaves;- when we know all this, and see nine-tenths of all the intelligent men in the world alive to it, then indeed we are willing to

accept the title of enemies to religion, morals, and legitimacy, and hope to do our duty with all becoming profaneness accordingly.

This prepares the reader for Byron's *The Vision of Judgment*, which makes delightfully creaky stage machinery out of the medieval version of Christianity cynically propagated in Sunday Schools for social control of the working classes, including the whole notion of judgement and the threat of hellfire 'that immortal fry/ Of almost every body born to die' (xv).

Anticipating outrage from both radical and Tory extremes at the piquant alliance in *The Liberal* between a radical journalist and an aristocrat poet, Hunt's preface alludes to Byron: 'We have a regard for certain modern barons' who identify with those 'who got the Great Charter for us' not the supporters of 'every feeble King John' (p. viii). The editor claims inspiration from a whole British tradition of such poets, including many aristocrats, who have 'thrown light and life upon man' by their oppositional stance towards tyranny and contempt towards the sycophantic writers and turncoats who nourish it (like Southey). He salutes: 'the WICKLIFFES, and the CHAUCERS; – ... not the slaves and sycophants of King HENRY the Eighth (whose names we have forgotten) but the HENRY HOWARDS, the SURREYS, and the WYATTS.' He goes through the centuries in similar fashion, castigating flatterers and praising 'ye BUCHANANS and ye WALTER RALEIGHS ... the HERBERTS, the HUTCHINSONS, the LOCKES, the POPES, and the PETERBOROUGHS ... ye MILTONS and ye MARVELLS, ye HOADLEYS, ADDISONS and STEELES, ye SOMERSETS, DORSETS, and PRIORS ...' (p. viii).

The title *The Liberal* was the first recorded example of the word being used in English as a noun. Hunt explains that it must be 'taken in its largest acceptation, old as well as new': the writers are 'advocates of every liberal knowledge' but politically 'go to the full length in matters of opinion with large bodies of men who are called LIBERALS' (p. ix). Hunt here has himself interrupted by an 'old club-house gentleman, in a buff waistcoat and red face', in other words a Whig. This boozy placeman claims he too is a Liberal because he wants a sensible balance between both parties which will 'let Governments go on as they do, have done, and will do for ever'. He is so liberal he sees the Tory point of view, even to the extent of justifying Castlereagh's treatment of Ireland and refusing to criticize the King, his ministers and the Duke of Wellington. But self-serving moderation is quite different from the active radicalism of true Liberals as defined by Hunt. A full-scale attack follows on the Duke of Wellington who has 'confounded the rights of nations with those of a manor', and on Lord Castlereagh with 'his famous Six Acts ... his patronage of such infamous journals as the *Beacon*, his fondness for imprisoning, and for what his weak obstinacy calls his other strong measures'. Probably anticipating outrage at the black humour of Byron's three scurrilous epigrams on Castlereagh's suicide, which closed the number, he quotes the *Courier's* gloating comment on the death of 'Shelley, a writer of infidel poetry', promising wrathfully: 'The force of our answers will always be proportioned to the want of liberality in the assailant'.

Hunt concludes by ranging history and geography in selecting litera- ture for our 'homage' and 'worship'. He abjures the sterile classicism versus romanticism debate, then raging in Europe. He points out that liberalism in literature is neither the monopoly of an atheistic French scepticism nor of the German sentimentalists; that there is room to admire Voltaire as well as Goethe and Schiller, Boccaccio and Ariosto as well as Dante and Milton. Contributors to *The Liberal* will set up no idols but, in its humanist creed, will pay tribute 'Wherever ... we see the mind of man exhibiting powers of its own, and at the same time helping to carry on the best interests of human nature'.

The Vision of Judgment

Byron was much more critical of Romanticism than Hunt and Shelley. He regretted that his own early poetry had contributed to Romanticism ('the wrong revolutionary poetical system'), which he now associated with solipsism and the political conservatism of the Lake Poets. As usual, Byron was more effective at personal attack than coherent literary the- orizing. He was currently fervently prosecuting a literary feud with Robert Southey. Byron believed that Southey was responsible for the rumours which had circulated that, in 1816, he, Mary Godwin, Percy Shelley and Godwin's stepdaughter 'Claire' Clairmont had participated in a 'league of incest' (*L&J*, vi. 76, 82–3). Though he had been forced to suppress the Dedication of *Don Juan* to Southey, and satiric shafts against Southey in Canto III of *Don Juan*, doubtless Southey knew of them through Murray's coterie. Robert Southey had written to the *Courier* replying to Byron's attack on him in a note to *The Two Foscari*. The Poet Laureate also reciprocated with a stinging attack on what he termed 'the Satanic School' in the preface to his poem on the death of George III, *A Vision of Judgment*, published on 11 April 1821:

> ... men of diseased hearts and depraved imaginations who, forming a system of opinions to suit their own unhappy course of conduct, have rebelled against the holiest ordinances of human society, and

hating that revealed religion which, with all their efforts and brava-
does, they are unable entirely to disbelieve, labour to make others as
miserable as themselves, by infecting them with a moral virus that
eats into the soul![17]

Unfortunately for Southey, his own poem could not have made a better object of parody if it had been specially constructed for the purpose. Better far than his first thought of challenging Southey to a duel,
Byron's *Vision of Judgment* destroyed Southey's credibility as a poet
for all time. The Laureate's reverential account of the judgement of the
soul of the late king, his detractors shamed and enemies reconciled,
his beatification and meeting with the former monarchs and British
worthies (which included the nationalist British canon) and entry into
heaven needed only the geniality of Horatian irony to bring into focus
the sinister sectarian divisiveness underlying the original. The Byronic
narrator wishes that everyone, even George III, may be saved:

> I know this is unpopular; I know
> 'Tis blasphemous; I know one may be damn'd
> For hoping no one else may e'er be so;
>
> (XIV)

His admission of his own vulnerability ('God help us all! God help
me too! I am/ God knows, as helpless as the devil can wish', XV) brings
out to the full the contrasting arrogant brutality of Southey's prophecy
that writing *Don Juan* had damned Byron's soul:

> Whatever remorse of conscience he may feel when his hour comes
> (and come it must!) will be of no avail. The poignancy of a death-
> bed repentance cannot cancel one copy of the thousands which are
> sent abroad; and as long as it continues to be read, so long is he the
> pandar of posterity, and so long is he heaping up guilt upon his soul
> in perpetual accumulation.
>
> (Preface, *Vision of Judgment*, p. 204)

Ironically embracing Southey's label of 'the Satanic School', Byron
makes Satan the leader of the heavenly Opposition ('for by many stories,/ And true, we learn the angels are all Tories', XXVI), and accepts
critics of the monarchy like John Wilkes and 'Junius' as denizens of
Hell. Byron therefore enacts the role of shadow Laureate, exposing the

corruption and tyranny rife during George III's reign instead of lauding the monarchy:

> He ever warr'd with freedom and the free:
> Nations as men, home subjects, foreign foes,
> So that they utter'd the word 'Liberty!'
> Found George the Third their first opponent...
> (XLV)

A letter to the editor of *My Grandmother's Review*

As well as *The Vision of Judgment* and the epigrams on Castlereagh, another piece by Byron appeared in the first number of *The Liberal*. This was a high-spirited, boyish spoof addressed to William Roberts, editor of the *British Review*. Byron had joked in *Don Juan* (I, 209–210) that he was expecting good notices for his new poem from this Evangelical periodical, as he had sent the editor a hefty bribe. He could hardly believe his eyes when, in August 1819, Roberts published a pompous rebuttal, apparently having failed to detect any humour. Though Roberts had unintentionally made a fool of himself in public Byron could not resist tormenting him further. 'Wortley Clutterbuck', or 'W.C.' from Little Pidlington, 'a believer in the Church of England – to say nothing of the State', writes that he personally believes Roberts's denial yet wishes Roberts had taken the precaution of obtaining an 'affadavit sworn before the Lord Mayor'; then assures him he could not possibly agree with those, like the poet S[outhey], who interpreted the phrase 'My Grandmother's Review' as 'a mere figurative allusion to your supposed intellectual age and sex'; but concludes with the after-thought that if by any chance the bribe had indeed been sent, the best way to lay the matter to rest would be to return the money to Lord Byron again. Roberts' retirement that same year was doubtless has-tened by this further ridicule.

Other contributions

The first number also contained 'May-day Night', Percy Shelley's fine translation of the Walpurgisnacht scene from Goethe's *Faust*. Hunt's several contributions included a chatty travelogue, 'Letters from Abroad: A description of Pisa'; an Italian tale based on Marco Lastri's *L'Osser-vatore Fiorentino*, and the humorous piece 'Rhyme and Reason', which suggests that poets abandon all but the rhyme-words both as an economy and as a means of avoiding prosecution. He gives an example from 'A panegyrical address to a certain house':

> What
> Use
> Rot
> Abuse.

The *Morning Chronicle* would go on to fill in the blanks in a skit on the Constitutional Association:

> The Bridge-street Gang's I know not *what*
> Nor what its social *use*,
> Unless it be to favour *rot*,
> And patronise *abuse* ...[18]

No humour, however, characterized the Constitutional Association's indictment of John Hunt for 'gross, impious and slanderous' libel on the late George III on 2 December 1822, except for the plentiful quotations from the work in question, *The Vision of Judgment*. Byron offered to go and stand trial in his stead. When advised this was futile, he wrote to tell John that he would retain the famous lawyer James Scarlett, to see 'the question at least *fairly* tried – it is an important one in a general point of view – or there is an end of History' (*L&J*, x. 80). In fact, the trial was delayed until 1824, when John Hunt was found guilty but only fined £100.

In contrast to the long pedantic review-essays of the quarterlies, *The Liberal* was an entertaining miscellany. John Hunt printed 7000 copies at 5 shillings each, and a second edition, including the Preface to *The Vision*, was published on 1 January 1823. Over 4000 copies were sold altogether. This constitutes an enormous circulation for a new periodical. It was boosted, of course, by the controversy created by the outburst of unremittingly hostile reviews and then the prosecution itself. The whole panoply of a *cause celèbre* of the radical press followed. There were anonymous parodies by Tory wits such as *A Critique on 'The Liberal'*, *The London Liberal*, and *The Illiberal*, the latter sometimes attributed to Gifford. Extracts from these appeared in the newspapers. The indictment cleared the way for radicals like T.M. Rowe, William Dugdale and

W. Bumpus to pirate *The Vision* with impunity, sometimes cheekily including Southey's original as well.[19]

The second number

The second number, which came out on 1 January 1823, was half as long again as the first. It included contributions from William Hazlitt, Mary Shelley, Keats's friend Charles Armitage Brown, Shelley's friend Thomas Jefferson Hogg, as well as the original triumvirate. With Byron's approval, John Hunt paid them handsomely, at £1 a page. The leading item was Byron's poetic drama, *Heaven and Earth*. This play, even now underrated on account of its association with *The Liberal*, further develops *Cain*'s critique of authoritarian religion. Calvinist belief that only the small band of the Elect shall be saved is unmasked as an ideology of patriarchal tyranny, in an apocalyptic portrayal of the flood from which only the righteous Noah and his sons will survive. Noah tells Japhet to leave the majority to their fate:

> *Noah.* Son! son!
> If that thou would'st avoid their doom, forget
> That they exist; they soon shall cease to be,
> While thou shalt be the sire of a new world,
> And better.
>
> (Sc. iii. 493–97)

Byron's own brand of deity-defying humanism is embodied in the triumph over damnation of two female descendants of Cain, Anah and Aholibamah. Their human beauty of body and soul, unprized by the sadistic Old Testament God, draws down two angels from heaven to earth for love of them. Through profane transgressive love they are saved, swept by their immortal lovers from the rising waves and ascend to the heavens.

Had Byron's drama been accompanied, as was intended, by Shelley's 'Defence of Poetry', *The Liberal* would have been lauded by posterity. Unfortunately, the manuscript was not sent to Italy in time. Nevertheless, the journal still outclassed all rivals with this sparkling number. Percy Shelley's 'Song, Written for an Indian Air', Mary Shelley's short story 'A Tale of the Passions', and Hazlitt's brilliant demystifying of the mystique of the Crown, in 'On the Spirit of Monarchy' stand out,

but most contributions combined literary expertise with a newly infor-
mal, ironic or entertaining approach.

The Age of Bronze and *The Island*

Byron felt sufficiently committed to write two poems in January 1823
specifically for further numbers of *The Liberal*. He chose to revert to
genres reminiscent of his years of fame. *The Age of Bronze* was a topical
satire on the November 1822 Congress of the Allied Powers at Verona,
'in my early English Bards style' and 'calculated for the reading part of
the Million' (*L&J*, x. 81). *The Island* was a verse tale: a love story
between a mutineer from *The Bounty* and a native princess on a South
Sea island paradise. He wrote frankly to Hunt:

> I have two things to avoid – the first that of running foul of my own
> 'Corsair' and style – so as to produce repetition and monotony – and
> the other *not* to run counter to the reigning stupidity altogether –
> otherwise they will say that I am eulogizing *Mutiny*. – This must pro-
> duce tameness in some degree – but recollect that I am merely trying
> to write a poem a little above the usual run of periodical poesy – and
> I hope that it will at least be that; – You think higher of readers than
> I do – but I will bet you a flask of Falernum that the most *stilted*
> parts of the political 'Age of Bronze' – and the most *pamby* portions
> of the Toobonai Islanders – will be the most agreeable to the
> enlightened Public…' (*L&J*, x. 90).

It was ironic that though the second number of *The Liberal* would
receive many favourable reviews, only now did the ferocity of the attack
on the *first* number really filter through to Genoa. On 24 February
1823 Byron wrote to Mary Shelley of his astonishment at the 'continual
declamation against The Liberal from all parties – literary – amicable –
and political – I never heard so persevering an outcry against any work –
nor do I know the reason for not even dullness or demerit could autho-
rize the extraordinary tone of reprobation' (*L&J*, x. 108). Moore wrote
again deploring his friend's association with the Hunts, and meanwhile
Douglas Kinnaird took it upon himself to order John Hunt to suspend
the journal. Byron countermanded this instruction but he instructed
Kinnaird to withdraw his satire *The Age of Bronze* from *The Liberal* and
have it published separately. He would shortly afterwards withdraw *The
Island*. He had lost confidence not only in the journal but in his standing as a writer. He began to think of contributing to the liberal cause

through direct action, by travelling to Greece and supporting insurrection against the Ottoman empire. The writing was on the wall for the journal. The Hunts began to make contingency plans, such as launching a literary supplement to the *Examiner* or resurrecting *The Indicator*.

Byron requested detailed accounts from John Hunt. The second number had not covered its costs. Expenses had risen steeply because of the fees paid and the extra paper. Sales held up reasonably well, considering 2700 were sold by June. But because of over-production, 6000 having been printed, the number made a loss. Reviews acknowledged its literary quality, however, and had a more realistic number of copies been printed, and had Byron continued to support it and be seen to support it, *The Liberal* would have eventually succeeded.[20]

In his *Lord Byron and Some of his Contemporaries* (1828), written in a disaffected mood he later regretted, Leigh Hunt spitefully confirmed the allegations to which Murray referred that Byron 'expected very large returns from "The Liberal". ... He would have beheld in them the most delightful of all proofs that his reputation was not on the wane' (p. 50). Bearing in mind the precarious living the Hunts had always made from journalism, such an idea was fanciful in the extreme. In fact, Byron drew neither proprietor's profits nor writer's fees from *The Liberal,* and Leigh himself received all the profits such as there were. Moreover, by withdrawing from Murray, Byron had renounced his literary income which had been averaging about £2500 per annum. The result was that he had to make economies in his own living expenses, especially as he was settling many old debts of his youth at this time. He had sent Leigh £250 for the journey, and subsequently gave Hunt £150 or more. He paid for the family's relocation at Genoa in September 1822; offered to pay either their fare home to England or to Florence in 1823; and stood surety for John Hunt's bills which relieved his brother's debts in England (*L&J*, x. 66). Nevertheless, Byron set limits to his patronage and Hunt understandably felt humiliated by his dependent position. When the Pisan group disbanded in summer 1823, he would give vent to his resentment and Byron would reciprocate in anger.

The third and fourth numbers

The Liberal limped on for two more numbers. The third, published April 1823, featured Byron's *The Blues*, a short poem of Shelley's, and lively contributions from Leigh Hunt, Mary Shelley, Charles Brown and William Hazlitt, including the latter's 'My first acquaintance with poets'. Many reviewers thought *The Blues* too weak to be Byron's work and assumed he had pulled out. Reviewers then began to lose interest in *The Liberal*. But Byron had told the Hunts in March that he wanted to withdraw because it was his unpopularity which was causing *The Liberal* to fail: 'I am at this moment the most unpopular man in England', (*L&J*, x. 120); '...it appears that the two pieces of my contribution have precipitated that failure more than any other...The Journal, if continued (as I see no reason why it should not be), will find much more efficacious assistance in the present and other contributors than myself' (*L&J*, x. 123). Leigh Hunt himself agreed that Byron's previous poems had been too controversial: '[T]he failure of *The Liberal*, if it has failed, is no doubt partly owing to its having contained from your pen, *none* but articles of a certain character, however meritorious in themselves, and to a certain want of superinduced cordiality towards it on your part, which you unfortunately allowed to escape to the public'.[21] Leigh repeated this opinion in his *Lord Byron and Some of his Contemporaries,* though he judged *The Vision* 'the best piece of satire Lord Byron ever put forth' and moreover 'the most masterly satire that has appeared since the time of Pope' (p. 126). Byron also described it as 'one of my best things' (*L&J*, ix. 168).

Byron decided to test his popularity by publishing the two poems intended for *The Liberal* separately. Hobhouse and the Murray coterie were always trying to persuade him to revert to *Childe Harold* and the tales. But he had lost for ever his former popularity with the fashionable classes. *The Age of Bronze* sold only three thousand copies, just covering its costs. *The Island*, published on 26 June, sold better but it was not a second *Corsair*. Byron's only contribution to the fourth and final number of *The Liberal* was his translation of the first canto of *Il Morgante Maggiore* by Luigi Pulci. He had sailed for Greece before it came out at the end of July. Byron revalidated the *Childe Harold* persona by his decision to become both purse and figurehead for the Philhellenist cause. He embarked at Leghorn for Greece on 24 July 1823 to take part in the war of Independence.

John Hunt publishes *Don Juan*

Before he departed, however, Byron made arrangements with John Hunt to publish the rest of *Don Juan*. He knew this would bring him 'popularity' in terms of mere copies sold. But willing publication even by the most respectable of the radical press would put him beyond the pale for the critics, the magisterial quarterlies and the literary establishment. To underline the step he was taking, the Preface to Cantos VI, VII and

VIII made common cause with the radical press. He declared that not the latter but the Tory press were 'a dreaded Crew of Conspirators' for uniting to produce such hypocritical cant as their sympathy for Castlereagh's suicide. They would have been glad of the opportunity to bury radicals like Samuel Waddington (the diminutive clown of carnivalesque street-politics, sentenced in 1822 to a year's imprisonment for selling a deist tract) or James Watson (salesman for Carlile) at a crossroad with stake and mallet, should they have committed suicide. Byron links himself with the 'millions' who considered Castlereagh 'the most despotic in intention and the weakest in intellect that ever tyrannized over a country' (ll. 21–2). His Voltairean defence of the earlier cantos of *Don Juan* against charges of immorality leads straight into a reference to the infamous imprisonment from 1819–25 of 'the wretched Infidel', Richard Carlile, for selling the works of Thomas Paine. Though 'with his opinions I have nothing to do', the poet proclaims that the 'title of Blasphemer', as well as 'radical, liberal, Jacobin, reformer &c.' should be welcome to those who remember they were also bestowed on Socrates and Jesus Christ.

Cantos VI–VIII followed the libertine comedy of the Turkish harem with a blistering anatomy of the sexual politics of monarchical imperialism. The Turkish Sultan and the Russian Empress use their armies to prostitute others to their power as they do in their respective palaces full of sex-slaves. In depicting the Siege of Ismail (1790), Byron was also commenting specifically on the contemporary support Britain was giving dynastic imperialism including Russia in the 'Holy Alliance'. Though Dissenters like Anna Barbauld had expressed pacificist sentiments in their poetry in the Napoleonic period, Byron's depiction of the Siege of Ismail would be the first major anti-war poem in English literature. He used a combination of graphic realism and satire to demystify the ideology of militarist patriotism in this anti-epic published in all the self-congratulatory atmosphere of the years after Waterloo.

> The reeking bayonet and the flashing blade
> Clashed 'gainst the scymitar, and babe and mother
> With distant shrieks were heard Heaven to upbraid; –
> Still closer sulphury clouds began to smother ...
> (VIII, 69)

Byron had become thoroughly businesslike in preparing his poems for publication, making sure he systematically corrected the proofs of each canto of *Don Juan*. He delayed letting John Hunt publish *Don Juan* because he thought the firm too small to handle the large circulation he expected: 'The principal objections I believe may probably be want of Capital – and of that mercantile influence by which publishers on a large scale are enabled to (what they call) *"push* a work"...' (*L&J*, x. 160). He wanted to tap a mass readership. Unlike Murray, Hunt took seriously Byron's suggestion of a small cheap edition in addition to the octavo. It is obvious that Byron himself worked closely with John Hunt to tailor the production of *Don Juan* to an entirely new lower-class readership. He did not sell his copyright but took the risk himself. Though he offered John 50 per cent of any profits, the upright old radical would only take 15 per cent. Hunt entirely abandoned Murray's provision of Byron as a luxury commodity to the genteel classes. Each of the four volumes was brought out in three sizes: demy octavo at 9s 6d, foolscap octavo at 7s and 'the common edition' or 18mo. at the startlingly low price of 1s.[22] The latter was poorly bound in thin wrappers, and few have survived despite the immense numbers produced. When Cantos VI, VII and VIII came out on 15 July 1823, only 1500 were printed of the demy octavo, 3000 of the foolscap octavo, but 16,000 of the 'common edition'. They had presumably calculated their target readership fairly well, for when Cantos IX, X, and XI came out on 29 August, the quantity of the foolscap octavo was slightly reduced to 2500 and the 'common' increased to 17,000. Cantos XII, XIII and XIV would follow on 1 December, and XV and XVI on 26 March 1824, in similar fashion.

The new policy made the official copies seriously competitive with the piracies, but these nevertheless continued to flourish up to 1832. Only four days after publication of the first volume, Hunt was granted an injunction against Hodgson, and a fortnight later prosecuted William Dugdale. Dugdale, who specialized in publishing libertine literature, read out salacious passages from Canto VIII which persuaded the court to refuse the injunction and let him proceed to sell his edition in peace! [23] Pirates like Benbow and Sudbury also brought out the new cantos, and after the poet's death in 1824 others even offered the complete poem, which neither Hunt nor Murray could do while obeying the copyright law.[24] For *Don Juan* had taken its place as a radical classic and Byron's poetry in general now became an indispensable part of the library of the common reader.

Postscript

To Thomas Moore:

Sir,– With great grief I inform you of the death of my late dear Master, my Lord, who died this morning at ten of the Clock of a rapid decline and slow fever, caused by anxiety, sea-bathing, women, and riding in the Sun against my advice.– He is a dreadful loss to everybody, mostly to me – who have lost a master and a place – also I hope you – Sir – will give me a charakter. – I saved in his service as you know several hundred pounds – God knows how – for I don't, nor my late master neither – and if my wage was not always paid to the day – still it was or is to be paid sometime and somehow – you – Sir – who are his executioner won't see a poor Servant wronged of his little all.... He suffered his illness with great patience – except when in extremity he twice damned his friends & said they were selfish rascals – you – Sir – particularly & Mr. Kinnaird – who had never answered his letters nor complied with his repeated requests.... His nine whores are already provided for & the other servants – but what is to become of me – I have got his Cloathes & Carriages – & Cash – & everything – but the Consul quite against law has clapt his seal & taken an inven*tary* & swears that *he* must account to my Lord's heirs – who they are – I don't know – but they ought to consider poor Servants & above all his Vally de Sham.... Hope you are well Sir – am with tears in my eyes

Yours faithfully to command
Wm. Fletcher

P.S. If you know any Gentleman in want of a Wally – hope for a charakter – I saw your late Swiss Servant in the Galleys at Leghorn for robbing an Inn – he produced your recommendation at his trial.

(*L&J*, vi. 44–5)

There can be few writers who have attempted to describe their own passing, and fewer still with the uncanny knack of correctly predicting the malady which would carry them off, as Byron did in this spoof epistle sent to Moore in 1818 to protest at his friend's failure to answer his letters. Byron did die of fever but in the swamp-infested town of Missolonghi on 19 April 1824 during the Greek revolution. Fletcher, Byron's faithful valet, was not quite so self-obsessed in his actual account of his master's last instructions (recorded by Edward Blaquiere), and his dying master summoned up enough strength to tease him to the last:

I then said, 'Shall I go my lord, and fetch pen, ink, and paper? 'Oh! My God, no – you will lose too much time, and I have it not to spare, for my time is now short,' said his lordship; and immediately after, 'Now pay attention'; his lordship commenced by saying, 'You will be provided for.' I begged him, however, to proceed with things of more consequence, he then continued, 'Oh, my poor dear child! – my dear Ada! My God, could I but have seen her! Give her my blessing – and my dear sister Augusta and her children; – and you will go to Lady Byron, and say – tell her everything – you are friends with her.' His lordship appeared to be greatly affected at this moment. Here my master's voice failed him, so that I could only catch a word at intervals, but he kept muttering something very seriously for some time, and would often raise his voice and say, 'Fletcher, now if you do not execute every order which I have given you, I will torment you hereafter if possible.

(*Life*, iii. 1227–28)

Like many other Philhellenes, Byron succumbed to fever rather than warfare itself. As he himself mordantly prophesied, his actual demise was accomplished by the doctors, who purged him until he could not stand and then applied leeches to his temples all night long when he was asleep and could not protest. It was not a glorious death, yet the shock that this charismatic poet had been struck down at the height of his powers endowed the cause of Greek nationalism with an aura of heroism it had done little to deserve. It also had the effect of re-igniting the flame of Byronism even in his homeland, where his alliance with the radicals had put him beyond the respectable pale.

Byron had also imagined his own death in romantic terms when in conversation with Lady Blessington: 'Yes! A grassy bed in Greece, and a grey stone to mark the spot, would please me more than a marble tomb in Westminster Abbey' (*HVSV*, p. 367). Yet he had ironized his own sentimentalism in the presentation of the lyric 'The Isles of Greece'. This pastiche of modern patriotic songs by Greek nationalists like Athanasios Christopoulos and Konstantin Rigas, was originally composed in 1812 and when the Greek revolution began in 1821 it was revised, expanded and interpolated in *Don Juan* Canto III. It begins:

> The isles of Greece, the isles of Greece!
> Where burning Sappho loved and sung,
> Where grew the arts of war and peace, –
> Where Delos rose, and Phoebus sprung!
> Eternal summer gilds them yet,
> But all, except their sun, is set.
>
> (III, 689–94)

The Greeks are then taunted with the traditional Philhellenist accusation of having degenerated from the heroism of Marathon to their present-day servility. The poet concludes with his intention of dying 'on Sunium's marbled steep' like a swan while still singing, and thus inspiring his Greek listeners to throw down their wine and seize their 'native swords'. Byron contextualizes this romantic gesture however. The author of this call for freedom is described as an untrustworthy turncoat: a Greek Monti or Southey (III, 79). Indeed all poets are 'such liars' / And take all colours – like the hands of dyers' (III, 87). To complicate its emotional effect still further, stanzas III, 82–6 on the singer are bitterly self-referential and remind us of the author of *Childe Harold, Hebrew Melodies* and *The Prophecy of Dante* himself:

> Thus, usually, when he was ask'd to sing,
> He gave the different nations something national;
> 'Twas all the same to him...
>
> (III, 85)

In the event, the impassioned stanzas of the song advocating revolution to obtain liberty, enshrining its singer's deepest political beliefs which have so long lain dormant, are received as no more than a maudlin drinking song at Juan's and Haidée's court. The caustic irony of the fictional context of 'The Isles of Greece' is not merely cynical, however. For Byron places idealistic faith in the emotive power of the song itself to outlast its original context and to achieve political change, to outlive its author, whose inconsistency and personal failings are ultimately irrelevant:

> But words are things, and a small drop of ink,
> Falling like dew, upon a thought, produces
> That which makes thousands, perhaps millions, think...
>
> (III, 88)

In 1820 and 1821 it had indeed seemed that the writing was on the wall for the reinstitution of the *ancien régime* in Europe by the Congress of Vienna (1815). Sporadic nationalist uprisings broke out all round the Mediterranean: in Spain, Portugal, Naples, Piedmont, and Sicily. All were short-lived, however, like that in the Romagna in which Byron had himself participated. So when the Greek revolt began there was a feeling that this was the last but also perhaps the best chance to create a constitutional nation-state embodying those ideals which had inspired the French Revolution but derived their historical credibility from the classical republican tradition. Ex-Bonapartists, failed Italian revolutionaries and liberals from all over the West turned their eyes to Greece in 1821. P.B. Shelley composed *Hellas*, and Byron's earlier poetry was once more in demand.

In 1822, George Canning, who himself published a poem entitled *The Slavery of Greece* (1823), became foreign secretary and was more supportive to British campaigners than Castlereagh had been, from inclination as well as British self-interest. Philhellenism evidently could appeal across the political spectrum. Nevertheless, as William St. Clair has pointed out, there was only one Tory on the London Greek Committee, which was founded in March 1823.[1] There were men from every shade of Whig and radical opinion, but the leading lights were radicals or Benthamites such as Joseph Hume, Sir Francis Burdett, Edward Ellice, and John Cam Hobhouse. One of their first acts was to send a propagandist, Edward Blaquiere, to Italy with the object of persuading Byron to put his name to the cause.

As they had anticipated, Byron readily promised his assistance and his name henceforth became the primary means of attracting volunteers and raising funds. Hobhouse then encouraged him to visit the Ionian islands and the mainland itself prior to the expedition of the British Philhellenes with arms and skilled men which would sail in November.

The twin aims of Byron's journey were to be gathering information about the progress of the uprising for the Committee and giving moral support to the insurgents. The Committee made public Byron's acquiescence so that it would have been humiliating for him to change his mind. However, once in Greece he decided to stay until the outcome of the insurgence was determined.

Teresa's hotheaded young brother, Count Pietro Gamba, accompanied him as well as Edward Trelawny. The poet managed to raise 10,000 Spanish dollars in cash and obtained bills of exchange for 40,000 more from his personal wealth for the cause (*Life,* iii. 1087). He sailed from Leghorn on 24 July 1823 in his own 120 ton ship aptly named the *Hercules.* Like Hercules, and like his own tragi-comic hero, Sardanapalus, who called for a mirror before leading his troops to battle, Byron was both attempting to prove his masculinity as a warrior and absurdly concerned with his appearance. He, who had so effectively denounced imperial warfare in *Don Juan,* now had two gilt Homeric helmets made to his own ostentatious designs, embellished with his coat of arms and motto 'Crede Byron'. Other military equipage included: four scarlet full dress uniforms trimmed with gold lace, gold lace shoulder knots, sword knots, silver and gold epaulets, silk sashes, plumed dress hats, ornamented caps, various guns, ten swords and a swordstick (*Life,* iii. 1098). George Finlay, a British Philhellene and future historian, recalled the bisexuality of his character, 'It seemed as if two different souls occupied his body alternately. One was feminine, and full of sympathy; the other masculine, and characterized by clear judgment, and by a rare power of presenting for consideration those facts only which were required for forming a decision. When one arrived the other departed' (*Life,* iii. 1122).

Byron was particularly clear-sighted about the disparity between the dreams of Hellas inspiring classically-educated European volunteers like himself and the primitive tribalism of the actual Romaic inhabitants who only united temporarily to fight what they saw as a religious war of exterminating Mohammedans. When he landed at Cephalonia, he received confused accounts of the uprising. After the early successes of the insurgents and the election as first president of Alexander Mavrocordato there had been Turkish reprisals as well as internal division. Byron saw immediately that his first task was to raise a loan to finance the new government, but to be administered by the British. The news of the English lord's presence caused a storm of excitement, for the British support and money he represented was crucial to each faction jostling for precedence. When the poet arrived in Missolonghi in January 1824 he was greeted with cheers and a twenty-one gun salute, 'the sight of the fleet saluting &c. and the crowds and different costumes was really picturesque' (*L&J*, xi. 92). He put himself at the head of a brigade of fierce Suliotes (Albanians) attired in their traditional costume, but as time went on he became depressed by their unruly and mutinous behaviour, and the continual demands for money he met on all sides. William Parry, a working-class Navy firemaster employed to set up an arsenal, with whom Byron struck up a rollicking drinking friendship (and whom Augusta, when she met him in London, reported to be 'a most *vulgar rough Bearish* person'), perceptively described this period as 'the most ennobling, and perhaps the most humiliating period of his existence'.[2] Byron had no privacy and few aristocratic comforts, he lived in the same building as the other officers. Parry described him as typically rising at nine, and receiving reports and issuing orders for the day over breakfast. He then inspected the accounts meticulously with his secretary. Then he would ride out and practise pistol-shooting, before the daily visit of Prince Mavrocordato and the Primates. After dinner he drilled and exercised with the officers, before retiring with them for the evening, sometimes studying military tactics. From eleven until four in the morning he read and wrote in solitude (Parry, *Last Days*, pp. 77–80).

Parry's book on Byron was ghost-written by his friend the working-class activist Thomas Hodgskin, author of *Labour Defended against the Claims of Capital* (1825) and one of the founders of the London Mechanics' Institution. It was overtly hostile to the other agent appointed by the London Greek Committee, with whom Byron collaborated in organizing the expedition, and portrayed him as critical of the poet.[3] The Honourable Leicester Stanhope was a lieutenant-colonel in the British army yet paradoxically was also a paternalistic Utilitarian who prioritized the setting up of a free press, and schools and legal codes over immediate military success. But though he and Byron argued over strategy, both were of a type – the eccentric aristocratic republican Philhellene – and they always respected each other. Parry and Hodgskin's book mythologizing the supposed split between the Romantic poet Byron and the Benthamite Stanhope, was clearly a product of the radical artisans' own struggle for independence from paternalistic bourgeois liberalism. However, it demonstrates to what an extent the aristocratic poet had been already adopted as the symbol of freedom by working-class activists. Parry's book depicts Byron saying that the United States of America should form the model for the new government of Greece:

> I will not say a federation of republics; but a federation of states;
> each of these states having that particular form of government most

suitable to the present situation and wishes of its people...In the islands and on the Continent wealth and power are very differently distributed, and the governments are conducted on different principles. It would be absurd, therefore, and perhaps impossible, to give the islands and the continent the same sort of government....Each state might be represented in a congress, and a president elected every four years in succession, from one of the three or four great divisions of the whole federation....No system of government in any part of Greece can be permanent, which does not leave in the hands of the peasantry the chief part of the political power. They are warmly attached to their country and they are the best portion of the people.

(Parry, The Last Days, pp. 174–6)

By the time of his illness it was evident to Byron that there was every prospect of civil war breaking out and little sign of the Greeks acquiring any sense of unifying nationalism. The expedition would be a failure. After fighting depression and fever for several weeks he died on 19 April, just days before the arrival of Blaquiere with the first instalment of the loan he had arranged.

Byron wrote little poetry while in Greece. The poignant 'On This Day I Complete My Thirty-Sixth Year' is the best known of three agonized lyrics written out of the poet's unreciprocated 'Greek love' for his fifteen-year-old pageboy, Lukas Chalandritsanos.[4] Byron had rescued the boy's mother and sisters, refugees left destitute after fleeing savage warfare in Patras, and Lukas had later applied to join them. Byron had also rescued a little Turkish girl, Hataké, oddly replicating his hero's action in *Don Juan*. When questioned by the suspicious Hobhouse after the poet's death about Byron's relationship with Lukas, Pietro Gamba characterized it as an excess of aristocratic patronage *cum* paternal protectiveness:

During the voyage and the residence at Missolonghi he watched with [such] particular care over this youth that one might call it a weakness. He gave him splendid clothes, arms and money; and he passed some half-hour every day with him reading Modern Greek. He took him with us in the cavalcade, and in the end he gave him the command of 30 irregular soldiers of his own brigade. On one occasion when this boy had a somewhat dangerous illness, My lord was pleased to give up his own bed and slept in the common room with us on a Turkish divan for 3 or four days.[5]

The poem which was probably the last but one the poet wrote appears below. Each verse depicts an actual incident from Byron's life: the attack on the ship on their voyage to Missolonghi when Byron feared both for the boy's life and possible violation at the hands of the Turks (*L&J*, xi. 87); the storm which followed when they hit the rocks; Lukas struck down with fever; an earthquake that shook the town that February; and the fit that heralded Byron's fatal illness. The poem is an autobiographical expression of the pathos of middle-aged unreciprocated passion for youth and beauty and at the same time a re-enactment of the homoerotic bonding of the Greek warriors of old:

> I watched thee when the foe was at our side,
> Ready to strike at him – or thee and me
> Were safety hopeless – rather than divide
> Aught with one loved – save love and liberty.
>
> I watched thee on the breakers – when the rock
> Received our prow – and all was storm and fear,
> And bade thee cling to me through every shock –
> This arm would be thy bark – or breast thy bier.
>
> I watched thee when the fever glazed thine eyes –
> Yielding my couch – and stretched me on the ground –
> When overworn with watching – ne'er to rise
> From thence – if thou an early grave hadst found.
>
> The Earthquake came, and rocked the quivering wall –
> And men and nature reeled as if with wine –
> Whom did I seek around the tottering hall –
> For *thee* – whose safety first provide for – thine.
>
> And when convulsive throes denied my breath
> The faintest utterance to my fading thought –
> To thee – to thee – even in the grasp of death
> My Spirit turned, Ah! oftener than it ought.
>
> Thus much and more – and yet thou lov'st me not,
> And never wilt – Love dwells not in our will –
> Nor can I blame thee – though it be my lot
> To strongly – wrongly – vainly – love thee still –

Notes

Preface

1. Edward John Trelawny, *Records of Shelley, Byron and the Author*, Harmondsworth, 1972, p. 87.
2. Laura Marcus, *Auto/Biographical Discourses: Theory, Criticism, Practice* (Manchester, 1994), p. 29.
3. Michel Foucault, *The Archaeology of Knowledge* (London, 1972), p. 45.

Prelude

1. On the possibility of Captain Byron's incestuous love for his sister, see A.L. Rowse, *The Byrons and the Trevanions* (London, 1978), p. 151.
2. Quoted in *The Byrons and the Trevanions*, p. 124.

1. The noble poet and 'the Trade'

1. Quoted in Scott Bennett, 'John Murray's family Library and the Cheapening of Books in Early Nineteenth Century Britain', *Studies in Bibliography*, 29 (1976),139–66, 139.
2. Samuel Smiles, *Memoir and correspondence of the late John Murray with an account of the origin and progress of the house, 1768–1843* (London, 1891) i. 101. Henceforth referred to as *Smiles,* and cited within the text.
3. *Byron's Letters and Journals*, ed. Leslie A. Marchand, 12 vols (London, 1973–94), ii. 344–5. Henceforth abbreviated to *L&J*, and cited within the text.
4. *Lord Byron: The Complete Poetical Works*, ed. Jerome J. McGann, 7 vols (Oxford, 1980–1993) i. 32. Henceforth abbreviated to *CPW* and cited within the text.
5. R.C Dallas, *Recollections of the Life of Lord Byron* (London, 1825), p. 150. Henceforth abbreviated to *Dallas* and cited within the text.
6. Willis W. Pratt, *Byron at Southwell: the Making of a Poet* (New York, 1973), p. 29.
7. For details of the contemporary reviews of Byron's poems, see: William S. Ward, *Literary Reviews in British Periodicals 1798–1820: a Bibliography*, 2 vols (New York and London, 1972), i. 185–93.
8. *Eclectic Review*, 3 (November, 1807), 989–93. See William S. Ward, 'Byron's *Hours of Idleness* and other than Scotch reviewers', *Modern Language Notes*, 59 (December 1944), 547–50.
9. For example, on 16 September 1811, he wrote to John Murray: 'I return the proof, which I should wish to be shown to Mr. Dallas, who understands typographical arrangements much better that I can pretend to do. The printer may place the notes in his *own way*, or in any *way*, so that they are out of *my way*; I care nothing about types or margins' (*L&J*, i. 100).
10. Jerome J. McGann, *Fiery Dust: Byron's Poetic Development* (Chicago, 1968), p. 5.
11. Leslie A. Marchand, *Byron: a Biography*, 3 vols (New York, 1957), i. 16. Henceforth abbreviated to *Life* and cited within the text.

12. *Edinburgh Review*, 11 (January 1808), reprinted in Caroline Franklin (ed.), *The Wellesley Series IV: British Romantic Poets*, 6 vols (London, 1998) ii. 653–7.

13. *Medwin's Conversations of Lord Byron*, ed. Ernest J. Lovell Jr (Princeton, N.J., 1966), p. 142. Henceforth abbreviated to *Medwin* and cited within the text.

14. Gary Dyer, *British Satire and the Politics of Style 1789–1832* (Cambridge, 1997), p. 43.

15. Cawthorn had agreed to take on all the expense and risk in return for half the profits on an edition of a thousand copies, though Byron left all the profits to the publisher. The copyright was retained by the author. See Dallas, *Recollections*, p. 41.

16. Frederick L. Beaty, *Byron the Satirist* (Dekalb, Ill., 1985), p. 38.

17. He wrote to Dallas from Constantinople: 'I heard the other day that my Satire was in a third edition; that is but a poor progress, but Cawthorn published too many copies in the first' (*L&J*, i. 248).

18. The *Literary Journal*, 1:4 (19 April 1818), 49–50; article continued 3 May, pp. 86–7 and 10 May, pp. 98–9.

19. He wrote to Scott: 'The satire was written when I was very young & very angry, & fully bent on displaying my wrath & my wit, & now I am haunted by the ghosts of my wholesale Assertions' (*L&J*, i. 182).

20. Andrew Rutherford, *Byron: a Critical Study* (London, 1961), p. 23.

21. Mary Clearman, 'A Blueprint for *English Bards and Scotch Reviewers*: the First Satire of Juvenal', *Keats-Shelley Journal*, 19 (1970), 87–99, p. 89. See also William Christie, 'Running with the English Hares and Hunting with the Scotch Bloodhounds', *The Byron Journal*, 25 (1997), 23–31, p. 29.

22. See Lord Cockburn, *Life of Lord Jeffrey, with a Selection from his Correspondence*, 2 vols (Edinburgh, 1852), i. 67; and Walter Graham, *English Literary Periodicals* (New York, 1930), pp. 233–6.

23. The *Satirist* in July 1809 quotes the complaint of the *Edinburgh Review*: 'The various attacks of the Edinburgh Review, which have appeared during the last six months, partly in prose,* partly in *some other sort of writing not exactly resembling prose*, would, if collected, make a volume of no ordinary weight; and, as far as we have had patience to peruse these things, *considerably exceeding in stupidity* any equal mass of controversial matter formerly produced.'

    *Alluding to Mr. Wharton's pamphlet, reviewed in our seventeenth number (Vol.IV. p. 184.) – *Satirist*. The reviewer italicizes this passage as referring to *English Bards and Scotch Reviewers*, the subject of the selection of 'Comparative Criticism'.

24. Cockburn, *Life of Lord Jeffrey*, i. 280.

25. *Eclectic Review*, 5 (May 1809), 482–84. See also Peter J. Manning, 'Byron's *English Bards and Scotch Reviewers*: The Art of Allusion', *Keats–Shelley Memorial Bulletin*, 21 (1970), 7–11.

26. 'Art XIV. Don Pedro Cevallos on the French usurpation of Spain', *Edinburgh Review*, 25 (October 1808), 215–54.

27. Edgar Johnson, *Sir Walter Scott: the Great Unknown*, 2 vols (London, 1970), i. 300. *Letters of Sidney Smith*, ed. Nowell C. Smith (London, 1953), i. 152.

28. 'Review of *English Bards and Scotch Reviewers*', *Anti-Jacobin Review* 32 (March 1809), 301–306, reprinted in Donald Reiman (ed.), *The Romantics Reviewed*, Part B, 5 vols (New York, 1972), i. 5–8, p. 6.

29. The similarity of Jeffrey's and Byron's literary judgements and the possibility that Byron's satire was influenced by his reading of the *Edinburgh Review* are discussed by Muriel Mellown, 'Francis Jeffrey, Lord Byron, and *English Bards and Scotch Reviewers*', *Studies in Scottish Literature*, 16 (1981), 80–90; see also William Christie, 'Byron and Francis Jeffrey', *The Byron Journal*, 25 (1997), 32–43. For a detailed examination of the aesthetic philosophy of the *Edinburgh Review*, see James A. Greig, *Francis Jeffrey of the* Edinburgh Review (London, 1948); 'The *Edinburgh Review* and Poetic Truth', *Costerus*, n.s. 16 1978 (Amsterdam, 1979).

30. On 2 November 1808, he wrote to his mother: ' ... it is from *experience* not *Books*, we ought to judge of mankind. – There is nothing like inspection & trusting to our own senses' (*L&J*, i. 172–3).

31. McGann, '"My brain is feminine": Byron and the poetry of deception', in Andrew Rutherford (ed.), *Byron: Augustan and Romantic* (Basingstoke, 1990), pp. 26–51, p. 29; Robert F. Gleckner, *Byron and the Ruins of Paradise* (Westport, Conn., 1967), p. 29.

2. The traveller from the East meets the 'Emperor of the West'

1. Letter to George and Georgiana Keats, Friday 17 – Monday 27 September, 1819, *The Letters of John Keats*, ed. Maurice Buxton Forman (Oxford, 1947), p. 413.

2. Quoted by Allan Massie, *Byron's Travels* (London, 1988), p. 31.

3. Diego Saglia, *Byron and Spain: Itinerary in the Writing of Place* (New York and Salzburg, 1996), pp. 12–13.

4. See Harold Wiener, 'Byron and the East: Literary Sources of the "Turkish tales"', in Herbert Davis, W.C. Vane, and R.C. Bald (eds), *Nineteenth Century Studies Dedicated to C.S. Northup* (New York, 1940), pp. 89–129.

5. See Terence Spencer, *Fair Greece, Sad Relic: Literary Philhellenism from Shakespeare to Byron* (London, 1954), pp. 247–94.

6. On the relationship between Byron's travels 1809–1811 and his poetry, see William A. Borst, *Lord Byron's First Pilgrimage* (New Haven and London, 1948); and on Spain, Saglia, *Byron and Spain*; see also Gordon Kent Thomas, *Lord Byron's Iberian Pilgrimage* (Provo, Utah, 1983); Allan Massie, *Byron's Travels* (London, 1988).

7. James Kennedy, *Conversations on religion with Lord Byron and others, held in Cephalonia* (London, 1830), pp. 166–7. Henceforth abbreviated to *Kennedy* and cited within the text.

8. Leigh Hunt, *Lord Byron and Some of his Contemporaries* (London, 1828), p. 31. Henceforth abbreviated to *LBC* and cited within the text.

9. Murray wrote to George Canning as early as 25 September 1807 proposing to set up a rival publication to counteract the 'dangerous tendency' of the *Edinburgh*. Stratford Canning introduced Murray to William Gifford in 1808. On the setting up of the *Quarterly*, see *Smiles*, i. 91–124.

10. See A.H. Qureshi, 'The *Edinburgh Review* and poetic truth', *Costerus*, ns 16 1978 (Amsterdam, 1979); Peter Morgan, *Literary Critics and Reviewers in Early Nineteenth Century Britain* (London and Canberra, 1983), chapter 1.

11. See James Buzard, *Beaten Track: European Tourism and the ways to Culture 1800–1918* (Oxford, 1993); Peter J. Manning, 'Childe Harold in the marketplace: From Romaunt to handbook', *Modern Language Quarterly*, 52 (1991), 170–90.

12. Frank Arthur Mumby, *Publishing and Bookselling: Part One: from the Earliest Times to 1870* (London, 1930, repr. 1974), p. 174; *Smiles*, i. 1–29.

13. *The News of Literature*, 10 December 1825. Quoted by Tim Chilcott, *A Publisher and his Circle: the Life and Work of John Taylor, Keats's Publisher* (London and Boston, 1972), p. 199.

14. See A.S Collins, *The Profession of Letters: a Study of the Relation of Author to Patron, Publisher and Public, 1780–1832* (Clifton, 1928 repr 1973), p. 133.

15. Collins, *The Profession of Letters*, p. 136.

16. See Victor Bonham–Carter, *Authors By Profession* (London, 1978), i. 43.

17. Collins, *The Profession of Letters*, pp. 171–6.

18. Simon Eliot, 'Some trends in British book production, 1800–1919', in John O. Jordan and Robert L. Patten (eds), *Literature in the Marketplace: Nineteenth-Century British Publishing and Reading Practices* (Cambridge, 1995), pp. 19–43, p. 36.

19. See Richard D. Altick, *The English Common Reader: a Social History of the Mass Reading Public 1800–1900* (Chicago, 1957), pp. 260–2.

20. Charles Knight, *The Old Printer and the Modern Press* (London, 1854), p. 239.

21. Altick, *The English Common Reader*, p. 260.

22. See Collins, *The Profession of Letters*, p. 172, Bonham–Carter, *Authors By Profession*, p. 48.

23. Edward John Trelawny, *Records of Shelley, Byron and the Author* (Harmondsworth, 1973), p. 221. Compare 'I am like the tyger (in poesy), if I miss my first Spring, I go growling back to my jungle. There is no second. I can't correct.' (*L&J*, v. 120); but also his admission of the importance of reading to compositon in Countess of Blessington, *Conversations of Lord Byron*, ed. E.J. Lovell Jr. (London and New York, 1969), p. 207, henceforth abbreviated to *Blessington*.

24. Ian Jack, *The Poet and his Audience* (Cambridge, 1984), p. 67.

25. See Peter Manning, 'The Hone-ing of Byron's *Corsair*', *Reading Romantics* (New York and Oxford, 1990), pp. 216–37.

26. The best account of this relationship is Roy Benjamin Clark, *William Gifford: Tory Satirist, Critic, and Editor* (New York, 1930), pp. 201–10. See also J.D. Jump, 'Lord Byron and William Gifford', *Bulletin of John Rylands University Library of Manchester*, 57 (1975), 310–26.

27. A facsimile of the appendix is available in an article attacking McGann's editorial decision not to print it in full in *CPW*: Roger Poole, 'What constitutes, and what is external to, the "real" text of Byron's *Childe Harold's Pilgrimage, a Romaunt: and Other Poems* (1812)?' in *Lord Byron the European: Essays from the International Byron Society*, ed. Richard A. Cardwell (New York, Lampeter, and Queenston, Ont., 1997), pp. 149–208.

28. A more extended discussion of the way gender operates in the poem may be found in my 'Cosmopolitan masculinity and the British Female Reader of *Childe Harold's Pilgrimage*', in Cardwell, pp. 105–26.

29. Malcolm Elwin, *Lord Byron's Wife* (London, 1962), p. 106.

30. Louis Crompton, *Byron and Greek Love: Homophobia in Nineteenth-Century England* (London, 1985), pp. 158–95.

3. The acting of tragedy and the tragedy of acting

1. George Steiner, *The Death of Tragedy* (London, 1961), pp. 201–2.
2. John P. Farrell, *Revolution as Tragedy: The Dilemma of the Moderate from Scott to Arnold* (Ithaca, NY, and London, 1980); Jeffrey N. Cox, *In the Shadows of Romance: Romantic Tragic Drama in Germany, England and France* (Athens, Ohio, 1987).
3. Cox, *In the Shadows of Romance*, p. 25.
4. Thomas Moore, *Memoirs of the Life of the Right Honourable Richard Brinsley Sheridan* (London, 1825), ii. 368–9.
5. See Joseph Donohue, *Theatre in the Age of Kean* (Oxford, 1975), p. 2.
6. I am indebted to John Russell Stephens for this point.
7. Watson Nicholson, *The Struggle for a Free Stage in London* (New York, 1906 repr. 1966), pp. 189–91.
8. 19 November 1809, reprinted in: *Leigh Hunt's Dramatic Criticism 1808–1831*, edited by Lawrence Huston Houtchens and Carolyn Washburn Houtchens (London, 1950), p. 33.
9. Nicholson, *The Struggle for a Free Stage in London*, pp. 200–23.
10. The *Examiner*, 27 January 1831. Reprinted in: *Leigh Hunt's Dramatic Criticism 1808–1831*, p. 257.
11. Donohue, *Theatre in the Age of Kean*, p. 56.
12. Nicholson, *The Struggle for a Free Stage in London*, chapter 9.
13. The *Examiner*, 21 July 1811. Reprinted in *Leigh Hunt's Dramatic Criticism 1808–1831*, p. 50.
14. On Whitbread's plans for Drury Lane I am indebted to Richard Lansdown, *Byron's Historical Dramas* (Oxford, 1992), chapter 1.
15. See John Russell Stephens, *The Profession of the Playwright: British Theatre 1800–1900* (Cambridge, 1992), p. 30; Donohue, *Theatre in the Age of Kean*, pp. 57–8.
16. *Specimens of the Table Talk of the late Samuel Taylor Coleridge* (1835), i. 24.
17. On this proposal and reactions to it, see Lansdown, *Byron's Historical Dramas*, pp. 28–9.
18. *Medwin*, p. 92.
19. For a list of pamphlets and satires by and concerning the amateur committee, see: Robert W. Lowe, James Fullarton Arnott and John William Robinson, *English Theatrical Literature 1559–1900* (London, 1970), pp. 137–8.
20. *Medwin*, p. 138.
21. *The Collected Letters of Samuel Taylor Coleridge*, ed. Earl Leslie Griggs 6 vols (Oxford, 1959), iv. 580, hereafter cited as *CLSTC*.
22. *CLSTC*, iv. 598.
23. *CLSTC*, iv. 605.
24. *Life*, ii. 555.
25. *CLSTC*, iv. 222.
26. *Medwin*, p. 95.
27. Margaret J. Howell, *Byron Tonight: A Poet's Plays on the Nineteenth Century Stage* (Windlesham, Surrey, 1982), p. 148; 158.
28. Howell, *Byron Tonight*, p. 159.
29. John Russell Stephens, *The Profession of the Playwright*, p. 119. Byron's influence was probably responsible for the fact Murray's list concentrated on tragedy. He also persuaded Murray to publish *The Magpie, or, Maid*

of Palaiseau, a French melodrama translated by Concanen, promising, 'I won't ask you to publish any more for D[rury] L[ane]'and suggesting what good sales Murray will have from Sotheby's *Ivan* if it succeeds on the stage (*L&J*, iv. 315).

30. Cox, *In the Shadows of Romance*, p. 42.
31. For information on nineteenth-century performances of Byron's plays throughout this chapter I am much indebted to Margaret J. Howell, *Byron Tonight*; see also, *CPW*, vi. 579–96.
32. Michael Simpson, *Closet Performances: Political Exhibition and Prohibition in the Dramas of Byron and Shelley* (Stanford, California, 1998), p. 112.
33. See Thomas L. Ashton, 'The Censorship of Byron's *Marino Faliero*', *Huntington Library Quarterly*, 36 (1972–3), 27–44, to whom I am indebted for details of the censorship of the text which follow.
34. Howell, *Byron Tonight*, p. 20.
35. David V. Erdman, 'Byron's stage fright: the history of his ambition and fear of writing for the stage', *English Literary History* 6 (September 1939), 219–43.
36. *CPW*, vi. 582, Ashton, 'The Censorship of Byron's *Marino Faliero*', p. 40.
37. Howell, *Byron Tonight*, p. 30.
38. *Medwin*, pp. 120, 123, 135. American productions of *Marino Faliero* included a production in New York in 1821 which only ran for four nights (*CPW*, viii. 582). *The Two Foscari* was performed in Baltimore in 1822 and Philadelphia in 1842, but appears not to have been extremely popular. The play was transformed into a successful opera by Verdi, with a libretto by Franceso Maria Piave, and was first performed in Rome on 3 November 1844. In 1865, Charles Calvert successfully produced a condensed adaptation of *The Two Foscari* in Manchester with incidental music from Verdi's opera. This was a critical success but only ran for six nights.
39. For Byron's outline of a possible second part, see *Medwin*, p. 156–7.

4. From pilgrim to patriot: Byron as poet of exile

1. Hilary Fraser, *The Victorians and Renaissance Italy* (Oxford, 1992), p. 148.
2. Roderick Marshall, *Italy in English Literature 1755–1815: Origins of the Romantic Interest in Italy* (New York, 1934), p. 173; see also C.P. Brand, *Italy and the English Romantics: the Italianate Fashion in Early Nineteenth-Century England* (Cambridge, 1957).
3. Hester Thrale Piozzi commented, 'While they pretend to whine as if despotism displeased them, they detest every republican state, feel envy towards Venice and contempt for Lucca'. *Observations and Reflections made in the course of a journey through France, Italy, and Germany*, 2 vols (London, 1789), i. 302.
4. Jerome McGann, *The Poetics of Sensibility: a Revolution in Literary Style* (Oxford, 1996), p. 81.
5. See Marilyn Butler, *Romantics, Rebels, and Reactionaries: English Literature and its Background 1760–1830* (Oxford: Oxford University Press, 1981), Chapter 5.
6. *The Letters of Percy Bysshe Shelley*, ed. Frederick L. Jones, 2 vols (Oxford, 1964), ii. 363. Henceforth abbreviated to *LPBS* and cited within the text.
7. In 1822 Lady Noel died and, according to the terms of the marriage settlement, Byron received an inheritance of £10,000 a year provided he took the name of Noel.

8. Charles E. Robinson, *Shelley and Byron: the Snake and Eagle wreathed in fight* (Baltimore and London, 1976), pp. 421–4.
9. Robinson, *Shelley and Byron*, p. 23.
10. Edward John Trelawny, *Records of Byron, Shelley and the author*, p. 71.
11. Byron's 'Augustus Darvell: a fragment of a Ghost Story' is reprinted in *Lord Byron: the Complete Miscellaneous Prose*, ed. Andrew Nicholson (Oxford, 1991), pp. 58–63. Hereafter abbreviated to *CMP* and cited within the text.
12. *Medwin*, p. 194. Byron in turn recited Coleridge's *Christabel* to Shelley and doubtless discussed with him the poems he had encouraged Murray to publish.
13. Samuel Chew, *Byron in England, his Fame and After-fame* (London, 1924), pp. 122–3.
14. Lord Broughton, *Recollections of a Long Life*, ii. 24.
15. *LPBS*, i. 504.
16. *CPW*, ii. 299; *LPBS*, i. 514.
17. Lord Broughton, *Recollections of a Long Life*, ii. 11
18. Anonymous review of *Childe Harold's Pilgrimage*, Canto III; 'The prisoner of Chillon', 'A Dream'; and other poems, in the *Quarterly Review*, 16 (October 1816).
19. Lord Broughton, *Recollections of a Long Life*, ii. 35–37.
20. *His Very Self and Voice: Collected conversations of Lord Byron*, ed. Ernest J. Lovell (New York, 1954), p. 198. Henceforth abbreviated to *HVSV.*
21. *HVSV*, pp. 205; *Life*, ii. 668.
22. Byron's poem, itself conditioned by the picturesque tradition in art, fed back into this tradition. Nicholas Alfrey in 'A Voyage Pittoresque: Byron, Turner and Childe Harold', *Renaissance and Modern Studies: Byron and Europe*, 32 (1988), 108–26 has pointed out that J.M.W. Turner attached quotations from the later cantos of *Childe Harold* to six of his exhibited pictures, *Field of Waterloo* (exhibited 1818), *Childe Harold's Pilgrimage – Italy* (1832), *Modern Rome – Campo Vaccino* (1839), *Venice, the Bridge of Sighs* (1840), *Approach to Venice* (1844), and *Bright Stone of Honour (Ehrenbreitstein) and the tomb of Marceau* (1835). Turner's interest in Byron prompted Murray to commission seven watercolours to be engraved for an eleven-volume edition of Byron's works published in 1825, then seventeen designs for frontispieces for the seventeen-volume *The Works of Lord Byron, with his letters and journals, and his life, by Thomas Moore, Esq.* (1832–4). These were later joined by engravings of other leading landscape artists in *Finden's Landscape and Portrait Illustrations of the Life and Works of Lord Byron* (1832–4). Like Byron, Turner dispensed with the cliché of the cloaked wanderer, and gave his picturesque landcapes a frankly subjective colouring.
23. Hobhouse's *Letters Written by an Englishman* was savagely treated by John Wilson Croker in the *Quarterly* for January 1816. Hobhouse wrote to Murray to protest on 22 May, stating that he hoped that the review was not by Gifford. When Murray wrote about this to Byron, the poet regretted his friend's criticism of Gifford, and distanced himself from Hobhouse, declaring that they were 'very sparing of our literary confidences' and that he had refused to send Hobhouse an MS of *Childe Harold's Pilgrimage* Canto III, that they never read each other's journals and rarely read each other's unpublished works (*L&J*, v. 169).

24. Francis Haskell, Preface to Andrew Wilton and Ilaria Bignamini. *Grand Tour: the Lure of Italy in the Eighteenth Century* (London, 1996), p. 17.
25. James Buzard, *Beaten Track: European Tourism, Literature and the Ways to Culture 1800–1918* (Oxford, 1993), p. 120.
26. E.R. Vincent, *Byron, Hobhouse and Foscolo: New Documents in the History of a Collaboration* (New York, 1972).
27. For Nathan's account of his collaboration with Byron, see Isaac Nathan, *Fugitive Pieces and Reminiscences of Lord Byron* (London, 1829). Nathan eventually emigrated to Australia, where he collected and adapted the music of the Aborigines, and became the first celebrated composer of the colony.
28. This point is made by Thomas L. Ashton, *Byron's Hebrew Melodies* (London, 1972), p. 34. I am indebted to Ashton for details of publication.
29. Lord Broughton, *Recollections of a Long Life*, ii. 80.
30. See Peter Vassallo, *Byron: the Italian Literary Influence* (London, 1984), pp. 46–81; see also *Medwin*, pp. 140–1.
31. On 25 October, 1817, he had been astonished at the fluency of Tommaso Sgricci the *improvisatore*, whom he saw at La Scala, Milan, and then at Venice.
32. Marchand, *Life*, ii. 780.
33. *Medwin*, p. 25.
34. *Medwin*, p. 158.
35. *LPBS*, ii. 339.
36. Marchand, *Life*, iii. 944.
37. *LPBS*, ii. 376; *LPBS*, ii. 683.
38. *LPBS*, ii. 708.
39. *Medwin*, p. 160. On Byron and Dante, see Peter Vassallo, *Byron: The Italian Influence*, ch.2; Ralph Pite, *The Circle of our Vision: Dante Presence in English Romantic Poetry* (Oxford, 1994), chapter 6; Valeria Tinkler-Villani, 'Byron's Vision of Dante', in *Centennial Hauntings: Pope, Byron and Eliot in the year 88*, ed. C.C. Barfoot and Theo D'Haen (Atlanta, Georgia, 1990), pp. 203–14.
40. See J.B. Bullen, *The Myth of the Renaissance in Nineteenth-Century Writing* (Oxford, 1992); Wallace K. Ferguson, *The Renaissance in Historical Thought: Five Centuries of Interpretation* (Cambridge, Mass., 1948); J.R. Hale, *England and the Italian Renaissance: the Growth of Interest in its History and Art* (London, 1954).
41. On the other members of the Pisan group and their activities, see: C.L. Cline, *Byron, Shelley and their Pisan Circle* (London, 1952).
42. *Medwin*, p. 161.

5. The bookseller to the Admiralty and the Board of Longitude beset by pirates

1. For information on these measures I am indebted to: J. Ann Hone, *For the Cause of Truth: Radicalism in London 1796–1821* (Oxford, 1982), chapter 6.
2. See: William H. Wickwar, *The Struggle for the Freedom of the Press 1819–1832* (London, 1928), pp. 246–52.
3. On 9 November 1820, Byron wrote regarding his lack of participation in British radical politics to Hobhouse, recently elected radical MP, 'Yours is

now a more active life, I admit ... We will divide the parts between us of *player* and poet ...' (*L&J*, vii. 222).

4. Byron in 1822 asked Murray to tell Moore to try and collect past missives to Lady Caroline Lamb, Lady Cowper, Mr Long, Mrs Chaworth and other acquaintances to add to the volume.

5. *Byron's Bulldog: the Letters of John Cam Hobhouse to Lord Byron*, ed. Peter W. Graham (Columbus, Ohio, 1984), p. 231. However, when Byron wrote on 28 June that 'I shall positively offer my next year to Longman – and I have lots upon the anvil', Hobhouse replied that Longman's 'beef and carrots' was 'very poor grub indeed' compared to that of the 'humble servitor', Murray (p. 241).

6. See Edward John Trelawny, *Records of Shelley, Byron and the Author*, p. 85. Byron is quoted as complaining: 'All this morning I was in labour at a letter to John Murray. It will be made public in his back parlour, where the rooks meet and will caw over it. They complain of my showing letters; mine go a regular circuit'.

7. When he visited Venice in October, 1819, Moore collected the manuscript of 78 folio sheets of Byron's life up to 1816, together with his journal of 1814. In December 1820 Byron sent his friend the continuation of the *Memoirs*, the postal charge of the hefty packet being 46 and a half francs. Moore later told Hobhouse the second part contained all sorts of erotic adventures. Murray sealed the deal on the *Memoirs* by offering Moore a handsome 2000 guineas on condition he edited them and wrote an accompanying life, should he outlive his friend, as he informed Byron on 6 September 1821 (*Smiles*, i. 424) The *Memoirs* were to be published three months after the poet's death, but Moore showed them to many in MS.

8. Truman Guy Steffan, *Byron's 'Don Juan'*, vol.1, *The Making of a Masterpiece*, 104–5. Steffan gives a meticulous account of the composition of the poem.

9. Graham (ed.), *Byron's Bulldog*, p. 254.

10. Graham (ed.), *Byron's Bulldog*, p. 260.

11. Byron's note to I, 148 draws attention to the fact that Julia mentions as a rejected lover Count O'Reilly, a historical personage who died in 1794.

12. Byron mocked Leigh Hunt for his use of the word 'profession' in the preface to *Foliage*: 'I thought that poetry was an *art*, or an *attribute*, and not a *profession*' (*L&J*, vi. 4).

13. The latter Horatian phrase had punningly hinted at revelations about the separation scandal, while announcing the Tory administration as the poem's satiric target, and also suggested the relationship between sexuality and political ideology, as in the modern 'sexual politics'.

14. Jerome McGann has commented that the manuscripts show that 'Murray and his editors were altering Byron's corrected proofs as they saw fit, and that Byron had no hand in such late alterations, nor was he even aware that they were being made'(*CPW*, v. 664).

15. *Blackwood's Edinburgh Magazine*, 5 (August 1819), pp. 512–18.

16. *British Critic*, 12 (August 1819), pp. 195–205.

17. See also *Medwin*, pp. 164–5; the account of Leigh Hunt, in Ernest J. Lovell, Jr (ed.), *His Very Self and Voice: Collected conversations of Lord Byron* (New York, 1954), p. 332; and Lady Blessington, *HVSV*, p. 363, and Dr Kennedy, *HVSV*, pp. 442–3.

18. William H. Wickwar, *The Struggle for the Freedom of the Press 1819–1832*, p. 260.
19. See Samuel C. Chew, *Byron in England, his fame and after-fame* (London, 1924), pp. 22–3.
20. Kyle Grimes, 'William Hone, John Murray, and the Uses of Byron', in Stephen C. Behrendt (ed.), *Romanticism, Radicalism and the Press* (Detroit, 1997), pp. 192–202, p. 200.
21. For information on Byron's radical publishers, I am indebted to: Hugh J. Luke Jr, 'The Publishing of Byron's *Don Juan*' *PMLA*, 80 (1965), 199–209.
22. Iain McCalman, *Radical Underworld: Prophets, Revolutionaries, and Pornographers in London, 1795–1840* (Oxford, 1993), p. 211.
23. It seems that Murray's printer was not the radical Thomas Davison of 10 Duke Street, Smithfield, who edited and published the *Medusa, London Alfred*, and *Deists' Magazine*, and published the *Cap of Liberty* and *Theological Comet*.
24. In 1822 the mathematician Babbage told Hobhouse that, because of mechanical improvements in the printing process, an 'octavo volume cost, as far as types and ink were concerned, only eightpence' (Broughton, ii. 181). William St. Clair has demonstrated how quickly Byron lost his upper-class readership after 1816, in 'The impact of Byron's writings: an evaluative approach', in Andrew Rutherford (ed.), *Byron: Augustan and Romantic* (London, 1990), pp. 1–25.
25. Hugh J. Luke, 'The Publishing of Byron's *Don Juan*,' *PMLA*, 80 (1965), 199–209, 200.
26. The details are obtained from S. Stephen Bauer, 'Romantic poets and radical journalists', *Neuphilologische Mitteilungen*, 79 (1978), 266–75.
27. Wickwar, p. 263.
28. Marcus Wood, *Radical Satire and Print Culture 1790–1822* (Oxford, 1994), p. 268 and 'The Dedication to *Don Juan* and Nursery Rhyme parody: A new satiric context', *Byron Journal*, 20 (1992), 71–7.
29. See, McCalman, *Radical Underworld*, chapter 10. He lists pirated editions of *Don Juan* by Hone, Hodgson, W. Wright, W. Clarke, Griffin, Benbow, Dugdale and Duncombe.
30. Edward Royle and James Walvin, *English Radicals and Reformers 1760–1848* (Brighton, 1982), 132.
31. See Moyra Haslett, *Byron's 'Don Juan' and the Don Juan Legend* (Oxford, 1997). Haslett argues that Byron's poem should be read in the context of contemporary controversy over the fictional character, regarding his transformation into a sympathetic or comic character in Byron's poem and other Regency versions and travesties of the myth.
32. Haslett, *Byron's 'Don Juan' and the Don Juan Legend*, pp. 36–51.
33. Quoted by Frederick Beaty in 'Harlequin Don Juan', *JEGP*, 67 (1968), 395–405, 399.
34. Caroline Franklin, 'Juan's sea changes: class, race and gender in Byron's *Don Juan*', in Nigel Wood (ed.), *Don Juan* (Buckingham, 1993), pp. 56–89.
35. For a full account of other parodies and continuations of the poem, see Chew, *Byron in England*, chapters 4 and 5.
36. Quoted by Ethel Colburn Mayne, *The Life and Letters of Anne Isabella, Lady Noel Byron* (London, 1929), p. 283.
37. See Thomas W. Lacqueur, 'The Queen Caroline Affair: Politics and Art in the reign of George IV', *Journal of Modern History*, 14 (1982), 417–66;

J. Ann Hone, *For the Cause of Truth: Radicalism in London 1796–1821,*
pp. 308–19; McCalman, *Radical Underworld,* pp. 162–77; Marcus Wood,
Radical Satire and Print Culture, pp. 253–8.
38. He told Medwin, 'I left him in the seraglio. There I shall make one of the
favourites, a Sultana, (no less a personage,) fall in love with him, and carry
him off from Constantinople. Such elopements are not uncommon, not
unnatural either, though it would shock the ladies to say they are ever to
blame. Well, they make good their escape to Russia; where, if Juan's passion
cools, and I don't know what to do with the lady, I shall make her die of
the plague. There are accounts enough of the plague to be met with, from
Boccaccio to De Foe; – but I have seen it myself, and that is worth all their
descriptions. As our hero can't do without a mistress, he shall next become
man-mistress to Catherine the Great. *Queens have had strange fancies for more*
ignoble people before and since. I shall, therefore, make him cut out the ances-
tor of the young Russian, and shall send him, when he is *hors de combat,* to
England as her ambassador. In his suite he shall have a girl whom he shall
have rescued during one of his northern campaigns, who shall be in love
with him, and he not with her.
   You see I am true to nature in making the advances come from the
females. I shall next draw a town and country life at home, which will give
me room for life, manners, scenery, &c. I will make him neither dandy in
town nor a fox-hunter in the country. He shall get into all sorts of scrapes,
and at length end his career in France. Poor Juan shall be guillotined in the
French Revolution! What think you of my plot? It shall have twenty four
books too, the legitimate number.' *Medwin,* pp. 164–5. The sentence in
italics doubtless refers to the Queen Caroline affair.
39. *CPW* v. xix says the first edition was in quarto but I have found no evidence
for this.
40. See Luke, 'The Publishing of Byron's *Don Juan',* p. 202.

6. The eagle, the wren and the snake: Byron and *The Liberal*

1. See McCalman, *Radical Underworld,* pp. 80–1.
2. William H. Marshall, *Byron, Shelley, Hunt and* The Liberal, (Philadelphia,
Penn., 1960), p. 23.
3. This point is made by George Dumas Stout, *The Political History of Leigh*
Hunt's Examiner (Saint Louis, 1949), p. 41.
4. *Correspondence of Leigh Hunt, edited by his eldest son,* 2 vols (London, 1862), i.
170.
5. *Correspondence of Leigh Hunt,* i. 172.
6. Quoted by Marshall, *Byron, Shelley, Hunt and* The Liberal, p. 59.
7. Leigh Hunt, *Lord Byron and Some of his Contemporaries* (London, 1828), pp.
66–8. Henceforth abbreviated as *LBC* and cited within the text.
8. Ann Blainey, *Immortal Boy: A Portrait of Leigh Hunt* (London and Sydney,
1985), p. 128.
9. 'Shelley, the writer of some infidel poetry, for the republication of which
a man of the name of Clarke, either has been, or is about to be, prosecuted,

is dead', the *Courier*, no. 9,616 (5 Aug. 1822), p. 3; 'Mr. Byshh Shelly [sic], the author of that abominable and blasphemous book called *Queen Mab*, was lately drowned in a storm somewhere in the Mediterranean. His object in visiting that part of the world, it was said, was to *write down* Christianity. The visitation is, therefore, striking; and the termination of his life (considering his creed) not more awful than surprising', *John Bull*, no. 87 (11 Aug. 1822).

10. *The Journal of Thomas Moore*, ed. Wilfrid S. Dowden (London and Toronto, 1983), ii. 842.

11. Moore wrote to Byron January 1822: '*Alone* you may do anything; but partnerships in fame, like those in trade, make the strongest party answerable for the deficiencies or delinquencies of the rest, and I tremble even for *you* with such a bankrupt *Co*'. See Moore, *Life*, p. 553.

12. Leigh Hunt wrote an article 'Lord Byron, Mr Moore and Mr Leigh Hunt', a review of Moore's *Life of Lord Byron* in the *Tatler* (no. 114, Jan. 1831) in which he attacked the influence of Moore on Byron. Hazlitt took a similar point of view in *The Spirit of the Age* (1825).

13. Luther A. Brewer, *My Leigh Hunt Library: the Holograph Letters* (Iowa City, Iowa, 1938), p. 155.

14. Brewer, *My Leigh Hunt Library*, p. 157.

15. Letter to Elizabeth Kent on 22 November, 1822, *Correspondence of Leigh Hunt*, p. 200.

16. *Edinburgh Review* 53 (June 1831), reprinted in Caroline Franklin (ed.), *The Wellesley Series: Nineteenth-Century Sources in the Humanities and Social Sciences; British Romantic Poets*, 5 vols (London, 1998), ii. 736–57, 741.

17. *The Poetical Works of Robert Southey, collected by himself*, 10 vols (London, 1845), x. 205–6.

18. Quoted by Marshall, *Byron, Shelley, Hunt, and* The Liberal, p. 106.

19. For details of the parodies of *The Liberal* and piracies of *The Vision*, see Marshall, *Byron, Shelley, Hunt, and* The Liberal, pp. 118–34.

20. Leigh Hunt commented, 'Though *The Liberal* had no mean success, he unquestionably looked to its having a far greater; and the result … was that the interest he took in it cooled in proportion as it should have grown warm'. *The Autobiography of Leigh Hunt*, 2 vols (London, 1850, repr. New York, 1965), ii. 158–9.

21. Quoted by Marshall, *Byron, Shelley, Hunt, and* The Liberal, p. 169.

22. Details are obtained from Francis Lewis Randolph, *Studies for a Byron Bibliography* (London, 1979).

23. Luke, 'The Publishing of Byron's *Don Juan*', p. 207.

24. Luke mentions a piracy in 1828 of *Don Juan* by Murray's printer Thomas Davison of Whitefriars, whose name had appeared on Cantos I–V (p. 208). Davison had approached Kinnaird in Byron's lifetime with a scheme for publishing the poem, but Byron was suspicious that he was Murray's spy (*L&J*, ix. 199, 200, x. 96, 98, 104, 108).

Postscript

1. William St. Clair, *That Greece might still be free: the Philhellenes in the War of Independence* (Oxford, 1972), p. 145.

2. William Parry, *The Last Days of Lord Byron: with his lordship's opinions on various subjects, particularly on the state and prospects of Greece* (London, 1825), p. v. Augusta's remark is quoted by Doris Langley Moore, *The Late Lord Byron: Posthumous Dramas* (London, 1976), p. 169.
3. For information on Parry and Hodgskin, and their exaggeration of the split between Byron and the Benthamites, see F. Rosen, *Bentham, Byron, and Greece: Constitutionalism, Nationalism, and Early Liberal Political Thought* (Oxford, 1992), pp. 190–218.
4. Full a full discussion of these three poems and the possible destruction of another by Hobhouse, see Crompton, *Byron and Greek Love*, chapter 9.
5. Quoted by Moore, *The Late Lord Byron*, p. 180.

Index